THE HIGH-RISK PREGNANCY SOURCEBOOK

The High-Risk Pregnancy Sourcebook

by
Denise M. Chism, R.N., M.S.N., P.N.N.P.

Foreword by
Eleanor D. Sabin, M.D.

LOWELL HOUSE

LOS ANGELES

CONTEMPORARY BOOKS

CHICAGO

Library of Congress Cataloging-in-Publication Data

Chism, Denise M.
    The high-risk pregnancy sourcebook / by Denise M. Chism.
        p.   cm.
    Includes index.
    ISBN 1-56565-632-6
    ISBN 1-56565-858-2 (paperback)
    1. Pregnancy—Complications—Popular works.   I. Title.
  RG572.C48 1997
  618.3—dc21   97-9345
                                                                      CIP

Requests for such permissions should be addressed to:
Lowell House
2020 Avenue of the Stars, Suite 300
Los Angeles, CA 90067

Lowell House books can be purchased at special discounts when ordered
in bulk for premiums and special sales. Contact Department TC at the
address above.

Publisher: Jack Artenstein
Associate Publisher, Lowell House Adult: Bud Sperry
Director of Publishing Services: Rena Copperman
Managing Editor: Maria Magallanes
Text design: Janice Jenkins

Manufactured in the United States of America
10 9 8 7 6 5 4 3 2 1

CONTRIBUTING AUTHORS

Diabetes, Neurologic Disorders, Autoimmune Diseases, Multiples:

Anne Dill, R.N., M.S.N., C.N.M., P.N.N.P.
Perinatal Nurse Practitioner/Certified Nurse Midwife
Columbia Presbyterian/St. Luke's Medical Center
Denver, Colorado

Preeclampsia, Bleeding in Pregnancy, Breast-feeding:

Jeana M. Kelley, R.N., M.S.N., P.N.N.P.
Perinatal Nurse Practitioner
Columbia Presbyterian/St. Luke's Medical Center
Adjunct Faculty, Regis University
Denver, Colorado

Heart Disease, Kidney Disease, Rh Disease:

Karen J. Zimmerman, R.N., M.S.N., P.N.N.P.
Perinatal Nurse Practitioner
Family Health Center
Columbia Presbyterian/St. Luke's Medical Center
Maternal Health Services
Denver Health Medical Center
Private Practice, Douglas Kirkpatrick, M.D., P.C.
Denver, Colorado

Medical Advisor:

Eleanor D. Sabin, M.D.
Associate Director, Maternal-Fetal Services
Columbia Presbyterian/St. Luke's Medical Center
Denver, Colorado

To Mary,

*who started with a high-risk pregnancy and
is truly an example of motherhood at its finest.*

CONTENTS

Foreword by Eleanor D. Sabin, M.D.   xi

Acknowledgments   xiii

PART ONE: The Basics of Normal Pregnancy   1

   I.   Introduction   3

   II.   Normal Pregnancy: Normal Changes   9

PART TWO: Medical Conditions That Impact Pregnancy   55

   III.   Heart Disease   57

   IV.   Kidney Problems and Chronic Hypertension   93

   V.   Rh Disease   117

   VI.   Diabetes   131

   VII.   Neurological Problems   139

   VIII.   Autoimmune Diseases   149

   IX.   Twins, Triplets, and More   169

PART THREE: Diseases of Pregnancy   183

   X.   Premature Labor   185

   XI.   Gestational Diabetes   203

   XII.   Preeclampsia, Toxemia, and Pregnancy-Induced Hypertension   209

   XIII.   Bleeding with Pregnancy   225

PART FOUR: The Final Details   239

   XIV.   Breast-feeding and Your High-Risk Pregnancy   241

   XV.   Glossary of Pregnancy-Related Terms   249

Index   271

FOREWORD

There are few things in life more wondrous than the journey into motherhood. With pregnancy, however, comes many physical changes, questions, and even apprehensions. For many patients experiencing high-risk pregnancies such as multiple gestation and preexisting medical conditions including heart disease, kidney disease, and diabetes, the challenges can be even greater.

In *The High-Risk Pregnancy Sourcebook,* an experienced team of perinatal nurse practitioners provides valuable information on the basics of pregnancy, specific diseases that complicate pregnancy, diseases that occur because of pregnancy, concerns for mother and baby, anticipated prenatal management by the health care team, and expectations for labor, delivery, and postpartum. Through this comprehensive sourcebook, these highly trained caregivers will also empower you to ask questions and learn more about *your* special circumstances with pregnancy.

We are learning more and more about high-risk pregnancies every day. As a result, the success of healthy outcomes for mother and baby is on the rise. As medical treatments and therapies change, your physician should always serve as your ultimate source. Being well-informed and intimately aware of your health condition during pregnancy can make your pregnancy a positive experience. This sourcebook will be an invaluable aid as you journey into motherhood.

Eleanor D. Sabin, M.D.
Associate Director of Maternal-Fetal Medicine
Columbia Presbyterian/St. Luke's Medical Center
Denver, Colorado

ACKNOWLEDGMENTS

Kenny, I thank you for twenty great years together and for continued love and support in all I do. Your faith in me has helped me to have faith in myself, and I commit my love to you forever. Abby, you are the best little girl in the whole world! Thank you for kisses at the computer. J.D., my little guy, thank you for rumpling my hair saying, "Get writing mom." I am so proud of you and your sister—you are the light of my life. Eleanor, thank you for your knowledge, your patience, and your commitment to this project despite extraordinary life circumstances. Growing a perfect Rose is a miracle indeed. Thanks Mike and Charlie for sharing! Karen, Jeana, Anne, Eleanor, you will never realize what an honor it is to be associated with such women of integrity, intelligence, and compassion. My life is so enriched because of you. Rich, Kent, Greg, thank you for taking the time to teach and nurture. Diane and Janice, thanks for finishing up in the office when deadlines were tight and for praying for me. Finally, Lord Jesus, I thank you for your faithfulness, grace, and mercy in my life.
    —Love, Dede

    Tim—thank you for your love, encouragement, and belief in me. I am who I am because of your presence in my life. Molly and Zack—thank you for your hugs, love, and patience. You are truly the joy of my life. To my family and friends—thank you for your love and support throughout the completion of this project. Dede and Eleanor—thank you for your love and gentle guidance as these chapters have been written and rewritten. I grew and learned so much through this process. To all the folks at P/SL in Denver—thank you for sharing your knowledge so freely with me and always keeping the care of pregnant women and their families a priority. Most importantly, thank you God for your loving grace in my life, and who makes all life possible.

—Love, Karen

I thank my husband, Jeff, my son Jake, and my sweet friend Auggie. You are my strength and I am all yours now! My greatest acknowledgment goes to those who have taught me my specialty: Rich, Eleanor, Sharon, Kent, Shannon, Cyndy, and the obstetricians at P/SL. I dedicate my chapters to the women and their families whom I have cared for during their high-risk pregnancies, and I wish to acknowledge their spectacular triumphs and sorrowful losses. Dede, you are incredible, thank you.

— Love, Jeana

I would like to acknowledge Fairfield University for an outstanding undergraduate education, for teaching me to strive for excellence, and for planting the seed for advanced practice nursing. I thank my entire family for your love and ever present support. I thank Dr. Porreco, Dr. Sabin, and the nurse practitioners and staff with whom I have the privilege to work. And, thank you Father Steve and my church family for keeping me grounded in my faith.

—Love, Anne

PART ONE

The Basics of Normal Pregnancy

I

Introduction

The term "high risk" is frightening. It suggests danger, harm, and potential death, and the last thing a pregnant woman wants to hear is that she is classified as "high risk." You would not be reading this book if there wasn't cause for you to believe that your pregnancy is at risk.

What Makes a Pregnancy High Risk?

There are many factors that can influence the degree of risk when you are pregnant. Your health history, your family's health history, and your partner's health history all determine the risk for you and your pregnancy. Other factors such as age, ethnicity, social or financial disadvantage, and lack of prenatal care can also impact your pregnancy. You are considered high risk if:
- you are younger than seventeen or older than thirty-five
- you have had more than three previous miscarriages
- you have had a previous high-risk pregnancy

- you have a current health condition that requires ongoing care, such as diabetes, thyroid problems, heart disease, seizure disorder, or kidney disease
- you have developed disorders specific to pregnancy, such as preeclampsia, placental abruption, placenta previa, gestational diabetes, or Rh disease
- you or your partner have had a previous child with a genetic abnormality, such as Down syndrome, or have a genetic disorder in your family that could be passed on to your unborn baby
- you are carrying more than one baby (multiple pregnancy)
- you have a history of gynecological problems such as pelvic inflammatory disease (PID), endometriosis, or cancer
- you have a sexually transmitted disease (STD)
- you conceived through assisted reproduction (IVF, ZIFT, GIFT)
- you have had an abortion
- your mother took diethylstilbestrol (DES) when pregnant
- you have an IUD currently in place
- you have suffered or are currently suffering from psychological, abusive, or psychiatric difficulties

These factors are markers or "red flags" for your care provider. Women with any one of these factors are at greater risk for problems during their pregnancy. However, being aware of your risk will help you and your care provider prevent potential problems through anticipation, education, preventive medicine, and forestalling worsening conditions through early treatment. Identifying a high-risk red flag indicates to your care provider to pay extra attention to your condition. Having one or more of these factors in no way is a sentence to a gloom and doom pregnancy! It does not mean something bad is going to happen. In most cases, it makes an unfortunate circumstance much better through anticipation and preparation.

This book is divided into four parts: Part One contains an introduction to high-risk pregnancy and a thorough review of the normal pregnancy. It is important to have a good grasp on the normal changes of pregnancy in order to better understand when something out of the ordinary is occurring.

Part Two looks at preexisting medical conditions such as heart problems, kidney disease, chronic high blood pressure, thyroid disease, lupus, antiphospholipid antibody syndrome, seizure disorders, multiple sclerosis, spinal cord injury, Rh disease, diabetes, and multiple pregnancy (twins, triplets, etc.) which not only impact pregnancy, but are impacted by pregnancy.

Part Three explores the diseases of pregnancy. Preterm labor, gestational diabetes, preeclampsia, and bleeding during pregnancy are conditions unique to pregnancy. All of these conditions can significantly alter the health and well-being of your baby as well as yourself. It's important to realize that the conditions in Part Two can quickly become the conditions of Part Three. In some cases, the conditions of Part Three could potentially lead to some of the chronic conditions of Part Two. What this means is that problems often travel together, and the high-risk mom needs to be aware of the concerns. The purpose of this book is to inform, not to frighten. Information is valuable, and ignorance can be dangerous. Through understanding, it is my hope that you will be able to reach the ultimate goal of a healthy baby and a healthy mom.

Part Four takes a brief look at breast-feeding and the high-risk pregnancy. It also contains a thorough glossary of pregnancy-related terms.

In this book, I will refer to the life growing inside you as your "baby." When a baby is still inside, it is medically termed a "fetus"—not that there is anything wrong with the word "fetus," only that the word "baby" conveys the miracle of life. Miracles are just too awesome to let slide by with technical terms!

The majority of the high-risk factors will be addressed in the individual chapters. Factors such as age and race do not have specific chapters devoted to them because they usually lead to a condition that is already detailed in a chapter. For instance, if you are younger than seventeen or older than thirty-five, you are at risk for preterm labor, gestational diabetes, preeclampsia, or bleeding. If you have not had prenatal care or are financially disadvantaged, you are also at risk for preterm labor and birth, preeclampsia, or bleeding. Sexually transmitted diseases, in general, create the risk for preterm labor. And, if you are African-American, you are at risk for preterm labor and birth, preeclampsia, chronic high blood pressure, or twins or triplets.

Regardless of what specific factor makes you high risk, there are warning signs of which all pregnant mothers should be aware. I will repeat these warning signs throughout the book in addition to the warning signs for your specific condition.

Warning Signs

Call your care provider immediately if you experience any of the following symptoms:
- vaginal bleeding or spotting
- leaking or gushing of fluid from the vagina
- severe abdominal or pelvic pain
- pain or burning sensation while urinating
- persistent or severe headaches
- sudden or rapid weight gain
- sudden swelling or puffiness of the hands, feet, or face

- dizziness, lightheadedness, or fainting spells
- blurred vision
- chills, fever higher than 100 degrees F, or rash
- foul vaginal discharge
- an injury or accident that may affect you or your baby's well-being
- hot, reddened, swollen, or painful areas on your leg
- absent or decreased fetal movement (after nineteen weeks)
- frequent uterine contractions or painless tightening of your belly (twenty to thirty-six weeks)

Your pregnancy is just that—your pregnancy. Every woman is unique. Every pregnancy is different. Your pregnancy may be *labeled* "high risk," but you must normalize it for yourself. Embrace it; live it. You have a very special job to mother this baby, and you *will* succeed.

II

Normal Pregnancy: Normal Changes

The term high-risk pregnancy seems to carry the implication that there is nothing *normal* about it. All pregnancies, however, include the normal changes of pregnancy. What makes a pregnancy high risk is how these normal changes affect a preexisting condition or how the presence of these changes create a high-risk situation for some women.

The normal development and growth of a baby takes approximately 280 days from start to finish. This chapter includes a *general* overview of pregnancy. As you read and understand the changes of normal pregnancy, you can then flip to the sections that have specifically led your care provider to categorize your pregnancy as high risk.

Some Details

Your care provider will discuss your pregnancy in terms of weeks. Your family, friends, and coworkers may discuss it in terms of months. So just how pregnant are you?

It can be confusing to figure out exactly how far along you are in your pregnancy. The estimated due date for the arrival of your full-term infant is calculated by using the first day of your last period. For many women who struggle with getting pregnant, it can be frustrating because periods oftentimes are so irregular. The two weeks or so from the start of your period to ovulation is considered a part of the gestation (pregnancy) because your body is actually preparing itself for pregnancy. Considering the fact that it takes approximately 280 days for complete gestation, counting the two weeks before fertilization actually occurs, one only needs to count 280 days from the first day of your last period. Well, this could be pretty difficult, especially if you have a tendency to be interrupted in the middle of things. Therefore, a quick rule of thumb is to note the first day of your last period, count back three months, then add one week. This will be your due date by LMP, or Last Menstrual Period. If this date is confirmed by ultrasound or your care provider, you might as well put the date of your last period in memory because people will be asking you that date for the next nine and a half months!

In The Beginning

Once an ovary is fertilized by a sperm, cells begin to divide. This dividing bundle of cells is the microscopic beginning of your baby. It is called a blastocyst and contains the entire genetic makeup of the baby. Each time the cells divide they copy the same genetic material that was initiated by the joining of the sperm and the egg. The outer portion of the blastocyst will become the placenta, and the inner portion will become the embryo.

The uterine lining secretes enzymes that nourish the freefloating blastocyst. If you were to look at this tiny bundle under a high-powered microscope, you would find that nearly every cell is different. This is because each cell has a different job. It is a mystery how each cell knows what it will do. The bundle of cells that is your baby then divides into two parts. One part will be the embryo, which is the baby itself; the other part becomes the placenta. After implantation, the cells of the placenta get right to work forming a hormone called human chorionic gonadotropin (hCG), which is also the hormone that tells your ovaries not to release any more eggs for a while. The ovaries then respond by keeping you from having a period.

So what does this mean to me?

In order for the ovaries to prevent you from having a period, they must secrete a hormone called progesterone. Progesterone helps the endometrium grow, but it can also make you feel lousy. As early as the second week you might feel breast or nipple tenderness and be just a little under the weather, feeling tired and irritable. Some women notice a *slight* amount of brownish-tinged discharge. This is due to the implantation of the blastocyst into your uterine lining. Many women mistake this for a light period. It's a good idea to remember the type of bleeding—if it's lighter than, the same as, or heavier than usual—as it may clarify your actual last menstrual period.

Moving along

The capsule that held your egg prior to ovulation is called the corpus luteum. It is the corpus luteum that first nourishes your baby, and it continues to do so until about eight to ten weeks when the placenta takes over the job. Large amounts of hormones necessary for the growth of your baby as well as for you are being produced in your body.

In the early part of your pregnancy, the baby is called an embryo. The cells have formed three layers. The outer layer is called the ectoderm which will become your baby's skin, hair, and nerves. The middle layer is called the mesoderm and will form the bones, cartilage, muscles (including the heart muscle), blood vessels, kidneys, and sex organs. The inner layer is called the endoderm and will form your baby's respiratory system, digestive system, and urinary tract. As these areas develop they begin to coordinate together. Pretty impressive for someone who is less than a tenth of an inch long!

You may first realize you are pregnant around week five of your pregnancy, after you have missed your period. Even with a well-planned pregnancy, the shock of actually being pregnant can be a little overwhelming. It's natural to feel a little scared about the changes that are happening to your body which are totally outside of your control. The first change many women notice is with their breasts. This can range from a rapid change in size to tenderness or tingling in your nipples, and the area around your nipples, the areola, may darken.

By week six the uterus is still low in the pelvis but has grown enough to press against the bladder. This is why you may feel like you are spending the majority of your day in the bathroom, but only urinating a little bit. Do not, however, decrease the amount of fluid you are drinking. Good hydration (drinking lots) will help prevent urinary tract infections and premature labor. Your baby needs that extra fluid as much as you do, so remember to drink! Your urine should be a clear, pale yellow. The only exception to this is your first urination in the morning.

The level of estrogen increases causing an increase in the blood flow. There is more circulating progesterone relaxing smooth muscle. This will result in a lowering of your blood pressure. The lower blood pressure sometimes causes women to feel faint when standing for long periods of time. As your pregnancy progresses, remember to change positions frequently and avoid hot, crowded areas. This will help prevent fainting.

The increased blood flow results in a bluish color in your vagina and cervix. Estrogen also causes slight swelling in all mucous producing areas, including your nose. You may feel like your nose is stuffy all the time, and you may get frequent nosebleeds. Placing a cool mist humidifier in your bedroom may help the stuffiness in your nose. It is very important in this early stage of pregnancy that you avoid *any* unnecessary medications such as aspirin or cold medications, including nasal sprays. If you are currently taking medicine for an ongoing condition, such as diabetes or thyroid problems, continue to do so and see your care provider as soon as possible.

A word or two about nausea in pregnancy

Your growing uterus and the hormones being produced to maintain your pregnancy will cause nausea and vomiting, and it is during the sixth week that many women get hit hard with these symptoms. There is no rule for "morning" sickness. It can occur morning, noon, night, all day long, or not at all.

Unfortunately, there is no hard and fast cure for nausea during pregnancy. Small, frequent meals are a good rule of thumb throughout pregnancy. A high protein snack, such as a turkey sandwich, may help when your stomach isn't quite so empty because protein takes longer to digest. Try eating a couple saltine crackers or frozen fruit bars before getting out of bed. Avoid unpleasant odors whenever possible. Eat slowly and chew your food well. Decrease the fat from your diet. Experiment to find out if drinking fluids before, during, or after your meals works best for you. Sometimes avoiding liquids thirty minutes before and after meals works well. Extra vitamin B_6 may help as well as taking your prenatal vitamin at night. Peppermint tea, ginger capsules, and pressure point wrist bands help some women. Eat whatever will stay down. If you are vomiting so much that you cannot keep food or liquids down, you need to see your care provider before you get seriously dehydrated.

And the story goes on

By week seven, your baby has grown to almost a half inch long. At the start of this week, the baby's hands resemble little paddles at the end of the arms. By the end of the week, fingers are developing and the feet paddles are present. Eyes, nose, and mouth are beginning to be visible. The brain is developing at one end of the neural tube and the spinal cord is at the other end. Intestines are present and bulge into what will become the umbilical cord.

Between six and eight weeks, if you have an ectopic pregnancy, or are carrying a fetus in a fallopian tube instead of the uterus, you will begin to notice symptoms such as extreme nausea, abdominal pain, shoulder pain, or vaginal bleeding. As you can imagine, the growing embryo inside the tube causes pain. This can be an emergency and must not be ignored so call your care provider *immediately*.

As you reach week eight, your uterus is about the size of a pear. The surrounding ligaments are beginning to stretch. Blood flow has increased through your breasts preparing them for lactation, and you may notice the blood vessels in your breasts are much more obvious.

It is around week eight that most women have their first comprehensive exam with their nurse practitioner, nurse midwife, or physician. All women who are categorized as high risk should have a qualified obstetrician involved in their care. This does not discount the vital role that a nurse practitioner, midwife, and family physician will play in the pregnancy. You will find that it is a team effort to bring *your* pregnancy to the very best outcome—a healthy mom and a healthy baby. The most important person on this team is you so take care of yourself by getting plenty of rest; drinking plenty of water; avoiding unhealthy choices such as smoking, alcohol, and drug use for non-medical purposes; eating a balanced diet; and adopting a good attitude.

Your first visit with the nurse practitioner, midwife, or physician is a comprehensive exam that involves a discussion of your health history and an extensive physical exam. The history will be broken up into questions about your menstrual history: When did you first start your period? How long is your cycle? How many days do you flow? Is your cycle regular? Do you have pain with your periods? One important question will be: When was your last normal menstrual period? As discussed earlier, this will determine your estimated due date.

You will also be asked questions about your obstetrical and gynecologic history. These will include the number of pregnancies including miscarriages and abortions, previous sexually transmitted diseases, previous surgeries, urinary problems or infections, or anything that might complicate this pregnancy. You and your care provider will review any family history of genetic traits you or your partner may have. This includes twins and triplets or family members who may have had a disease or disorder that could be passed on to you or your baby. Your general health will be reviewed, going over every system from head to toe. Do you have any current conditions such as diabetes, thyroid disease, high blood pressure, problems with blood clots, or kidney problems? Are you allergic to anything?

This is a good time to discuss your questions or concerns. Ask your care provider what you can expect from his or her practice. What are the office hours? What should you expect at your appointments? Will you be seeing one care provider? Will you alternate between nurse practitioner at one appointment and midwife or physician at the next? When you call with an emergent question or concern, who will call you back and how long should you expect to wait before your call is returned?

Most care providers prefer that you call with non-emergency questions during office hours. However, many women stew over a concern all day and decide not to call the office until 10:00 P.M. If indeed you waited only to find out that you needed immediate attention, you could possibly endanger you or the baby. So remember to review the warning signs listed on pages 6 and 7, and call at any time you notice any of those symptoms. If you feel a question or concern can wait until your appointment, write it down. You don't want to forget any of your questions.

The exam itself is a thorough assessment of your entire body. Your care provider will assess your throat and mouth, lymph nodes, heart, lungs, breasts, abdomen, liver, kidneys, bladder, legs and arms, and reflexes. The internal exam will include a careful assessment of your pelvic bones, vagina, cervix, uterus, fallopian tubes, and ovaries. Be sure and ask questions throughout the exam and give any information you remember along the way.

Your first prenatal physical exam will probably include the following laboratory tests: urinalysis, blood tests for your blood type and Rh factor, a blood cell count, rubella (German measles) status, syphilis, hepatitis, and possibly, HIV. The pelvic exam includes a Pap smear and cultures for chlamydia and gonorrhea. Your specific condition may require further testing so review the individual chapters that address your specific high-risk condition for other tests that may be necessary.

By week nine your baby is a little longer than one inch. Primitive nerve pathways are being formed in your baby's brain, and the muscles are responding. From head to toes, your baby is moving, but you are unaware of these spontaneous actions. The heart is now developed, and blood is circulating through the body. During the previous week, structures of the ear were forming, and now the mechanisms for hearing and balance are developing. The lungs, liver, kidneys, spleen, pancreas, stomach, intestines, and reproductive organs are now present.

The increase in hormones affects your own skin, hair, and nails. Your skin may feel smooth, and it may have a bit more color. Some women develop a darkened, mask-like appearance on their face. The areola (the dark part around your nipples) will darken, and many women get a dark line that runs right down the middle of their belly. All of these skin changes are normal and vary with every mom. Your hair may seem thicker and more shiny, and fingernails may grow faster and be stronger.

The hormone progesterone, which has been produced by the corpus luteum since your egg was first released from your ovary, will now be secreted by the placenta. Progesterone is the primary hormone that keeps the inner lining of the uterus (endometrium) healthy and keeps your uterus from contracting excessively. The placenta is now responsible for producing all the necessary hormones that will maintain your pregnancy. It is also the communication station between you and your baby. This is the place where oxygen and nutrients transfer to your baby. A healthy placenta is essential for a healthy baby.

By week eleven, your baby has now graduated from an embryo to a fetus. This baby is about two inches long and weighs about one-third of an ounce. The eyelids are forming, the mouth opens and closes, the heart is beating between 110–160 times a minute, and fingernails are developing.

The hormone hCG has reached its peak and is beginning to decline. This hormone is largely responsible for causing nausea; therefore, your queasiness should begin to fade (no guarantees though, sorry!). Estrogen and progesterone continue to rise and stimulate your mammary glands for lactation (breast-feeding). The hormone relaxin causes the ligaments in your pelvis to widen and become flexible so that birth will be easier. You may notice your hips widen, and they may also feel a little floppy from the relaxin. Because relaxin increases flexibility, it is easy to injure yourself during exercise so be careful not to overstretch your joints.

A few words on sexuality, intimacy, and intercourse

The increase in hormones may make you feel more aroused and sexually excited than you may have been for some time. Often the stresses of infertility dampen the mood for making love. Pregnancy is a wonderful time to rekindle the sparks of romance.

Pregnancy often brings a sense of uncertainty regarding sexuality to both partners. Concerns about harming the baby or the pregnant mom top the list. Other feelings about being sexually attracted to your partner and about being sexually attractive yourself often surface. Both partners can struggle with these issues. During early pregnancy and late in the third trimester, it can be a little hard to feel sexy. If you're not throwing up or sleeping, then your belly just seems too much of a barrier.

Communication

Talking with your partner about what you are feeling, and hearing your partner's feelings, are very important. Intimacy begins with communication. This is the time to get past being embarrassed about your body and your sexual desires. Some women experience their first true orgasm while pregnant. This is a great time for great sex!

Erotic areas

As blood supply increases, you may find that your breasts, belly, and genitals are easily aroused. Tell your partner what feels good and what doesn't. Intercourse is not necessary to feel warm, content, and sexually satisfied. However, there are a few reasons to abstain from intercourse (see below). If it is necessary for you to abstain, explore other ways for you and your partner to be sexually fulfilled. Massage with scented oil and oral sex are both ways to reach fulfillment and are fine in pregnancy. Special note: *Never* allow air to be blown into the vagina as this could be harmful to you and your pregnancy.

Positions

Be creative! Look at your belly as a blessing for creative sex rather than a burden to no sex. Since you won't want your partner's weight fully on your belly, try positioning yourself tilted to the side, lying sideways, and of course, being on top.

What about the baby? Sex does not hurt the baby. The heart rate increases for a while after an orgasm, but it is not harmful and shortly returns to normal. The baby may also move from the physical activity.

Reasons to avoid sexual intercourse

- If you are at risk for or are threatening a miscarriage
- If you are at risk for premature labor
- If you have abdominal or vaginal pain

- If you have placenta previa or any vaginal bleeding
- If you have increased or unusual pressure in your uterus
- If your membranes have ruptured (your bag of water has broken)

Your care provider will discuss with you and your partner if you are at risk and need to avoid sexual intercourse. If your care provider advises against sexual intercourse but cannot provide you with a reason, discuss it further until you have a clearer understanding, or seek a second opinion.

Completing the First Trimester

Week twelve marks the end of the first trimester. It is amazing how much you have already accomplished. Your uterus is no longer tucked beneath your pubic bone. It has grown past that bony pelvis and can now be felt in the lower part of your belly just above the pubic hair. You may also notice a little less pressure on your bladder. As the uterus grows it begins to contract intermittently. A contraction is noted by the tightening of the uterus. This tightening is the way the uterus keeps in shape during the incredible stretching that is occurring. Some women notice this tightening once or twice a day, but it may actually occur as often as once an hour. Any more than this could indicate a problem. All high-risk mothers should read Chapter X on premature labor for more information about contractions and the complications associated with them.

As your uterus grows over the next several weeks, you may notice a change in your sense of balance. Your back may begin to have a slight sway and this change in posture often leads to a nagging backache. It is easy to force your growing belly forward, but this just makes the backache worse, so it is important to practice good posture technique when sitting and standing. If you are standing for long periods of time or are experiencing back problems, try tucking your bottom under and tilting your pelvis forward. You can do this by pressing your lower back against a wall or the floor or as an exercise on your hands and knees. Try tilting for a few seconds and then release. This is an exercise to remember throughout your pregnancy as well as later when your back is aching from carrying a baby, chasing a toddler, and tying little shoes.

As this first trimester ends, your baby has made tremendous strides in development. The skeletal system is developing with actual bone formation. Bone marrow is beginning to form and will be responsible for the production of red blood cells. Fingers and toes are more distinct. Blood is beginning to circulate through the umbilical cord, to the placenta, and back again. Your baby can now respond to touch.

The baby's head is still large compared to the rest of the body, but this disproportion starts to even out as the growth of the head slows down. The eyes and ears are closer to their final position. The mouth is beginning to make sucking and swallowing movements. The beginnings of tooth buds are forming, but teeth don't actually begin to erupt from the gums for another year. The liver and pancreas are also functioning and actively excreting bile and insulin. Your baby's stomach and intestines are now closed inside the abdomen. The kidney system is being refined with the process of swallowing and, subsequently, urinating.

If you're wondering what the baby swallows, it's the surrounding amniotic fluid which has been accumulating since conception and is now up to about four tablespoons. By the end of your pregnancy there may be as much as a whole liter of fluid surrounding the baby.

Amniotic fluid has many functions. It protects the baby from harm with its cushioning effect; it regulates temperature; and because it is all around the baby, it allows equal growth on all sides and allows strengthening, growth, and development of the baby's muscles and bones. It also functions to mature the baby's lungs. The amniotic fluid that the baby swallows passes through the kidneys and is eliminated as urine, which contributes to the volume of fluid.

The Second Trimester: Weeks Thirteen Through Twenty-seven

Increased blood in the vaginal area causes an increase in vaginal secretions or discharge. An increase in irritable vaginal discharge may be present. However, if you notice a foul odor or itching, or if the discharge has a yellow or green color to it, a vaginal infection may be present and you should notify your care provider. A curdy white discharge with itching is probably a yeast infection and is treatable. A foul smelling discharge, or one that is yellow or green could indicate a more serious infection that could lead to premature labor if untreated.

If you have genital warts, they may begin to increase in number and in size. Moles, like warts, are also nourished through the hormones that increase in pregnancy, and they can grow in size, number, and color. You may notice a change in your existing warts and moles, and these warts and moles could spread to your vaginal and rectal area. Spreading warts may be treatable depending on the type. *Any changing mole needs to be checked.*

Progesterone depresses the central nervous system and may cause moodiness or depression. You may feel unpredictably teary or cranky. If you experienced mood swings prior to your periods before you got pregnant, you can count on some moodiness during pregnancy. Moodiness may be a good reminder to talk about your feelings, excitements, and fears with your partner, family, and friends. Oftentimes pregnancy will open the door to stronger relationships as you experience these phenomenal changes in your life. Don't let things build up inside, and don't try to analyze every emotion. Let insignificant showers roll off your back like a duck.

If your pregnancy brings up issues such as rape, abuse, or incest, professional counseling will help you and your partner work through these issues. Dealing with these head-on, before you face the out-of-control scariness that labor can sometimes bring can be emotionally and spiritually healing.

The hormones that have slowed down the intestinal tract have also relaxed the sphincter between the stomach and esophagus, allowing stomach juices to flow up into the esophagus. When the stomach juices flow back into the esophagus, this causes a burning sensation in the middle of your chest which is heartburn (it has nothing to do with your heart). As the uterus grows, it crowds the intestines, and heartburn may get much worse.

Heartburn can sometimes be prevented or relieved through a few different measures:

- Identify the foods that make it worse and avoid them.
- Eat several small meals a day.
- Avoid greasy or spicy foods.
- Avoid lying down right after eating; or, lie on your right side to improve your stomach emptying. Sleep propped up to keep the stomach fluids from flowing back into the esophagus.
- Avoid taking baking soda for heartburn.
- To stimulate digestion, try a small amount of fatty food, such as toast with butter, buttermilk, or yogurt about thirty minutes before you eat.
- Consult with your care provider about the use of antacids.

Moving along

By week fifteen your baby weighs almost 2 ounces. The bones are growing and the muscle movement is increasing. You probably don't feel the baby moving yet, but when you do, the first movements feel like flutters. A soft, very fine hair called lanugo covers the baby. The neck is getting longer and the head can move. The arms move freely in front of the body and the hands can grasp one another. Ultrasound has picked up babies actually sucking their thumbs by this time.

You may begin to notice that you are gaining weight. This is a very good sign. The following breakdown is an approximation of how weight is distributed during pregnancy. This will vary with each mother and will increase with twins, triplets, and quadruplets. Keep in mind that with multiple babies, the weight of each baby will be smaller. See Chapter IX for an expanded explanation on weight gain with multiple babies.

Table 1. Where Does the Weight Go?

Mother (at term)	
Uterus	2–3 pounds
Breasts	1–3 pounds
Blood volume	3–5 pounds
Body fluid	1–3 pounds
Fat, protein, etc.	5–8 pounds
Baby (at 9 months)	
Baby	7–8 pounds
Amniotic fluid	2–2.5 pounds
Placenta	1–1.5 pounds
Total	22–32 Pounds

Common screening tests done between fifteen and eighteen weeks

Between fifteen and eighteen weeks, you will have the option of a blood test done to screen for birth defects and to assess placental function. The maternal serum alpha fetoprotein test (MSAFP) screens for your risk of having a baby with Down syndrome, abdominal wall defects, or neural tube defects, such as spina bifida and anencephaly. Spina bifida is a disorder characterized by an open spine. It is a defect of the spinal column and has many variations. Normal development of the child with spina bifida is possible, but paralysis of the lower limbs sometimes occurs. These children can also have chronic urinary tract infections, hydrocephaly (water on the brain), mental retardation, and the inability to control bowel and bladder function. Anencephaly occurs when the brain, the head, and sometimes the spinal cord do not develop normally. These children usually die shortly after birth.

It is important to note that MSAFP is only a screening test and is not 100 percent reliable. It *can* be a predictor though, and many couples want to know if there may be a serious problem with their baby. The decision to screen for these defects can be difficult. You may ask yourself why you would want the information. You may also feel that your preparation for this child will be unaffected by whatever information this test may reveal. On the other hand, you may choose to have the blood test if the information you receive will influence your preparation for the baby.

MSAFP can help your care provider assess placental function. Abnormal values may place you at risk for pregnancy problems that are not related to the baby. Alerting your care provider to these potential problems can help you and your baby *stay* healthy.

As you approach nineteen to twenty weeks, the midpoint of normal pregnancy, you might marvel at all the changes that have occurred over the last four-and-a-half months. Many things are happening with you, your baby, and your prenatal care.

The amount of blood circulating throughout your body and especially in the areas of your vagina and rectum continues to increase. New vessels form, but they are not as strong as the ones you have had. They are very sensitive and often bulge or swell in the vaginal area as well as the rectum and legs. You may notice varicose veins around your labia, vagina, and legs. When these vessels in the rectum swell, hemorrhoids develop. They may protrude out the rectum with strenuous bowel movements. For the most part, varicose veins are inherited, and there is little you can do to prevent them. However, there are things you can do to keep them from getting worse and from aching, including:

- resting with your legs elevated
- not crossing your legs when sitting
- exercising regularly
- moving around a bit after sitting or standing for any length of time
- resting in bed on your side
- wearing support hose *every day*

Hemorrhoids can continue to worsen throughout pregnancy, labor, and birth. For now, take care of your hemorrhoids by:

- avoiding constipation (drink plenty of liquids; increase your fiber through fruits, vegetables, and bran) and
- doing Kegel exercises (this will tighten the muscles around your vagina and rectum and increase circulation; if you've been slacking off in doing your Kegel exercises, or never really learned what a Kegel exercise is, it's not too late)

How to do Kegel exercises

- Practice, first, by stopping the flow of urine. You won't routinely do these exercises while going to the bathroom, but it will help you "feel" the muscles you need to use. (It is important to always empty your bladder completely to help prevent urinary tract infections.)
- Slowly tighten these muscles as if you are raising them up from the floor, until you have raised them as high as you can.
- Now, slowly release the muscles as if you are gently placing them back on the floor.
- At first, it may be easiest to do this while sitting, but soon you'll be doing Kegels almost anywhere! Some women use "reminders" such as talking on the phone, stopping at a traffic signal, or television commercials to remember to do Kegels.
- Do at least twelve Kegel exercises, three times a day.

Just as in the vagina and legs, tiny blood vessels develop in your mouth and gums from the large amounts of estrogen flowing through your body. This increases the sensitivity in your mouth. You may experience bleeding gums every time you brush your teeth and perhaps sore gums while chewing.

It is very important to keep your regularly scheduled dental checkups. (Remember to tell your dentist you are pregnant.) Floss and brush your teeth to keep them healthy. Resist the temptation to put off good dental hygiene because your mouth hurts or bleeds easily. Good hygiene will also decrease bacteria in your mouth that can lead to infection. Rinsing your mouth out with an antiseptic mouthwash or mild salt water may make your mouth feel less sore and more fresh.

In addition to changes in your blood vessels, the glands in your vagina are very active. They produce a thick vaginal discharge. This is one way the body protects itself against infection.

By midpoint in your pregnancy, you will have noticed that your belly is "pooching out" as the top of your uterus has risen to your navel. It is not unusual to have gained about 8 to 13 pounds already. Sixty-two percent of this weight gain is water, 30 percent is fat, and 8 percent is protein. Remember, your baby still weighs less than one pound. Expect to gain about one pound a week for the remainder of your pregnancy. If you started out this pregnancy underweight, it is recommended you gain a little more. If you started out this pregnancy overweight, it is recommended you gain a little less.

By virtue of your growing belly, your pregnancy is now more public. If you have enjoyed the privacy of your pregnancy, people may start inquiring about your changing body. This attention can be special, or it can be annoying. Many people assume it is okay to touch your belly and invade your "space" or ask extremely personal questions. Many people find the miracle of pregnancy and childbirth truly an awesome happening so asking questions and touching your belly may be their way of being "touched" by this also. Without your permission, however, this is not okay. Your health, your body, and your baby are *your* business. You may want to share information about your pregnancy, or your may want to be more private. Your response can encourage or discourage further inquiries.

Midway through pregnancy—what's up with the baby?

By twenty-one weeks, your baby weighs almost one pound and is nearly 10 to 11 inches long. Every system is progressing in development. The primitive structures of the brain have been developed for some time. Now, the fine details of the nerve pathways in the brain are forming. Nerve cells that will allow your baby's brain to receive and transmit messages are forming layers in the brain. This process will continue at a much slower rate for another three months.

T-cells and B-cells are essential for every human's immune system. These are the cells that fight off germs, and your baby's immune cells are already reaching adult proportions.

Your baby is able to hear sounds from outside of your body. She is used to the constant rhythm created by your beating heart as well as the switching and gurgling of fluids inside your body. When a loud noise occurs close to your body, she may jump or wiggle to get away from the noise. Her eyes remain fused shut. By the end of week twenty-one, the layers of the retina will be developed. Her skin is developing a white coating called vernix caseosa, a fatty film that protects your baby's skin from breakdown in the amniotic fluid. Vernix also prevents the loss of water and electrolytes from the baby into the amniotic fluid. The permanent ridges that form the fingers, hands, and footprints are now developed and the fingernails and toenails are getting harder.

Your baby is swallowing over 2 teaspoons of amniotic fluid per day. (By the end of your pregnancy he will be swallowing nearly 2 *cups* of amniotic fluid per day.) The digestive system is developed, and the digestive processes are beginning. Stool is being formed in the bowel. This little baby poop is called meconium.

The little air sacs in the lungs called alveoli are beginning to emerge. These are essential for your baby to be able to breathe on her own. They will be functioning by your due date. If you develop problems, your care provider may give you medication to help them function sooner. The oxygen your baby uses at this time is between 1.5 and 2 times greater than the amount the average adult uses.

The ultrasound examination

Ultrasound is a method of visualizing soft tissue, bones, and fluid inside the body, and it is a medical procedure that provides valuable information about your pregnancy. This information includes the baby's gestational age; how fast the baby is growing; where the placenta is located; the baby's position, movement, breathing, and heart rate; the amount of amniotic fluid around the baby; the number of babies in your uterus; and certain birth defects. Ultrasound can often tell the sex of your baby, but this is not 100 percent accurate, and it is certainly not a medical indication for having an ultrasound. Many health care providers want their pregnant patients to have an ultrasound evaluation, and most high-risk pregnancies require several ultrasound evaluations.

When you come in for your ultrasound wear comfortable, loose-fitting clothing that can easily expose your abdomen. The ultrasonographer will have you lie on a bed and will apply mineral oil or a special gel on your belly prior to placing a hand-held device called a transducer. A picture is produced on a screen similar to a television screen through the transmission of fast sound waves passing through the transducer. The sound waves bounce off tissue and bones producing a picture of the baby, parts of the baby, or whatever else is being evaluated.

Many ultrasound machines have the capability of videotaping the procedure. Ask your care provider if this is a possibility and if you need to provide the videotape. If it is not possible, you may be able to get an instant photo of part of the ultrasound. Ultrasound can be very interesting, but it can also be confusing to the parents. Be sure to ask questions and have the person performing the ultrasound explain what is being done.

During the last part of the second trimester, you may start to notice your digestive system more. As your baby grows, your diaphragm flattens, changing the angle of your esophagus. The combination of the angle change and a decreased pressure in the lower esophagus allows gastric juices from your stomach to enter your esophagus. The medical term for this is gastric reflux, commonly referred to as heartburn. Review the list on page 23 for help with heartburn.

The hormone progesterone slows down the digestive process. You make less stomach acid, and overall movement in your intestines is slower. This is actually a benefit because it allows you to better absorb calcium, sodium, water, and iron. Your calcium requirements increase as much as 50 to 75 percent during pregnancy. Some research has shown that adding calcium to your diet may reduce the risk of preeclampsia. High-risk mothers may want to consider additional calcium supplementation. Use moderation when consuming foods high in phosphorus, such as processed meats and snacks as well as soda.

The progesterone that has slowed your digestive system has affected your gallbladder in much the same way. It takes your gallbladder a longer time to empty, allowing bile salts to accumulate in your system and absorb through your skin. This causes significant itching which is sometimes only noticeable around the navel. Often, women notice it over their entire belly, chest, neck, face, and sometimes their hands. If massage oils and lotions don't seem to help, ask your care provider for a prescription to alleviate the itching. It is important not to scratch so hard that you bleed, as this could lead to infection.

Your growing uterus and the little baby inside are now putting a lot of pressure on the two main blood vessels that lead into and out of your heart. These vessels are called the vena cava and aorta. Pressure from your uterus and baby primarily occurs when you are lying flat on your back. Picture these two big vessels as two garden hoses placed side by side, water flowing full blast from and to your heart. Now, imagine placing a large rock on top of them: The water is unable to flow! This is similar to what happens to your blood when you lie flat on your back. Blood and oxygen are unable to flow to your brain, your body, your baby, and back to your heart. Even if you seem to tolerate this poor blood flow, your baby will not! A small pillow or towel roll placed under one hip will tilt you just enough to allow blood to flow freely.

Capillaries are the very tiny blood vessels that are close to the surface of your skin. As your pregnancy progresses, these capillaries have a tendency to leak water. When the capillaries leak water, the result is an increase in water retention, or edema. You will notice this as a puffiness or tightness in your hands and feet. Some edema is normal in pregnancy, but if this increases all over your body, particularly your legs, arms, lower back, and face, it could indicate a serious problem. *A rapid increase in swelling of your legs, arms, and face may also indicate a serious problem with your kidneys. If you notice a rapid change or a large weight gain within a few days, call your care provider immediately. See Chapters IV and XII on kidney disease and preeclampsia for more information.*

Following are suggestions to ease the discomforts of swelling:

- Drink plenty of fluids to stimulate your kidneys.
- Avoid tight fitting clothing, especially socks, hose, pant legs, and waistbands.
- Avoid standing or sitting in one place for long periods of time.
- Rest with your legs elevated on a chair or pillow.
- Lie down on your left side to increase kidney function.
- Increase your protein intake to pull the fluid back into your vessels.
- Exercise such as walking and swimming increases circulation and movement of water back into your vessels.
- Do *not* take diuretics for water retention in pregnancy.
- Again, drink plenty of fluids.

Your renal system—the system that is made up of your kidneys, ureters, bladder, and urethra—is changing. The kidneys produce more urine. Your bladder has decreased tone and the urethra, the tube from the bladder to the outside of your body, changes also. The same progesterone that has altered your other systems influences the urinary system to be less efficient. As a result, many pregnant women have a tendency to develop urinary tract infections. Urinary tract infections can become very serious and cause not only pain and discomfort, but also preterm labor. If untreated, a mild urinary tract infection can lead to a serious bladder or kidney infection that could require hospitalization and treatment with IV antibiotics.

Warning signs of urinary tract infection:
- increased frequency of urination (usually very small amounts of urine)
- pain or burning sensation with urination
- urgency or sense that you need to urinate all the time
- pain in the lower abdomen or back
- visible blood in the urine
- fever and chills
- rapid heart rate
- nausea and vomiting

Suggestions to decrease chances of urinary tract infections:
- Drink plenty of fluids.
- Lie on your left side to increase kidney efficiency and output.
- Wear cotton panties.
- Avoid tight fitting clothes.
- Keep the vaginal area clean: Always wipe from front to back after urinating or having a bowel movement.
- Avoid perfumed soaps and panty liners.

And the beat goes on

As you complete the second trimester your baby is at a milestone in development. The eyes are no longer fused shut as the fine details of optic nerve development, peripheral vision, and focus are present. Hearing is completely developed. The brain is functioning at a higher level as all of your baby's senses—sight, auditory, taste, touch, and smell are present. Your baby has his own schedule of sorts—moving while awake and being still while asleep. A very early sucking reflex is present, although the ability to suck and swallow will not be present until about thirty-four weeks. Your baby is practicing the motion of breathing in his lungs. Although he doesn't actually move air in and out, this motion moves fluid through the lungs, which will eventually prepare them for breathing outside the uterus.

The Third Trimester: Weeks Twenty-eight Through Forty

The third trimester marks the beginning of the end. Unfortunately, many high-risk pregnancies never make it through this trimester. However manifest healthy babies make it partly through the third trimester and deliver early.

Sleep patterns are significantly altered during pregnancy. There are two phases of sleep: rapid eye movement (REM) (the time when we dream), and non-rapid eye movement (NREM) (the period of sleep when healing and rest take place). During the next several weeks of your pregnancy, the periods of REM sleep will increase and NREM sleep will decrease. While your sleep phases are changing, your ability to stay asleep for long periods of time changes as well. You may awaken several times throughout the night and you may have wild dreams or nightmares that you can remember in detail. Dreams are more easily recalled when you awaken frequently. They are not premonitions and do not mean you are mentally unstable. They may only be manifestations of your own apprehensions and worries about labor, childbirth, your ability to parent, your relationship with your partner, or perceptions about yourself. Dreams are safe avenues for the subconscious to deal with our worries so that we are not overcome by them when we are awake.

Take time before going to bed to unwind. After a busy or stressful day, it is easy to want to plop in bed right away, but it may be more restful to take a warm bath first, stretch your legs, and write in a journal before you actually settle into sleep. Sleep with plenty of pillows—the more fluffed you are, the longer you'll stay comfortable. Talk to your partner about your concerns. You may be surprised to find that your partner shares the same worries and perhaps even the same types of dreams.

The relaxed ligaments of your spine and the pull of your uterus create a deeper curve in your lower back. Postural changes and edema can also effect the nerves in your arms, hands, and fingers. Carpal tunnel syndrome, a condition that can cause numbness in your hand or burning up your arm, is usually worse at night when your hands are more swollen. If this gets extremely bothersome, your care provider may have you wear a wrist brace at night.

Lower backaches are very common in pregnancy, especially if you have been on your feet for any length of time. When your uterus presses against the sciatic nerve, you will notice a sharp pain down your bottom and leg. Pressure on other nerves may create a tingling, pins-and-needles feeling in your hands and feet. Another reason for this may be due to hyperventilation which occurs when you breathe too fast and too deeply. Sometimes when you feel short of breath or anxious, you may want to overcompensate by breathing more. This over-breathing causes the tingling feeling.

During the third trimester the structures of your eyes will slightly change. Just as you develop some edema in your hands and feet, you also develop edema in the cornea of your eyes, which alters the ability of the eye to focus. Many women experience significant changes in their ability to see far or close, and this seems to be a bigger problem for women who already wear contact lenses or glasses. Contact lens wearers may have difficulty with tears and increased sensitivity to the contacts themselves. You may find that you're unable to wear your contacts at all. Additionally, corneal edema causes sensitivity to light, dust, and wind.

Accumulating estrogen levels contribute to a chronic stuffy nose and feeling of fullness in the Eustachian tubes deep within your ear. Fluid can accumulate, increasing the pressure in the middle ear, making you feel slightly off balance with the sensation that your ears are plugged up, and you may have a slight temporary hearing loss. Mild edema can also occur around your vocal cords causing a hoarseness in your voice and a dry cough.

Around weeks twenty-eight to thirty, your baby develops "brown fat." This fat is essential for maintaining body temperature without shivering. Weighing over 3 pounds, your baby is making purposeful movements rather than the uncontrolled movements made in the past weeks. This movement builds muscle tone, first in the legs followed by the arms. Even with all of these changes, by thirty-two weeks this baby is still 80 percent water! The water is continually transferring between baby, amniotic fluid, and placenta. The baby urinates about a teaspoon of urine every hour, making up the majority of the amniotic fluid.

Weeks thirty-three to thirty-eight

Your body now allows you to generate 35 percent more heat due to an increase in your metabolic rate. Your tolerance for heat is decreasing, and your tolerance for cool temperatures is increasing. This increased metabolic rate may make you want to eat constantly, especially if you are eating small meals. You may feel that you are perspiring significantly more because your sweat glands have also increased their activity. Your total blood volume is now at its highest point.

Provided that you don't develop pregnancy-induced hypertension or preeclampsia, this blood level will remain constant throughout the rest of your pregnancy. If you stand too quickly or lie flat on your back, you may become dizzy or nauseated because all the blood has pooled in your legs and it doesn't get to your brain very quickly. Control your movements and keep them slow to avoid rapid drops in your blood pressure. Remember to rest with a towel roll under one hip so that you are tilted.

This high blood volume plus high estrogen level can create many surface blood vessels. You may notice small red blood vessels resembling little spiders on your neck, shoulders, and upper chest. These will fade away about four to six weeks after delivery. Your skin temperature is also higher from the increased blood flow to your skin. The bluish veins in your breasts are more pronounced and your breasts are larger and may be slightly tender as they were at the beginning of your pregnancy. The increased pressure in your pelvic area is compounding the congested vessels in your vagina and rectum. Varicose veins may appear on your labia, and new hemorrhoids may appear around your anus.

By week thirty-six, your uterus begins to get more irritable than it has been in the past as the levels of circulating oxytocin, the hormone that causes contractions, increases. Your body has a built in counter enzyme called oxytocinase which balances with oxytocin to keep you from going into labor. Oxytocinase is beginning to decrease. Your placenta is beginning to age causing a decrease in progesterone (remember that progesterone has kept you from contracting). You may experience painless irregular contractions known as Braxton-Hicks contractions. As long as your contractions are irregular in length, strength, and timing they can be false labor pains. These pains, usually at the top of your uterus and along the sides, will often stop after a couple of hours or if you change what you are doing. Lie down, drink a glass of water, take a bath, or just rest. They will often start at the same time each day, often late in the afternoon or early evening.

True labor usually starts with regular contractions that are far apart and gradually get closer together, stronger, and last longer. They will not go away with a change of activity or by drinking fluids. The pain begins in the lower back and comes around to the lower front of your belly just above the pubic bone. They are regular and rhythmic, with a definite beginning and end. Most important, true labor creates a thinning (effacement) or opening (dilation) in your cervix. When you are in labor, your care provider will describe your cervical exam in terms of dilation, effacement, and station.

Dilation refers to the amount your cervix has opened. It is measured in centimeters from closed, or 0 centimeters, to completely dilated, meaning the cervix is no longer present and has opened completely. This is usually about 10 centimeters.

Effacement is the shortening or thinning of your cervix. The cervix is the bottom necklike portion of your uterus. Effacement is measured in percentages from 0 to 100 percent and generally occurs to some degree before dilation. First-time mothers almost always efface 90 to 100 percent before dilation occurs.

Station refers to the descent of the baby in relation to bony landmarks in your pelvis, which can be felt by the examiner. When the baby's head is above the bony landmarks, the baby is said to be at -3, -2, or -1 station. As the baby's head moves past the landmarks, the baby is at +1, +2, or +3 station. When your baby moves into these "plus" stations, you will feel an incredible amount of pressure. At the +4 station, your baby's head is bulging out of your vagina, which means you will soon meet this little one.

By thirty-seven weeks, estrogen levels increase and progesterone levels decrease. The common discomforts you have gotten used to are now a little worse. Your nasal congestion and runny nose will increase. You may notice a little more swelling in your hands and feet. Leg cramps become more frequent. Contractions may become stronger as your body tries to find that rhythm of a regular pattern. If you have had to take medication for preterm labor, your care provider will have you stop. The collagen that has kept your cervix tightly shut is breaking down and now softening, or ripening, your cervix.

The finishing touches on the baby

Your baby makes tremendous strides in growth and development between thirty-three and thirty-eight weeks. During these last few weeks, fat is building beneath the skin, and your baby will continue to get a little chubby from now until birth. Her skin is less red and more pink-tinged in color. The immune system is functional and has the ability to fight off many infections. She swallows one-and-a-half to two cups of amniotic fluid per day. When she practices breathing movements and swallows at the same time she will get the hiccups. This is the quick rhythmic jerks you feel for brief periods of time. She produces over three teaspoons of urine per hour. She will gain about one half pound per week during these final weeks. So, if she weighs 4 pounds at thirty-three weeks, she will weigh around 7 pounds at forty weeks.

The baby will settle in your pelvis in the position which he plans to be born, a term called lightening. Most babies will settle into the pelvis with their head down. Occasionally, a baby will settle with the buttocks, foot, or another part of the body in the pelvis. If the buttocks or feet are in the pelvis, the baby is considered to be in the breech presentation. If the head is not in the pelvis it can alter your ability to have a vaginal delivery. If your baby is in the breech presentation, your care provider may have you practice an exercise to try and encourage the baby to turn. This involves getting on your hands and knees, then resting your head on a pillow with your bottom high for fifteen minutes, three times a day. If the baby does not turn, your care provider may then try and turn the baby, a procedure called an external version.

Although very crowded, the baby continues to move, swallow amniotic fluid, and practice breathing movements. The lungs are almost ready for the outside world as they are developing the necessary substance for breathing known as surfactant which keeps the lungs inflated after your baby takes his first breath. If you have been treated in anticipation of an early birth, your care provider may give you medication to speed up the production of surfactant.

By thirty-eight weeks, the lungs are mature, and every organ is developed and ready to function outside the uterus. The baby is sloughing off the flaky skin that contains the oily properties of the cernix caseosa. These skin flakes are just floating around in the amniotic fluid. Your baby wants to help you get into labor as her adrenal glands are also secreting estrogen into the amniotic fluid through the placenta to start the process of labor from inside the amniotic sac.

Labor

Your uterus has a peak blood flow of about one-half liter flowing through it every minute. Your body is now prepared to safely undergo the physical trauma of birth. The increased blood volume and clotting abilities protect you from losing too much blood, and the increased blood flow allows both you and your baby to get the necessary amount of oxygen during contractions. The muscle cells in your uterus have increased in size and number, and every muscle fiber is enhanced so that muscle contractions can occur more consistently.

You may lose the plug of mucus that has tightly sealed the inside of your uterus from the vagina. This mucous plug looks like a big glob of slime and is usually brownish in color. Most women notice it on toilet paper or in their panties. This does not necessarily mean you will begin labor immediately, it is just one of the stepping stones. When labor is about to begin, women will often notice a small amount of bright red bleeding, much less than the bleeding with a period but certainly noticeable and it may require a panty liner.

About 15 percent of women will start the labor process with their water breaking. This is the amniotic sac leaking fluid. When this occurs you may notice either a large gush of fluid or a small trickle of fluid. Sometimes the only thing a woman notices is that her panties are wet. Amniotic fluid should not have a foul odor and should be clear. If your water breaks, it may catch you a little off guard. Notice what color the fluid is and if it has an odor. Call your care provider immediately, describe the amount of fluid and its characteristics. Your care provider may have you come to the hospital at this point.

Pay close attention to the activity of your baby. His movements may be a little different in the confined uterus, but they should still be present. If they seem to be decreased, or if you don't recall feeling the baby move, eat and drink something, lie down on your side, and begin counting movements for an hour. You may stop at ten movements. If the baby does not move ten times during that hour, call your care provider.

Amniotic fluid that has a foul odor or is yellow or green indicates infection or the presence of meconium. Remember that meconium is "little baby poop." If babies get stressed, they will have a bowel movement. This will require close evaluation of the baby during labor and thorough attention to protecting the baby from breathing the amniotic fluid into the lungs during the birth. The care providers for you and your baby will suction the baby's mouth, nose, and throat before stimulating the baby to cry.

Contractions will begin slowly with the hardening or balling up of your uterus. You can feel the strength of the contraction by placing your hand on the top of your belly. The pain will come from the back, down around to the front of your belly, and just above the pubic bone.

If your water does not break, but your contractions begin, perhaps every twenty minutes, then increase to every fifteen minutes for a couple of hours, then every ten minutes for the next hour, it may be a good idea to call your care provider and describe what's happening. At this point, if it is during office hours, your care provider may have you come in to check your cervix for dilation. If contractions begin after office hours, you may be asked to go to the hospital and have the nurses check your cervix. The nurses will also check your blood pressure, pulse, respirations, and temperature. They will have you lie down so that they can evaluate the baby's heart rate and your contractions with a fetal monitor which gives a constant reading of the baby's heart rate. It traces the heart rate onto a strip of paper. The people caring for you in the hospital will evaluate the readout of the baby's heart rate pattern as these patterns can provide some indication of how the baby is doing at a given point. The fetal monitor cannot tell everything, but it can tell how your baby is tolerating labor, whether or not the placenta is working well, and if the umbilical cord is getting pressed. If there has been no change in your cervix, they will probably have you walk around for a couple of hours and then recheck your cervix. If there still has been no change, they may even send you home for a while. Don't get discouraged if this happens. Many women make several trips to the hospital before the real thing. Sometimes the excitement of going into the hospital stops the contractions and sometimes getting to the hospital and rehydrating with fluids will also stop contractions. Labor is an "all or nothing" game. All the pieces need to be in place before it will actually happen.

A few words about inducing labor

The process of inducing labor involves stimulating the cervix to soften and dilate and the uterus to contract. Many high-risk pregnancies must be induced for the safety of the mother or baby, and many women ask to have their labor induced around thirty-eight weeks primarily because they are too big, too tired, and too stressed about waiting for something to happen. This is *not* an acceptable reason for induction. Medical reasons, such as high blood pressure or diabetes, or if you are past your due date, are reasons for induction of labor.

If your cervix is not soft and starting to thin out and open, a prostaglandin preparation may be applied directly on your cervix, or a small tablet may be placed at the very back of your vagina. These will initiate the breakdown of the collagen that is keeping your cervix tightly closed. You will need to have an intravenous catheter, better known as an IV, in your hand or forearm. When your cervix is soft, thinning, and starting to open, an IV preparation containing the hormone oxytocin (Pitocin is the trade name) will be started. As the levels of oxytocin rise, your contractions will begin. Your nurse will continue to increase the amount of oxytocin infusing until your contractions are strong, two to three minutes apart, and lasting about sixty seconds. This combination will help dilate your cervix. Patience, perseverance, and pleasant thoughts will be a blessing right now.

Labor is divided into three stages. The first stage begins with the onset of contractions and the dilation of your cervix and ends with complete cervical dilation. This stage is further broken down into three phases: early, active, and transition. In early labor, your contractions are regular but still quite far apart. Cervical dilation in early labor is from 0 to 4 centimeters. During the active phase of labor, your cervix will dilate from 4 to 8 centimeters. Transition is the shortest phase of labor, beginning when your cervix is about 8 centimeters. It usually takes less than two hours for complete dilation to occur once you have reached this point. The second stage of labor is the pushing stage through to the birth of your baby. The third stage of labor is the delivery of the placenta.

In early labor, you probably won't *need* to breathe through your contractions in a focused way. However, you may want to try some relaxation breathing techniques before the pain becomes too strong. Begin and end every contraction with a deep, cleansing breath. When you breathe during a contraction, try using your belly muscles. Practice by putting your hand on your belly and letting it rise and fall with your breaths. This forces the muscles that instinctively tense with a contraction to relax. Some women find this method of breathing helpful throughout their entire labor. You may want to establish a visualization meditation during your contractions.

Visualization/relaxation technique

- Begin with a deep cleansing breath.
- Close your eyes.
- Relax every part of your body: head and neck, shoulders, arms, hands, fingers, chest, back, belly, hips, bottom, legs, feet, toes.
- Picture a place in your mind where you feel warm and safe (this may be in your home, a place where you went as a little girl, or a warm sandy beach on an island with the breeze blowing and the rhythmic sound of the water in the background). Formulate the details in your mind, so that when a contraction gets closer, you can call on this image and have all the details in place.
- Slowly breathe with your contraction.
- When the contraction ends, take a deep cleansing breath and return to reality.
- Open your eyes.

As your labor progresses and your cervix opens, you may find your contractions are stronger and longer lasting. They may also occur more frequently. You may notice that the bloody mucous plug from your cervix and your membranes eventually break. Focused breathing will make a tremendous difference in your ability to deal with contractions. If you feel that you would like medication or an epidural, be sure to communicate your wishes to your nurses and care providers. It is everyone's goal to help you get through this labor, and medication use or an epidural may actually help your labor. Listen to your body, and it will tell you what it needs in the way of breathing, pain relief, and rest.

The pressure of the contraction inside the uterus increases 100 percent during the active phase of labor. When you are sitting up, rocking, walking, squatting, or kneeling, your abdominal wall relaxes and allows the top of your uterus to fall forward. This directs the baby's head toward your cervix, increasing pressure, allowing it to stretch, and reducing the length of labor. Lying on your side is a good position when laboring as your heart is more efficient, your uterus gets more blood flow to it, and your baby gets more oxygen. Positions that reduce the length of labor but allow the contractions to be most efficient are best for the baby.

Transition is the last phase of labor before you begin to push out your baby. The uterus is working extremely hard, and it is very difficult to relax. You may feel nauseated, cold, trembly, restless, discouraged, and scared. You will notice an increase in bleeding from your vagina and an almost unbearable pressure in your rectum. You may find that you want to stop breathing during your contraction and grunt or bear down as with a bowel movement. Let your nurse know what you are feeling. Try to stay focused with your contractions; keep breathing. Only think of one contraction at a time; each contraction is one less than you will ever feel again. If you feel the urge to bear down and push, try blowing quick breaths as if you are blowing out a candle.

When your cervix is completely dilated or your premature baby is squeezing out of your cervix, your care provider will tell you to go ahead and push. Rest between the contractions, but when the contraction begins, take a couple of deep, cleansing breaths. Keep your face relaxed and your eyes open during pushing. All energy should be focused on your bottom. A wrinkled up face, eyes squeezed tightly shut, a mouth losing air through screams all take precious energy that need to be used to push out your baby. Premature babies are under much stress at this point so it isn't a good idea to prolong the pushing phase. If you need to cry or scream, it will be better for both you and your baby to cry or scream between contractions. As the contraction grows in strength, take a breath and hold it. Now, while holding your breath, bear down straight into your bottom with all of your might. Hold that push long and strong. It may be helpful to count to ten in your head if possible. Quickly grab more air, hold it, and bear down again, long and strong. Try to repeat this one more time during your contraction. Now let this contraction go, letting your whole body sink into the bed. Take a deep cleansing breath. You may want to have an ice chip and rest, even sleep, between contractions. As your baby's head is crowning, bulging on your perineum, you may want to reach down and touch your baby's head for the first time. If a mirror is available, it may be motivational for you to see your baby's head and even watch it move as you push.

If the skin and muscle around your vaginal opening does not stretch enough to allow the baby's head to come out, your care provider may make the opening larger by cutting an episiotomy. This small incision and any tears that occur are repaired with stitches after the birth of your baby, and they generally heal quickly.

After the baby's head is out, your care provider will tell you not to push while the baby's mouth and nose are being cleaned out. This is done to prevent your baby from breathing in anything left in his mouth when he takes his first breath. When you push again, you will give one final push. *Open your eyes and see your baby enter this world.* The baby will be quickly dried off and handed to the specialized nursery staff who will take care of this precious miracle. If both of you are stable, you may be able to hold your baby right away. Many babies of high-risk mothers need to be in the neonatal intensive care nursery. You will be unable to accompany your baby to the intensive care nursery immediately after delivery, therefore you may want your partner or another family member to stay by your baby's side and ask questions.

The remainder of your recovery and postpartum period will be similar to that of a mother who gave birth to a full-term infant. The biggest difference is being separated from your newborn.

A few thoughts on cesarean birth

For many high-risk mothers, surgical delivery is necessary. This is most commonly referred to as a cesarean section (C-section) delivery, and the baby is delivered through an incision made in the lower part of your abdomen and uterus. This, of course, is done under anesthesia so that you do not feel any pain, only the pressure of the doctors removing the baby.

If a cesarean birth was necessary, your recovery will be a little different from a mother who gave birth vaginally.

- You may have a catheter in your bladder for several hours after surgery.
- You will be encouraged to change positions frequently, take deep breaths, and cough to help keep your lungs clear of fluid. The nurses will show you how to position a pillow over your incision for support and to decrease discomfort. This is so important because high-risk moms who require surgical delivery are generally at very high risk for developing fluid in their lungs.
- You must not begin to eat until you are passing gas. This is a sign that the bowels are working. Eating too soon can be harmful and extremely painful. Walking around will help get the gas moving.

Do not let this surgery keep you from mothering your baby. If your baby is in the intensive care nursery, have instant snapshots taped to your bed. Talk with nursery personnel frequently for updates on your baby's condition. If you are stable, you should be able to visit the nursery very soon. You may need some extra help, but plan to hold, feed, and care for your baby.

Postpartum: The First Few Days

After labor, your heart is still functioning at a higher level even though you lost blood, but if you recall, your blood volume had been increasing in preparation. Your uterus is much smaller and should remain firm. The first day the uterus will rise above your navel, and every day after that it decreases in size. By the end of this week it will be almost half way between your navel and pubic bone. When you breast-feed, oxytocin is released into your system. This will stimulate your uterus to remain firm through contractions and return to its prepregnancy size. Your chest wall, which had expanded for the growing baby, returns to normal allowing you to breathe deeper. By the end of the week your breathing will be as though you were never pregnant. The sodium and water retention that had caused swelling in your hands and feet will be reversed and is most obvious on days two and five after delivery. If the bladder was traumatized by the baby's head or by forceps during delivery, you may experience a temporary loss of feeling in the bladder. Your digestive system and immune system slowly return to normal, and your white blood cell count drops within a week. Whether you are breast-feeding or bottle feeding, the hormone prolactin is being released causing the production of milk in your breasts. The injured tissues in your vaginal and perineal area will be swollen and bruised at the start of the week, but new tissue growth and healing of the area will be present by the end of the week.

Your baby is adapting to life outside of you. Her heart is functioning in a more effective way as she is now using her own lungs to transport oxygen to her blood. Her nervous system and senses are working; she can see, hear, smell, taste, and feel pain. She has reflexes of rooting (turning the mouth toward touch on the cheek), sucking, startling from loud sounds or movements, and grasping with her fingers. The eyelids may be slightly swollen. The kidneys are functioning, but for the first few days after delivery, the baby will not have many wet diapers. The frequency of wet diapers increases by the end of the week. The digestive system is working and the first bowel movement will be the sticky, dark, tarlike stool called meconium. Stools after this will change to a greenish brown. Within a few days, your breast-fed baby will have very loose yellow "seedy" stools after your milk has come in, and you may notice this seedy bowel movement with every diaper change. This is normal. Breast-fed babies will have at least two to four stools a day. The formula-fed baby will have stools less frequently, and the stools will be more yellow-brown in color and more compact. Your baby's umbilical cord will initially have a clamp on it immediately after delivery. The clamp will be removed the next day. Over the next few weeks the cord will dry up and fall off, leaving a tiny little belly button.

Most moms expect to feel considerably good during this first week after delivery. They are often surprised when some part of their body feels lousy all the time. Worse yet, several parts of your body may hurt *all* at the same time. It's hard to glow with happiness over your new baby when you hurt. Here's what to expect during this first week after delivery.

Days 1–2:

- If you are Rh negative and your baby is positive, you will receive a Rhogam shot before you leave the hospital.
- Your uterus will cramp intermittently. When you breast-feed

your baby, you will notice the cramping in your uterus is much stronger. This cramping is known as afterpains and it plays a crucial role in keeping you from bleeding too much, and it will help your uterus return to its prepregnancy size.

- Blood flow from the vagina after delivery is called lochia. In the first twenty-four hours it will seem much heavier than a menstrual period. The blood will be bright red, and you may pass some small clots. In the days that follow, the bleeding will taper to that of a normal period, and the blood will be more of a pinkish brown by the end of the week.
- When the sodium and water shifts in your body, you will begin to urinate large amounts. A decrease in bladder sensation will increase this amount even more. Some women with decreased bladder sensation will urinate without control, oftentimes when they stand or lift heavy objects. This is called urinary incontinence. This will usually go away as your bladder sensation returns over the next few weeks. It is not uncommon for the postpartum mom to urinate as much as a half to full liter of urine every time this first week.
- If you had epidural anesthesia for vaginal or cesarean delivery, you may experience itching in the first couple of days.
- You will experience many awakenings at night, especially during the first week. These are usually caused by a variety of things, including going to the bathroom, feeding the baby, and pains and discomforts.
- The discomforts you experience may include headaches; breast and nipple tenderness; afterpains; incision pain from surgery; vaginal pain from episiotomy, tearing, or swelling; and painful hemorrhoids. You should *not* have painful or warm reddened areas on your legs.

Days 3–7:

- Bowel function slowly returns, but you should be able to have a bowel movement around day three or four. This first week you will probably lose about 12 pounds. The rest of the weight will slowly come off over the next six to twelve weeks.
- The congestion of pregnancy is usually gone by the end of the first week.
- The fluid changes often contribute to a postpartum headache that usually goes away by the end of the week.
- All of the hormonal changes in addition to being tired and experiencing birth (whether or not it went the way you had planned it), contribute to depression during the first two weeks after delivery. This is often referred to the baby blues or postpartum depression. It usually goes away after the first two weeks. It is *not* normal for this to continue for a prolonged period of time making you unable to care for yourself and your baby.

Your baby will develop sleep pattern changes, as well. She may sleep a lot during the day and then be awake at night. She may want to eat every two hours and then go a stretch of four or five hours. If you are breast-feeding, expect her to eat at least eight to twelve times in a twenty-four hour period. If she is formula fed, she will eat 1 to 4 ounces every two to five hours.

Here are some ideas for the different aches and pains you have this first week:

Afterpains/cramping

Try lying on your stomach with a heating pad and pillow under your abdomen while you rest. Keep your bladder empty. An over-the-counter pain medication such as acetaminophen or ibuprofen taken thirty to sixty minutes before you breast-feed may help.

Headaches

Drink plenty of fluids. Rest must be a priority. Acetaminophen or ibuprofen may also help. If you have a headache that gets progressively worse and does not get better with either of these medications, call your care provider.

Perineal pain from episiotomy, tears, swelling, and hemorrhoids

Ice packs applied directly on your perineum will help decrease the swelling. Alternating cold packs with warm baths will also help. You can create a sitz bath by rolling up two bath towels and setting them side by side on the tub floor. As you sit down, squeeze your bottom cheeks together to avoid pulling on your stitches. Sit with the towels under each side of your bottom so that the tender vaginal area doesn't get all the pressure. Let the hot water in the tub swirl around your sore bottom. Wash your perineum with a squirt bottle from front to back every time you urinate and pat it dry. When you wipe after urinating or having a bowel movement, always wipe from front to back to prevent germs from your rectum getting to your episiotomy, vagina, or urinary tract. There are sprays, creams, and witch hazel pads that can ease perineal and hemorrhoid discomfort. If perineal pain persists, increasing as the week progresses, notify your care provider.

Constipation

The slowing of your digestive system through labor and delivery, medications, a decrease in food, and fear of the pain from straining to have a bowel movement all contribute to constipation.

Stool softeners may help, but *avoid laxatives*. Increasing your intake of fruits and vegetables, eating bran cereals, drinking eight to twelve glasses of water and fruit juices, and getting out of bed and taking short walks will all get your bowels in working order.

Postpartum depression/baby blues

Seventy-five percent of women experience some type of mood swings after delivery. Remember that it is normal to be emotional. Your life is changing; you hurt in places you didn't know exist; and being a mom is hard, tiring work despite the blessings. Talk to your partner, friends, and care provider about all the things you are feeling. These often range from happiness to sadness, to anger, to anxiety and fear. It is made worse by not getting enough rest. Give yourself time to heal physically as well as emotionally as your role in life changes from being a pregnant woman to being a mother. You have been mothering this baby already for a long time. Now you are able to mother more completely. Seek professional help immediately if you feel that you want to hurt yourself or your baby or if you are unable to care for yourself or your baby.

Congratulations on your accomplishment. Through your willingness to mother your baby while she was still inside, you have achieved success. Continue to listen to your instincts and be in touch with changes in your body as well as changes in your baby. Good luck!

PART TWO

Medical Conditions That Impact Pregnancy

III

Heart Disease

Overview

$\mathbf{A}$s we begin this discussion of heart disease and pregnancy, it is important to begin with some basic but essential information. Even if you don't have a particular heart problem, you may want to read this entire section as it will help to make the topics at the end of the chapter more understandable.

Heart structure and function

The heart is a hollow organ made up of muscle walls, nerve fibers, valves, and blood vessels (both arteries and veins). It is about the size of your fist and lies just left of your sternum, or breastbone, behind your ribs and left breast.

Several thousand cardiac muscle fibers lie side-by-side, making up the strong muscular walls of the heart, or myocardium. When you think of individual muscle fibers, think of a rubber band. As a rubber band is stretched, its natural response is to snap back to its original, relaxed state. Thus, the further it is stretched, the harder or stronger it will snap back. It takes more force to stretch the band to its maximum length. Myocardial fibers are much like this: The greater the fill of the chambers of the heart, the greater is the subsequent snap back, or contraction, of the heart. This protective mechanism saves a person's life in times of great stress, keeping blood and oxygen flowing to the vital systems when needed.

Embedded in these muscle walls are nerve fibers. These nerve fibers are responsible for carrying the impulses to and through the myocardium and stimulating it to contract in a wonderfully coordinated manner. As these impulses are fired, nerve fibers transmit them along nerve branches or paths, and then, in a wavelike or ripple effect, the impulse is transmitted from one cell to the next simply by being in contact with another receptive muscle cell. The result is a rhythmic stimulation of the entire heart muscle, allowing for a rhythmic pumping action of blood through the heart and lungs.

Four separate chambers lie within the heart: the right atrium, the right ventricle, the left atrium, and the left ventricle. The right and left sides of the heart are divided by the septum, which extends from the base to the apex. In the normal adult heart, the septum should be intact, without openings or blood flow between the right and left sides of the heart. This design allows for a double pumplike mechanism of the heart. The right side of the heart pumps blood to the lungs and helps maintain a pressure that continues to move blood from the lungs back into the left side of the heart. The left side of the heart then pumps blood out the rest of your body and sustains a pressure that eventually moves the same blood back into the right side of the heart to start the process all over again.

Additionally, there are four valves in the structure of the heart. The purpose of the valves, much like that of garden hoses, is to ensure a one-directional flow of fluid, in this case the blood. The valves of the heart help to minimize turbulence and backflow of blood, especially during a time of increased pressure in the chambers or blood vessels of the heart.

Between the right atrium and right ventricle lies the tricuspid valve. Its job is to prevent blood from flowing back into the right atrium, particularly during the time of right ventricular contraction.

The next valve, moving from right to left, is the pulmonic valve which is located in the pulmonary artery. Leaving the right ventricle, this large blood vessel is responsible for carrying blood from the right side of the heart into the lungs. This valve keeps blood moving through the blood vessels of the lungs, preventing a backflow into the right side of the heart. In the lungs, individual red blood cells drop off their waste product of carbon dioxide and pick up fresh oxygen. Pressure from the right side continues to push blood on into the left side of the heart, specifically the left atrium. From here, blood is squeezed into the left ventricle.

Between the left atrium and left ventricle lies the mitral valve. This important valve has a big job. It is responsible for preventing backflow of blood from the left ventricle into the left atrium, and potentially back into the lungs. It is a difficult job, because the intense pumping action of the left ventricle is essential in maintaining blood flow toward all other parts of the body.

As blood leaves the left ventricle it passes into the aorta through one more valve, the aortic valve. The aorta is a very large blood vessel which carries freshly oxygenated blood from the left ventricle into the general circulation. This important valve keeps blood flowing away from the heart, preventing a backup of blood and a subsequent increase in pressure in the left ventricle.

The heart cannot do its work without the blood vessels to transport the blood around, and the blood vessels cannot do their job without the heart to pump blood through the miles and miles of blood vessels. Blood vessels in the body are much like branches of a tree. Both arteries and veins start off big in diameter, much like a tree trunk, and then become progressively smaller as they move toward the tissues of the body for which they're responsible. A simple way to remember the difference between the two types of blood vessels is that "arteries" are those blood vessels which carry blood away from the heart, and "veins" are those blood vessels which carry blood toward the heart. Arteries have a greater capacity for dilating (becoming larger), resulting in a decrease in blood pressure, or for constricting (becoming smaller), causing an increase in blood pressure.

Systolic blood pressure (the top number in a blood pressure reading) is a measure of the pressure exerted against the walls of the arteries when the heart is contracting. Diastolic blood pressure (the bottom number of a reading) measures the pressure exerted on the walls of the arteries when the heart is at rest. Arteries have an incredible ability—in response to hormones, chemicals, or nerve impulses—to dilate and constrict, constantly adjusting our blood pressure to meet the immediate needs of the body. If we're exercising, our heart rate goes up, and our arteries dilate near the parts of the body doing the work while others may constrict to maintain an adequate blood pressure. At rest, our blood pressure is stable and consistent. But even standing up from the couch and walking to the kitchen causes our blood vessels and heart rate to adjust to accommodate the change of position; otherwise we would pass out every time we stood up.

Another essential characteristic of blood vessels is their ability to keep blood cells and plasma proteins inside the vessel walls; yet allow other fluids and particles to flow easily back and forth across the vessel walls. This is an important concept to remember as I discuss heart problems in this chapter and high blood pressure problems in the following chapter.

Imagine a closed system, responsible for transporting fluid and gases to several locations and needing to bring back the "garbage" so that it doesn't pile up in the outlying areas. Required is a strong pump and a branching hose network that reaches every destination on the route, but one that can maintain enough pressure to get the fluid and garbage back to the refueling station. So now, let's trace some fluid and its cargo through this closed system.

Table 2. The Path of a Blood Cell

<u>unoxygenated blood</u> → into veins → into superior/inferior vena cava → into right atrium → through tricuspid valve → into right ventricle through pulmonic valve → into pulmonary artery → into small capillaries of lungs
*carbon dioxide is exchanged for oxygen here

<u>freshly oxygenated blood</u> → into left atrium → through mitral valve into left ventricle → through aortic valve → into aorta → into arteries into small capillaries of the body's tissues
*oxygen and carbon dioxide are exchanged here

<u>unoxygenated blood</u> → into veins → and we begin again

Normal Changes of Pregnancy

Pregnant women have an increased amount of circulating blood, and their blood vessels are dilated and relaxed. These normal changes bring about hemodynamic changes. Hemodynamics refers to blood volume and the changing resistance of the blood vessels and heart structures. Carrying a baby from conception to term puts significant stresses and strains on the cardiovascular system. The cardiovascular system has the ability to adapt to pregnancy demands by increasing its volume and decreasing its resistance. This achieves a healthy outcome for you and your baby.

Circulating hormones of pregnancy—estrogen, progesterone, and prostaglandins—are responsible for many of the necessary changes. Primarily, these hormones help to dilate most of the maternal blood vessels, allowing for adequate distribution of oxygen and nutrients via the cardiovascular system. The uterus, placenta, and subsequently, your baby are in many ways responsible for and benefit from this vasodilatation, promoting good blood flow to and carrying waste products away from your baby. Additionally, the balance of hormones in pregnancy encourages a nearly constant state of relaxation of the uterus itself. A soft, noncontracting uterus allows for the consistent flow of blood through the uterine blood vessels and to the placenta which supports your baby.

The following is a list of changes in the cardiovascular system that occur with normal pregnancy. As you browse through this list, think about the "normals" discussed earlier, and then think about how a heart problem might impact some of the adaptive changes necessary for a successful pregnancy:

- increase in total blood volume
- increased risk for developing a blood clot
- increase in the amount of blood pushed out of the left ventricle in one minute (cardiac output) and increase in heart rate by fifteen to twenty beats per minute; overall, the heart requires 20 to 30 percent more oxygen to do this increased work
- decrease in blood pressure begins to fall early in first trimester, often reaching the lowest point at the midpoint of pregnancy, gradually returning to nonpregnant levels by the due date

During labor, many factors may influence the cardiovascular system and its response. Anxiety, pain, and regular, strong contractions will affect cardiovascular function. With every contraction, 300 to 500 milliliters of blood (1 to 2 pints) is expelled from the uterus into the general circulation.

As discussed in the chapter on normal pregnancy, your body's position has a significant influence on blood flow to your vital organs as well as to your baby. Lying flat on your back allows the weight of your uterus to compress your aorta (which is carrying oxygenated blood to you and your baby) as well as the inferior vena cava (which is bringing blood back to the heart for reoxygenation and recirculation). In many pregnant women, this often results in a decreased heart rate and blood pressure. You will be able to tell when this is happening because you may become lightheaded, sweaty, nauseated, dizzy, and weak. Simply repositioning to the left or right side restores blood flow through these large blood vessels and corrects the problem. This phenomenon is called supine hypotensive syndrome of pregnancy—a long word for a fixable condition.

Anesthesia during labor can alter some of the normal, protective physiologic responses to labor and delivery, such as increased heart rate, increased blood pressure, and increased cardiac output. Epidural anesthesia seems to minimize some of these significant changes.

The postpartum period is a time of great hemodynamic shifts, due to blood loss at delivery, the stress of delivery itself, and the large shift of blood back into your general circulation. This can be a time of potential instability as the body works at restoring its balance. During a vaginal delivery, blood loss averages 500 milliliters (about 2 pints) compared with a cesarean section which averages about 1,000 milliliters. Just after delivery, the cardiac output increases by 60 to 80 percent, lasting maybe ten minutes, then stabilizes to prelabor levels over the next several hours. It takes two to four weeks for the cardiac output to return to prepregnant levels. Overall, the cardiovascular changes that occur with pregnancy return to the nonpregnant state in about six to eight weeks.

Specific Heart Problems

The incidence of heart disease in pregnant women is 0.5 to 2 percent, but this is steadily increasing for several reasons. Women with significant heart disease, who in the past may have been counseled against or encouraged to terminate a pregnancy, are now able to sustain a pregnancy due to an increased knowledge base and improved technical capabilities in the medical community. Children born twenty and thirty years ago with complicated heart disease (who might have died as infants as recently as forty years ago) are now choosing to become mothers themselves. Further, women who wait until their thirties and forties to begin having children have an increased risk for heart disease related to their age.

Causes of heart disease in pregnant women vary. Many people have heart disease from an acquired condition, or something occurring after birth. This is most often as a result of rheumatic fever and subsequent heart valve damage caused by group-A streptococcal infection. Coronary artery disease can result in a type of heart disease referred to as ischemic, meaning without blood flow or circulation to a part of the heart structure. An example of ischemic heart disease is a myocardial infarction, which is the death of part of the heart muscle due to obstruction of blood flow.

The most common reason for heart disease is a congenital cause, meaning it was a condition or problem present at birth. Congenital problems include atrial septal defects (ASD), ventricular septal defects (VSD), patent ductus arteriosus (PDA), Eisenmenger's syndrome, and tetralogy of Fallot. There are several conditions that fall into an "other" category for heart disease.

These include peripartum cardiomyopathy and Marfan's syndrome.

The following New York Heart Association (NYHA) list of guidelines are currently utilized extensively to help determine how a woman might tolerate the stresses associated with pregnancy.

Class I

Uncompromised. No limitation of physical activity. No signs or symptoms of heart disease even with activity.

Class II

Slightly compromised. Slight limitation of activity. No signs or symptoms of heart disease at rest, but becomes symptomatic with heavy or strenuous physical activity.

Class III

Markedly compromised. Considerable limitation of physical activity. No signs or symptoms of heart disease at rest, but becomes easily symptomatic with minimal physical activity.

Class IV

Severely compromised. Severe limitation of activity. Significant signs and symptoms of heart disease with any physical activity, sometimes even at bedrest.

Women with Class I and II classifications have a good prognosis for pregnancy. However, pregnant women classified with Class III and IV heart disease have a 30 to 50 percent risk of significant morbidity, meaning a worsening of their heart disease, and a 25 to 50 percent risk of death. In addition, women with Class III or IV disease have a 20 to 30 percent risk of fetal death. The more severe the symptoms are for the mother, the greater the risk for a poor fetal outcome. I know these statistics are scary, but that's why you're reading this part of the book, so you have the knowledge up front to make smart and informed decisions about your health and your current or future pregnancy.

Okay, let's continue and we will discuss each of these heart conditions individually, including what this means for your pregnancy, your baby, and things you might anticipate if this is *your* heart problem. Remember to refer back to the discussion of *normal* cardiac function and blood flow, as well as normal *changes* of pregnancy to help you understand how each specific heart condition might cause problems. Please take the time to read about all of the following heart disorders, as many of them are interrelated or share common symptoms, treatments, and outcomes.

Valve Problems

The following problems primarily involve valvular disorders or stenosis, which is a "stiffening" of an opening. A stenosis limits the amount of blood that can pass through the valve. The degree of obstruction determines the severity of the problem.

Mitral stenosis

Remember, the mitral valve sits between the left atrium and the left ventricle. Stenosis here results in a backup of blood and an increase in pressure in the left atrium and in the pulmonary (lung) veins and capillaries, resulting in pulmonary congestion—not the kind of congestion you have with a cold, but congestion of the tissues of the lung due to high pressure in the blood vessels of the lungs. Mitral stenosis is acquired and usually caused by rheumatic fever.

What this means for your pregnancy

This pressure pushes fluids out of the blood vessels into and around the cells of the lungs. Pregnancy, with its increase in fluid volume as well as its increase in heart rate and cardiac output, may worsen the symptoms of pulmonary congestion. This can sometimes lead to a decrease in cardiac output, a decrease in uterine blood flow, and potential heart failure. The primary symptom is increased fatigue with minimal activity, but can include shortness of breath and lightheadedness or fainting. During pregnancy these symptoms are worse between twenty and thirty weeks, but can be exacerbated at the time of delivery and in the postpartum period due to the increase in heart rate and blood volume. Additionally, any valvular disease can put a pregnant woman at increased risk for developing blood clots around the involved valve, presenting an increased risk for a traveling blood clot which can lodge in any smaller blood vessel, particularly in the brain or the lungs.

Implications for the baby

Because mitral stenosis is an acquired problem, there are no additional genetic risks for this child, but there are some environmental risks with a decreased blood supply. Adequate blood flow with well oxygenated blood (also called perfusion) to the uterus is essential for normal fetal development. Anything that interferes with blood flow of the uterus, placenta, and ultimately your baby can interfere with fetal growth. For these reasons it is important to closely monitor your baby and its growth, taking into consideration how changes or modifications in your care will affect your baby. In cases of significant heart disease (those who are symptomatic), it is common for your primary obstetrician/gynecologist

(OB/Gyn) to consult with a maternal-fetal medicine specialist (also called a perinatologist) to evaluate the baby via ultrasound. This physician may make recommendations regarding care of mom, as well as ongoing surveillance of the baby.

Anticipated management and care

Patients with valvular heart disease are commonly treated with antibiotics to prevent further infection of the affected valve. The medical term for this therapy is called sub-bacterial endo-carditis prophylaxis, or SBE prophylaxis for short. Depending on the severity and extent of the damage to the valve, women are placed on antibiotics throughout pregnancy. Other women with less severe disease are simply treated with intravenous antibiotics at the time of labor and delivery. As pregnancy progresses, both mother and baby will be monitored closely for signs and symp-toms of worsening disease which can include fatigue, shortness of breath, or lightheadedness. If symptoms develop, you may be encouraged to limit your activity in order to minimize the stress on your heart, and to restrict your sodium or salt intake in order to decrease the amount of fluid retained by your body. Your care provider may consider adding diuretic medications or heart med-ications if symptoms persist. If there is evidence that a blood clot has developed, heparin injections (a medication to prevent blood clotting) may be used to help minimize further formation of blood clots. In severe cases of heart failure, surgery to repair or replace the valve may be suggested. Decisions regarding care and medical management will most often be made in consultation with the pri-mary OB/Gyn, the perinatologist, and the cardiologist (or heart specialist). Continuing care with your cardiologist is essential.

Mitral regurgitation or insufficiency

The mitral valve sits between the left atrium and the left ventricle. When this valve is weak and unable to stay closed during the time of left ventricular contraction, blood is pushed backward into the left atrium, causing a prolapse of the valve leaflets (called mitral valve prolapse) toward the left atrium and a turbulence, regurgitation, or backflow of blood. This acquired defect is sometimes due to rheumatic fever, but there are several other conditions which can cause this to develop.

What this means for your pregnancy

Fatigue is the primary symptom, and if severe, pulmonary congestion can result (see mitral stenosis). There is also an increased risk for some irregular or very fast heartbeats of the atria, as well as a possibility of forming blood clots. However, most women with mitral regurgitation tolerate pregnancy very well.

Implications for the baby

As an acquired condition, this child is at no greater genetic risk but is at some risk for environmental problems if the condition is severe. It is crucial for adequate fetal growth to have well oxygenated blood flowing to the uterus and through the placenta. In most cases, mothers tolerate mitral regurgitation very well with minimal effects on the baby. If, however, you are symptomatic, your baby should be closely monitored for growth and normal development in consultation with a perinatologist.

Anticipated management and care

Antibiotic therapy is an expected part of the management plan. If you are without symptoms, nothing further needs to be done. However, if there is evidence or a history of blood clot formation, heparin therapy may be initiated. Many of these decisions will be made in consultation with the primary OB/Gyn, the perinatologist, and the cardiologist.

Mitral valve prolapse

When the mitral valve is weak and unable to stay closed during left ventricular contraction, blood is pushed backward into the left atrium. This can cause a prolapse of the valve leaflets toward the left atrium and a turbulence or regurgitation of blood. This congenital disease is found in about 12 to 17 percent of women of childbearing age.

What this means for your pregnancy

Mitral valve prolapse (MVP) can vary from mild to moderate or severe and is generally tolerated well in pregnancy. In fact, it may even improve during pregnancy due to the generalized dilation of blood vessels. Most women have no symptoms of heart disease with mitral valve prolapse. In rare instances, complications such as chest pain, palpitations or a sense of a racing heartbeat, and possibly fainting can arise.

Implications for the baby

Mitral valve prolapse may be caused by a congenital condition, or by a weakening of the valve due to recurrent injury and repair. Regardless of the cause, the risk for your baby inside your uterus is minimal. Most moms and babies do very well with mitral valve prolapse. However, if you become significantly symptomatic and the blood flow to your uterus, placenta, and your baby are decreased, your baby will be at risk for growth problems. In these cases, a perinatologist may evaluate your baby via ultrasound to assess his tolerance of the symptoms you are experiencing.

Anticipated management and care

Prophylactic antibiotic therapy is controversial in cases of uncomplicated mitral valve prolapse. If chest pain or heart palpitations are significant, an additional medication might be added to help control the feeling of a racing heartbeat. If there is evidence or history of blood clot formation, heparin injection therapy may be initiated.

Aortic stenosis

Aortic stenosis, a narrowing or stiffening of the aortic valve, creates resistance to blood flow out of the left ventricle. The result is a potential for backup on the left side of your heart. It can be acquired due to rheumatic fever, but it may also be congenital.

What this means for your pregnancy

Pregnant women with only mild to moderate stenosis often are without symptoms and do quite well. If, however, your stenosis is severe enough to cause a significant narrowing of the aortic valve, the result can be a very inefficient heart. Anytime cardiac output is compromised, both you and your baby are at risk for decreased blood flow to your vital organs, including your brain, heart, and uterus.

In moderate to severe disease, symptoms may occur even with minimal exertion. These include chest pain, fainting, irregular or rapid heart beats, heart failure, and sometimes sudden cardiac death. The greatest risk is at the time of delivery when sudden, rapid shifts in fluid volume occur requiring your cardiac system to adapt, and it is sometimes difficult for your body to handle these adaptive changes.

Implications for the baby

There is some risk that your child may develop a cardiac problem because this problem is most commonly congenital and may be inherited. Additionally, in cases of severe disease, if there is a decrease in good blood flow to the uterus during important times of fetal development, overall organ system development may be adversely affected, including your baby's heart. Later in gestation, your baby continues to be at risk for poor growth due to a decrease in blood flow through your uterus.

Decisions regarding the care management and monitoring you and your baby's status will involve the primary OB/Gyn, the perinatologist, the cardiologist, and in cases of anticipated early delivery, the neonatologist.

Anticipated management and care

If you are without symptoms, only close monitoring of both you and your baby is necessary. However, in cases where significant symptoms (as those previously described) are present, physical activity is strictly limited to maximize adequate blood flow. Additionally, close monitoring for any infection is necessary, including prompt recognition and treatment.

It is important to know that if symptoms persist, even with strict bedrest, surgical intervention may be necessary. If your heart condition worsens early in your pregnancy, your care provider may suggest that you terminate your pregnancy to ensure your safety. However, many of the severe symptoms often do not develop until later in pregnancy. In these cases, valve replacement or surgical enlargement of the existing valve (called valvotomy) can be done. Another option, depending on the severity of disease, may be the use of a balloon catheter. This device is threaded through a large blood vessel, into the aortic valve itself, and the balloon on the end of the catheter is inflated to enlarge the opening.

Labor and delivery are often the time of greatest risk, particularly if stenosis of the aortic valve is severe. In these instances, it is necessary for you and your baby to be closely monitored throughout labor and delivery, as well as immediately postpartum. During labor, you can expect to have intravenous fluids; antibiotics; close monitoring of your baby's heart rate and your contractions; a specialized intravenous line (called a Swan-Ganz catheter) that can monitor fluid volume, pressures, and cardiac output; pain relief with intravenous narcotic administration or epidural narcotics; and avoidance of actually pushing during delivery by use of forceps instead. Additionally, the time immediately after birth is critical and requires close monitoring of total blood volume and pressures to avoid a significant drop in blood pressure or an overload of fluid. In circumstances of even moderate blood loss, it might be necessary to replace what blood was lost. Management of complex cases will require the collaborative work of you and your family, your primary OB/Gyn, the perinatologist, the cardiologist, and the neonatologist, who may need to make decisions regarding delivery prior to the due date. In sick pregnant women, decisions are often made by weighing the risks and benefits to both mother and baby. Does the benefit of keeping baby inside a little longer outweigh the risk to mom? Many variables play into these difficult decisions. If early delivery is anticipated, the physicians may suggest giving you steroid injections to help prepare the baby's lungs for a preterm delivery (see the section on preterm labor further on).

Aortic regurgitation or insufficiency

Aortic insufficiency is the backflow of blood, just after contraction of the heart, from the aorta back into the left ventricle. Chronic or long-term insufficiency results from a congenitally weak valve, or from a condition such as Marfan's syndrome (see Marfan's Syndrome). It can be acquired as a result of rheumatic fever but is more commonly a congenital problem. Often, these conditions result in an enlargement of the left ventricle and potential for a backup of blood, not just on the left side of the heart, but back into the lungs and into the right side of the heart.

What this means for your pregnancy

If pregnancy causes a worsening of heart disease, symptoms are similar to those of congestive heart failure, including tiredness, shortness of breath, and edema in the legs.

Acute (meaning sudden or rapid) aortic insufficiency can be due to bacterial endocarditis, which is a rapidly progressing infection of the lining of the heart and particularly of the valves of the heart. Another acute cause can be the result of aortic dissection, or a tear at the root of the aorta as it leaves the left ventricle. Both of these conditions can be very serious and are often difficult to anticipate.

In general, aortic insufficiency is tolerated well in pregnancy. In many instances it may improve with pregnancy related to the generalized dilation or enlargement of blood vessels and the decrease in resistance to blood flow out of the heart.

Implications for the baby

Because this is often a congenital problem, your baby is at some risk for inheriting this valvular weakness genetically. But the greater risk is related to inadequate blood flow to the uterus, placenta, and your baby during times when your symptoms are present. If you are having symptoms of low oxygenation (fatigue, shortness of breath, etc.) your baby probably is, too. The baby is also at risk for growth delays while still in your uterus.

Anticipated management and care

If you are without symptoms, simply follow the well-being of you and your baby. However, if symptoms of congestive heart failure develop (fatigue, shortness of breath with minimal exertion, and significant swelling), then you and your baby will be very closely monitored. Activity will probably be restricted, including strict bedrest, as well as a sodium restricted diet to minimize fluid retention, and diuretic medication to get rid of excess fluid and decrease the fluid load on your heart. Oftentimes, epidural anesthesia is recommended. In all cases of aortic insufficiency, antibiotic therapy is given intravenously while you are in active labor to prevent subacute bacterial endocarditis.

Valve replacement

Many adults with valvular disease have undergone valve replacement surgery. There are two distinct types of valves used for replacement, one is called a mechanical valve, the other is called a porcine valve. Most pregnant moms with artificial valves do very well but are at risk for developing some minor and some serious complications. Additionally, pregnancy can shorten the life of the artificial valves, requiring replacement sooner than expected.

Mechanical valves present a greater risk to the pregnant woman than do porcine valves, because of increased blood volume and increased risk for blood clotting during pregnancy. The greatest risk is formation of blood clots near and around the valve itself. These can then be dislodged and sent into the general circulation causing a blood clot in a vein, or a stroke, or a blood clot in the lungs. Additionally, there is a risk for infection to develop near the artificial valve causing the entire heart and body to not function well. Porcine valves, because they're more like human tissue than mechanical valves, have fewer risks with pregnancy and fewer risk for increased blood clotting or infection. However, pregnancy can stress the valve enough that it needs to be replaced much sooner.

If you have an artificial mechanical valve you will be put on an anticoagulant medication, including warfarin (Coumadin) pills, and heparin injections, much like when you are not pregnant. Warfarin carries a risk for developmental problems with the baby's organ systems and therefore is not used during the first trimester. Both drugs carry an increased risk for bleeding during pregnancy, labor and delivery, and postpartum. However, it is important to find a good balance between the drug levels and the need to prevent the development of blood clots. In addition, you will also be given intravenous antibiotics during labor and delivery to prevent cardiac infection.

Congenital Problems

Congenital heart disease affects about 8 out of 1,000 live-born infants in the United States, with about one-third of those infants suffering from critical problems requiring intervention. As discussed earlier in this chapter, therapies to treat children with congenital heart disease have improved greatly over the past twenty to thirty years, resulting in many young women growing to adulthood and bearing children. For this reason, the medical community is beginning to care for pregnant women who in the past were either unable to become pregnant or did not live to childbearing age.

We've already discussed a few congenital heart problems involving the valves of the heart: mitral valve prolapse, aortic stenosis, and aortic insufficiency. The following congenital problems are related to development of the heart structures themselves, including the wall (or septum) separating the right and left atria and ventricles, the continuation of fetal heart structures that persist even after birth, and the abnormal development of the blood vessels which leave the heart.

Atrial septal defects

An atrial septal defect (ASD) is an opening in the wall or septum of the heart muscle which separates the right atrium from the left atrium. Remember that unoxygenated blood moves into the right atrium from the vena cava, going into the right ventricle, to the lungs for oxygenation, back into the left atrium, then into the left ventricle and out through the aorta to the general circulation. In an ASD, oxygenated blood from the left atrium flows through the hole or opening in the atrial wall into the right atrium and into the lungs. The result is an increase in volume in the right side of the heart, and potentially in the lungs. These congenital defects are the second most common heart abnormality in adults.

What this means for your pregnancy

The most common complication is the risk of developing an arrhythmia (irregular heartbeat). There is small risk for pulmonary hypertension, or an increase in the blood pressure of the lungs, making it difficult to circulate blood through the lungs to be reoxygenated. In general, though, ASD in pregnancy is tolerated very well, unless the opening or lesion is very large.

Implications for the baby

Risks for your baby are few, as long as you remain without symptoms. But anytime blood flow to the uterus is compromised there is a risk for poor fetal growth.

Anticipated management and care

If you are without symptoms of congestive heart failure (fatigue, shortness of breath, edema) or heartbeat irregularities, routine prenatal care is appropriate. If symptoms develop, specific problems will be addressed as they arise, such as bedrest for tiredness; sodium restriction to decrease fluid retention; diuretic medication to aid in getting rid of excess fluid; and heart medication to help control arrhythmias.

Ventricular septal defects (VSDs)

These congenital defects are the most common heart problem found at birth. Most are small and close spontaneously by age ten. VSDs can occur as isolated problems or along with other congenital heart disorders such as tetralogy of Fallot, transposition of the great vessels, or coarctation of the aorta (to be discussed later). Most are repaired in childhood if they don't close on their own, or if pulmonary hypertension (high pressure in the lungs that prevent blood flow into the lungs for reoxygenation) develops. This hole in the wall of the ventricle lies between the left and right ventricles, resulting in a mixing of oxygenated and unoxygenated blood on both the left and right sides of the heart. Remember, the ventricles are the workhorses of the heart, responsible for moving blood through the lungs, the heart, and the systemic circulation to the rest of the body. The right ventricle sends unoxygenated blood from the right side of the heart into the pulmonary circulation to pick up oxygen, then back into the left side where the left ventricle pushes oxygenated blood into the general circulation through the aorta. An opening between these two chambers means a lot of blood is mixing around in the heart but not necessarily getting to the lungs and body tissues.

What this means for your pregnancy

An important point to remember is that as long as the shift of blood is from left to right, meaning that *oxygenated* blood is being distributed both to the aorta for general circulation as well as to the right side of the heart for recirculation to the lungs, pregnancy is well tolerated. If, however, the shift of blood begins to change direction and begins moving from right to left, meaning *unoxygenated* blood is moving into the left ventricle and is then being squeezed through the aorta into the general circulation and to the tissues, then problems will occur. Clearly, it is the size of the ventricular wall defect that determines how well pregnancy is tolerated. The larger the defect, the greater the risk for developing a right-to-left movement of blood (or shunt) and for developing pulmonary hypertension. This condition is called Eisenmenger's syndrome and carries a 30 to 50 percent mortality rate (to be discussed later).

Implications for the baby

There is an increased risk for your baby developing congenital heart disease. However, additional risks for your baby are minimal if you remain without symptoms. If you begin to develop symptoms, particularly those that might indicate a progression toward Eisenmenger's syndrome, your prognosis and the prognosis for your baby can be quite poor (see Eisenmenger's syndrome).

Anticipated management and care

You and your baby will be closely monitored for signs of worsening disease. You will be seen frequently to evaluate your status and how well you are tolerating pregnancy with a preexisting VSD. Also, your baby will be monitored via ultrasound to evaluate growth, including an assessment of the heart structures. In labor, you will probably be on fluid restriction in order to prevent changing from a stable left-to-right movement of blood to a less stable and more dangerous right-to-left shunt, which sends unoxygenated blood into the circulation. As with many heart disorders, antibiotic prophylaxis will be administered in labor.

Patent ductus arteriosus

The patent ductus arteriosus (PDA) is a special blood vessel that we all have as babies in our mother's uterus. The ductus is responsible for transporting blood from the right side of the heart, bypassing the nonfunctioning lungs of the baby, and putting it directly into the aorta for circulation to the baby's tissues and organs. This mechanism is essential for survival while the baby is in the uterus. However, shortly after birth, it is important for the ductus to close, which then directs blood to the now functioning lungs for oxygenation. If this closure doesn't occur, some unoxygenated blood gets sent to the lungs like its supposed to, and some unoxygenated blood gets pumped directly into the aorta.

What this means for your pregnancy

Most PDAs close shortly after birth. Women with repaired PDAs do well in pregnancy. Unrepaired PDAs are usually tolerated well, also. However, tolerance is dependent on the size of the opening. Some women are at risk for developing pulmonary hypertension (high pressure in the lungs which prevent adequate oxygenation of blood) as well as heart failure.

Implications for the baby

There is some risk that your baby will have a congenital heart condition, but beyond that, most babies do well with growth. If you have symptoms of worsening disease, such as turning blue with activity, shortness of breath, or excessive tiredness, then the baby might be at risk for poor growth.

Anticipated management and care

As long as you show no symptoms of the worsening problems listed above, you can expect routine prenatal care. The baby will be evaluated by ultrasound for normal growth. During labor and delivery you will most likely be given antibiotics to avoid a bacterial infection of the heart. The greatest risk for you if you are without significant symptoms, is a sudden drop in blood pressure before, during, or after delivery which could result in you and your baby having a lot of unoxygenated blood in your circulation. For these reasons, epidural anesthesia during labor should be given with great care to avoid drops in the blood pressure.

Eisenmenger's syndrome

This congenital defect is associated with other heart problems, primarily ventricular septal defects and patent ductus arteriosus, which cause severe pulmonary hypertension (high pressure in the lungs which prevents blood from being reoxygenated). This is a serious condition in which a right-to-left movement of blood occurs, resulting in unoxygenated blood coming into the left side of your heart and being pumped into the general circulation.

Without oxygen, the tissues die, including important organs like your heart, brain, kidneys, lungs, and uterus.

What this means for your pregnancy

Without oxygenated blood going to your uterus, the placenta and baby can die, as well. In addition, the normal changes of pregnancy, particularly the great increase in blood volume, can put even greater stresses on your heart. Your body tries to respond by making more oxygen-carrying red blood cells, so that the blood becomes thicker than normal. Irreversible changes occur such as enlargement of the heart, worsening pulmonary hypertension, and chronic cyanosis (turning blue from lack of oxygen in the blood). All of these together put you at tremendous risk for a heart attack, heart failure, stroke, and death. The risk for death is quoted between 30 and 65 percent.

Implications for the baby

With this severe form of heart disease the expected outcome for your baby is very poor. Remember, the more symptomatic you are, the more your baby is at risk. Often, women with such serious heart disease are strongly counseled against ever becoming pregnant. If pregnancy does occur, mom will most likely be counseled to terminate the pregnancy in order to avoid a truly significant risk of death. If she decides to go for it and attempts to carry her baby to term, then both mom and baby will be monitored extremely closely for signs of worsening disease.

Anticipated management and care

With this condition it is common for you to be hospitalized early in pregnancy, often by twenty-six or twenty-eight weeks. You will usually be on oxygen to help increase the amount of oxygen in your blood. You will be monitored closely for signs of heart failure, including worsening cyanosis (bluish-colored skin from lack of oxygen), heart beat irregularities, and swelling in your legs and lower body. Your baby will have frequent ultrasounds to determine how well he is growing. Possibly, you will have an amniocentesis early in the pregnancy to determine if any chromosome problems exist, and again later in pregnancy to determine if the baby is becoming mature enough to be delivered early, especially if your condition is beginning to deteriorate. During labor it will be necessary to have a special intravenous catheter, called a Swan-Ganz catheter and/or hemodynamic monitoring, placed into a large blood vessel in the neck or near the collarbone to closely monitor blood volume and pressure in the heart, lungs, and blood vessels. Labor and delivery is a precarious time of rapid fluid changes, and it is extremely important to avoid big shifts in fluid and blood volume. The physicians will prefer to allow you to go into spontaneous labor and avoid inducing labor with medications. However, your condition will often determine when delivery will need to take place. During labor, you and your baby will be *very* closely monitored. Intravenous antibiotics will be administered to avoid an infection of the heart. At delivery, you will be encouraged not to actually push your baby out, and forceps may be used to deliver the baby. Immediate postpartum is still a critical time for you, and you will be closely watched, often in an intensive care unit, depending on your condition.

All of the decisions regarding care of both you and your baby will be made in collaboration with several specialists including the perinatologist, the cardiologist, the neonatologist, and sometimes an intensivist (physician who cares for critically-ill patients in an intensive care unit). Women with Eisenmenger's syndrome can be some of the very sickest people to care for, especially when pregnant.

Tetralogy of Fallot

This congenital condition includes a combination of ventricular septal defect, stenosis of the pulmonic valve, right heart enlargement, and abnormal placement of the base of the aorta as it leaves the left ventricle. Surgical correction of this problem is usually done shortly after birth.

What this means for your pregnancy

If you have undergone repair as an infant, the potential outcome for your pregnancy is very good. If the problems have not been corrected, however, some of the normal changes of pregnancy can worsen the condition. The opening between the right and left ventricles causes unoxygenated and oxygenated blood to mix. There is stenosis, or narrowing and rigidity of the pulmonic valve. The aorta is somewhat displaced as it leaves the left ventricle carrying blood into the general circulation. The normal enlargement of the heart due to normal changes of pregnancy can cause an increase in the amount of blood remaining in the heart chambers. The total result is a lot of unoxygenated blood in the right side of the heart which is supposed to go into the lungs through the pulmonic valve. But it is narrow and rigid; so much of the unoxygenated blood takes the path of least resistance and goes through the opening in the ventricular wall to the left side of the heart. Here it is squeezed out into the circulation where it does no good because it isn't carrying any oxygen.

In response to the decreased oxygen, the body tries to make more oxygen-carrying cells, or red blood cells, in order to improve the amount of oxygen getting to the body tissues. However, this only makes the blood thicker, putting you at greater risk for developing blood clots. Due to the increased blood volume with pregnancy, movement of blood directly from the right side to the left is often made worse in unrepaired tetralogy of Fallot. The long-term prognosis for mom in this circumstance is unfortunately poor.

Implications for the baby

After repair of tetralogy of Fallot, moms usually do fairly well during pregnancy, so their babies usually do, too. In instances where defects were never repaired, babies develop problems with growth when mom becomes significantly symptomatic, such as cyanosis (becoming blue) with activity, shortness of breath, fainting, or swelling due to heart failure. Because this is a congenital problem, the baby is also at risk for inheriting a heart defect, as well as for other problems that may occur due to inadequate oxygenation during the time when organ systems are developing early in pregnancy.

Anticipated management and care

In cases where repair has already occurred, only close monitoring of you and your baby are required. Most moms do well, but you may require observation for signs of problems such as shortness of breath, fatigue, or water retention.

When repair has not occurred, you and your baby are watched much more closely because of the significant risk for inadequate oxygenation of vital body organs and tissues. Your baby will have several ultrasounds to frequently assess its growth. You may be placed on oxygen to increase the amount of oxygen being circulated in your body and to the baby. Also, you will be watched closely for signs of worsening disease and you may require hospitalization early in pregnancy.

During labor, the greatest emphasis will be placed on avoiding a significant drop in blood pressure or drop in blood volume (as in hemorrhage or too much bleeding). This can cause tremendous problems and lead to having no oxygenated blood circulating in your system with only unoxygenated blood being pushed into the general circulation. For this reason, fluid volume is closely monitored, and epidural anesthesia is avoided. It is important for a pregnant woman with a complex heart disease such as this to have her care managed collaboratively by a perinatologist, cardiologist, and neonatologist.

Other Heart Problems

Several other heart problems can occur in pregnancy including myocardial infarction, or heart attack, aortic problems, and heart disease actually caused by pregnancy.

Myocardial infarction

Myocardial infarction (MI), or heart attack, are different names for the same problem: inadequate blood flow to a part of the heart muscle causing a part of the heart tissue to die.

What this means for your pregnancy

This is rare in pregnancy, but can occur if there are underlying risk factors for heart attack already present such as smoking, high blood pressure, high cholesterol levels, obesity, or diabetes. Sometimes the normal changes of pregnancy put enough stress on the heart to unmask an already present but undiagnosed heart condition, resulting in a heart attack.

In those women who have had a previous heart attack prior to pregnancy there is controversy regarding whether pregnancy is advisable or not. If the initial heart attack is related to high blood pressure or significant coronary artery disease, pregnancy is usually not recommended. If, however, a previous heart attack was due to trauma or another problem it is appropriate to have a thorough heart workup before attempting pregnancy.

Implications for the baby

With an acute, or sudden, heart attack the risk for stillbirth is high. If mom can be stabilized in a short period of time and delivery can be delayed for up to two weeks, the potential outcome for the baby is better.

Anticipated management and care

The first priority for management will always be the stabilization of the mother. Beyond that, the baby's status will be monitored and evaluated. Depending on the age of the baby, delivery will be delayed as long as the mother remains stable. If the mother is close to her due date, delivery will be delayed for up to two weeks to allow her to truly stabilize before proceeding with the work of labor. During labor and delivery, she will often be placed in a side lying position to reduce the strain on her heart; she will be placed on oxygen to maximize oxygen in the blood; she will probably be encouraged to have an epidural to reduce pain and the stress on her heart; and she will quite probably have a special intravenous catheter to assess her fluid volume and pressure.

Decisions for care will be made in collaboration with the woman and her family, the perinatologist, the cardiologist, the neonatologist, and an intensivist (critical care specialist).

Marfan's syndrome

This is a genetically inherited connective tissue disorder, which results in problems and weakness of the specialized body tissues that provide elasticity to our muscles, bones, tendons, and ligaments; the walls of our blood vessels; the heart and its valves; our lungs and kidneys; the gel-like substance in our eyes; and the synovial fluid around our joints. People with Marfan's syndrome are usually quite tall, lanky, and thin. The most serious heart problem is enlargement of the base or root of the aorta as it leaves the left ventricle. Because the normal changes of pregnancy increase blood volume, relaxes or enlarges blood vessels, and enlarges the heart slightly, a woman develops an increased risk for worsening her heart condition if she has Marfan's syndrome. Often, women with Marfan's syndrome already have some mitral valve prolapse (MVP) and regurgitation (see the section on mitral valve prolapse and regurgitation). Pregnancy can often worsen their MVP or regurgitation and subsequently worsen their risk for heart failure.

In addition, the base or root of the aorta becomes widened and stretched. In Marfan's syndrome the inherent general weakness of blood vessels and of the aortic root in particular, can result in a dissection or separation of the three layers which make up the wall of the aorta. Together, these three layers are strong enough to withstand the high pressure of blood as it is squeezed out of the left ventricle. However, if these layers are separated, they become weak and vulnerable to those same high pressures and can result in an aneurysm or bubble in the wall of the vessel close to the base of the aorta, which will eventually rupture under increased pressure. Or it can result in a complete tear in the wall of the blood vessel. Either way, the outcome is severe because all the blood being pumped out of the left ventricle fills the chest cavity rather than circulating out to the rest of the body. Very few people survive a ruptured aortic aneurysm, especially so near the heart as is the aortic root.

What this means for your pregnancy

The defining criteria of how well pregnancy may be tolerated depends on how dilated or enlarged the root of the aorta is, which can be measured by echocardiogram (an ultrasound of the heart). If the diameter is less than 40 millimeters (or 4 centimeters), then pregnancy is usually tolerated fairly. If, however, it is greater than 4 centimeters, the risk for death during pregnancy is at least 50 percent. With this significant dilation of the aorta, pregnancy is not recommended. On the other hand, in cases of only mild or moderate dilation, without other significant heart problems, the prognosis for a positive pregnancy outcome is good.

Implications for the baby

Because this is a genetically inherited disorder, your baby has a 50 percent chance of developing this condition also. As discussed before, if you remain without symptoms, your baby will generally do well. If, however, you have symptoms of heart failure (fatigue, shortness of breath, fainting, chest pain, or water retention) then your baby is at risk for problems with growth.

Anticipated management and care

An echocardiogram is recommended early in pregnancy to assess the diameter of the aortic root, as well as mitral valve involvement. Additionally, an echocardiogram is recommended monthly throughout pregnancy. Both you and your baby will be closely monitored for signs and symptoms of worsening disease. You will be watched for any of the above mentioned symptoms, as well as worsening heart changes. Your baby will be watched closely via ultrasound for adequate growth. Additionally, the baby will be evaluated after birth to see if she has inherited Marfan's syndrome.

If there are any indications of problems regarding your tolerance of pregnancy, your activity will most likely be significantly restricted. Also, you may be placed on medications to prevent high blood pressure and a racing heartbeat in order to reduce stress on your aorta. During labor and delivery, a special intravenous line may be placed to monitor volume and pressure closely. Epidural anesthesia is carefully administered during vaginal and cesarean deliveries due to the risk of a significant drop in blood pressure. As with other heart conditions involving valve problems, prophylactic antibiotics will be used to prevent risk of a heart or valvular infection. If repair of the aorta is indicated during or after pregnancy, it is recommended that surgery be delayed, if possible, until four to six weeks after delivery.

Peripartum cardiomyopathy

This is a disease of the heart, not related to any other previous heart condition or problem, developing within the last month of pregnancy or during the first six months after delivery.

What this means for your pregnancy

The greatest challenge of this condition is proper diagnosis. Symptoms include fatigue, shortness of breath, and water retention in the lungs or other parts of the body. Further diagnostic studies may also reveal an enlarged heart, extra heart sounds when someone is listening to the beats of your heart, congestion in the lungs, and sometimes a blood clot in the lungs or other parts of the body. Because these symptoms are common to many other diseases, as well as to underlying heart disease, it is important to rule out all other possible causes before diagnosing peripartum cardiomyopathy. Some of the risk factors associated with this condition include multiple gestation (twins, triplets, or more), pregnancy induced hypertension or preeclampsia (see Chapter XII), older women with a history of several previous pregnancies, and African-American women who are statistically at greater risk.

Implications for the baby

If you remain without symptoms, the baby often does well. However, in this condition, evaluation of the baby may be one of the first indicators that something is wrong. Because the baby is so dependent on good blood flow to the uterus and placenta, she may begin to show signs of inadequate oxygenation by slowed growth. This might trigger further investigation to discover heart disease. If you become ill at or near your due date, the baby will most likely look very bad on a fetal monitor and on ultrasound. If, however, you become ill shortly after delivery, your baby will be fine because she would have been born prior to the crisis.

Anticipated management and care

If this condition occurs prior to delivery and all other possible causes have been eliminated, treatment will be initiated as soon as symptoms appear. Some of the treatments will include medications to improve heart function, medications to decrease swelling, as well as medications to prevent blood clots. During delivery it may be necessary to have a special intravenous line placed in order to monitor blood volume and pressure both in the heart and in the rest of the body. The prognosis for a good outcome is often related to the size of heart enlargement and early accurate diagnosis of the problem. If the heart is greatly enlarged, the outcome can be poor for you and your baby. After delivery, aggressive management is used to stabilize you and prevent your condition from worsening. This condition tends to recur in subsequent pregnancies, and is often worse, occurring earlier in the next pregnancy than in the first. For this reason, another pregnancy is not recommended, especially if enlargement of the heart has persisted beyond six to twelve months after delivery.

In Conclusion

You've plowed through a lot of material about normal heart function, normal changes of pregnancy, and heart disease occurring in pregnancy. Remember, the most important points are accurate and early diagnosis, close monitoring of both you and your baby, and prompt action with any significant changes. Management of complex disease in pregnancy, and heart disease can be *very* complex, especially with the added stress of pregnancy, which requires the collaborative work of *you*, your family, primary OB/Gyn, perinatologist, cardiologist, and neonatologist. It may also require input from a genetic specialist, pediatric cardiologist, hematologist (blood disease specialist), or any number of other specialists, depending on the problem.

This may seem a bit overwhelming, but information can only help you make informed decisions about your care and the care of your baby. If the information presented to you is too technical, or too much to process, or it simply doesn't make sense to you and your family, ask for clarification. There are a few instances where decisions need to be made quickly, but most often you will have time to ask lots of questions and get good answers in return. That doesn't mean you'll always have great choices as some decisions may be very difficult indeed, but it does mean you have a choice in what happens—it is your body, your baby, and your family. The job of the medical team is to provide information and good care, and your job is to be informed, get good prenatal care early and often, and then make the best choices for you and your family.

IV

Kidney Problems and Chronic Hypertension

Overview

It may seem odd to combine the discussions of kidney problems with chronic high blood pressure, but in fact the two can be closely linked to one another. We will begin this chapter by looking at the basic structure of the kidney and its purposes. Why is it so vital and important in our bodies? What does it do normally, and how does it change in normal pregnancy? And what happens if it doesn't do its job? Hopefully, by the end of this chapter you will have a better understanding of your particular risks as a pregnant woman experiencing kidney problems and possibly high blood pressure.

This chapter will address some common kidney problems in pregnancy, namely, recurrent bladder infections and kidney infections. I will also briefly discuss pregnancy and kidney failure, both chronic (long-term or long-lasting) and acute (sudden). Lastly, I will address the issue of chronic high blood pressure (hypertension) in pregnancy.

Basic kidney structure

The kidneys, a matched pair, are about the size of a small fist and sit just beneath the diaphragm (the thin muscle separating the abdomen from the chest cavity). They are somewhat dense, heavy organs made up of many blood vessels and specialized kidney cells. You have one on the left and one on the right; both sit just slightly tucked up under the lowest ribs at your back.

Ureters are tiny tubes which drain urine from the kidneys into the bladder, the collecting site for urine. Generally, the bladder can hold about a pint, or a half liter, of urine, which is expelled from the bladder through a larger tube called the urethra.

The urine in the kidneys is sterile, meaning that it is without infection-causing bacteria, viruses, or other organisms. As it moves from the kidneys, through both left and right ureters, into the bladder, and out of the body through the urethra, it remains sterile. So, all of these structures are also considered sterile.

Purposes of the kidney

The overall purpose of the kidneys is to maintain homeostasis, a constant state of balance in the internal environment of the body. This dynamic process is constantly shifting and adjusting to accommodate changes in and around the body. Specifically, the kidneys are responsible for the following functions:

- cleaning and maintaining a balance of body fluids by excreting the waste products and foreign substances in the urine;
- regulating the balance of water and electrolytes (such as sodium or salt, potassium, and chloride) in the body;
- producing renin, a key player in the maintenance of blood

94

pressure, as well as overall kidney function;

- formation and production of erythropoietin, the hormone required to make new red blood cells; and
- metabolizing vitamin D into a usable form.

An overresponse by the kidneys to "balance" things, as well as some of the normal changes of pregnancy can sometimes create problems.

Normal Kidney Changes During Pregnancy

Pregnancy is a time of many changes and adaptations by the female body, most of which are caused by the changes in our hormone balance. All of these adaptations are necessary to accommodate a successful pregnancy and maintain a healthy mom and growing a healthy baby. The hormone progesterone is primarily responsible for a relaxation of smooth muscle cells throughout the body, including those in the heart muscle and in the walls of the hundreds of miles of blood vessels that carry blood to and from our vital organs and tissues. The result of circulating progesterone is an overall enlarging of these vessels, including the vessels of the kidney. Both kidneys actually become larger during pregnancy by about 1 to 2 centimeters. In addition, the ureters from both kidneys and the bladder relax somewhat and can hold more urine during pregnancy. Throughout pregnancy, the uterus continues to grow and put pressure on the ureters. This increased pressure, along with the general dilation or enlargement of the ureters, can cause urine to be held in the ureters and potentially back up into the kidneys. The bladder nearly doubles in capacity, able to hold almost a quart, or about a liter, of urine. With all of this going on, frequent urination is very common in pregnancy, and women often feel the need to get up in the middle of the night to urinate. Another hormone of pregnancy, estrogen, can cause a weakness in the musculature of the bladder, sometimes allowing a backflow of urine upward toward the kidneys through the ureters.

Overall blood volume increases by 30 to 50 percent, and the kidney is one of the many organ recipients of that increased blood flow through the renal (kidney) artery. The result is a 50 percent increase in the filtration of the blood which occurs in the kidneys, beginning as early as six weeks after conception. The kidneys work harder during pregnancy, continually adjusting and adapting to the increased blood flow. They need to hold onto vital substances like sodium, glucose, potassium, and water, while still excreting the waste products of normal body metabolism. During pregnancy, increases of some of these substances show up in the urine, such as glucose and protein.

Why are the kidneys so vitally important? What if they cannot do their job?

The kidneys are critically important to the process of maintaining homeostasis, or balance. More simply, without the kidneys, there is no balance. No other systems in the body can pick up the slack and, thus, no way to maintain fluid balance, no way to adjust our blood pressure to accommodate the change from sitting to vigorous exercise, no way to trigger the formation of new red blood cells, and most importantly, no way to get rid of the waste products that can quickly build up in our circulation and tissues if the kidneys are unable to their job.

Without the kidneys to do these jobs we begin to show signs of kidney damage and potential kidney failure. Too much fluid may accumulate in our bodies putting us at risk for heart failure or stroke. If we get rid of fluids too fast, we can become quickly dehydrated. Our blood pressure can go haywire, becoming too high rather than too low, thus putting us at risk for stroke or rupture of a blood vessel somewhere else in the body. We can become anemic, with too few circulating red blood cells, which are required for oxygen delivery to all the cells in the body. And the buildup of waste products can result in bone and muscle pain, mental confusion, stomach and bowel problems, and coma.

With pregnancy, the key for optimal fetal growth is a stable mother, so the primary goal in caring for a mother with any kind of illness or disease is to have her get better, or at least work toward her equilibrium in order to maximize the baby's chances of doing well.

Bladder and Kidney Infections

The medical term for bladder infection is urinary tract infection, or UTI for short. The definition for UTI is really a laboratory one: the presence of more than 100,000 bacteria, per milliliter of urine, of the same species in two consecutive specimens. Clinically, a UTI is an infection of the lower urinary tract involving the bladder and urethra. In the nonpregnant woman a UTI is often accompanied by signs and symptoms of a bladder infection. These include urgency, or the need to go to the bathroom immediately; frequency, or the need to go to the bathroom all the time, often producing only small amounts of urine; or pain above the pubic bone when walking, pain in the back by your ribs, or pain when actually urinating. The difficulty during pregnancy is that many of these symptoms are *not* present at the time of a UTI.

A kidney infection, pyelonephritis in medical terminology, is an infection of the kidneys which is accompanied by bacteria in the urine, fever, chills, back pain at the lower border of the ribs, and sometimes nausea and vomiting. In pregnancy, these symptoms are often present all at once and very suddenly when the infection is usually quite serious.

What puts pregnant women at higher risk?

Primarily, it is the normal changes of the kidneys, ureters, bladder, and urethra during pregnancy which put a woman at greater risk for urinary tract infections than when she is not pregnant. All of these structures, as discussed earlier, are somewhat enlarged and dilated, holding more urine than they would in a nonpregnant state. The result is stasis of urine, or urine that may sit for longer periods of time in all of these structures. Remember, too, that the urine potentially has an increased amount of glucose (sugar) and protein present in the pregnant woman because of the increased filtration that is occurring.

Bacteria, in this warm environment, with plenty of glucose to feed on, can grow quite rapidly. The bacteria adheres to the walls of the structures in the urinary tract, climbing upward from the opening of the urethra, into the bladder, up into the ureters, and then into the kidneys. Bacteria can also be pushed toward the kidneys from the bladder during urination by the backflow of urine which can occur normally in pregnancy. It is this movement of bacteria-rich urine toward the kidneys that can result in sudden kidney infection.

In a nonpregnant woman, symptoms of both bladder and kidney infections can be sudden and painful. Symptoms such as urgency, frequency, pain, fever, and chills are the by-product of the body fighting off infection or disease. Pregnancy, however, is a time when the immune system (the part of the system that fights infection and disease) is somewhat suppressed, a protective mechanism for the growing baby that allows a little more tolerance for the presence of "foreign" structures such as a placenta and a fetus. Unfortunately, it also means that in order for a pregnant woman to become symptomatic, there must be an abundant growth of bacteria before her body begins to show signs of the fight—urgency, frequency, pain, fever, and chills.

How do you get a urinary tract infection?

The most common bacterial culprit in UTI is *escherichia coli (E-coli)*. This is an organism that is present in the colon of humans, as well as many other organisms that can cause UTI. These bacteria thrive in the glucose and protein-rich environment of warm urine. These organisms can be transmitted to the urethra by simple common things such as wiping your bottom from back to front after going to the bathroom or having sexual intercourse.

Why is UTI and kidney infection a concern in pregnancy?

Often, the greatest concern with infections of the genital tract and urinary tract during pregnancy is the risk for preterm labor. Labor is considered preterm if it occurs prior to the thirty-seventh week of pregnancy (see Chapter X regarding preterm labor). Medical studies that have researched UTIs and preterm labor are inconsistent and controversial because they have failed to show a direct link between the two. However, the risk of a UTI progressing toward a kidney infection is quite significant, and preterm labor has been shown to be highly correlated with kidney infection in the pregnant woman.

So, beyond the risks to the pregnancy itself, there is a risk for kidney infection and subsequent chronic (long-term) kidney disease and kidney failure. Additionally, a kidney infection can put you at risk for developing septic shock (a result of an overwhelming infection which is difficult to reverse) and respiratory failure (or difficulty with breathing). The risk for the pregnancy is that you can begin having contractions as the kidney infection worsens, which can result in early cervical dilation, the defining characteristic of labor.

Your baby, then, is at risk for all the problems associated with a preterm birth. While still in your uterus, however, your baby can show signs that the kidney infection and fever is affecting her, too. One of these signs is an increased heart rate in response to your fever. The baby can also have a concerning or nonreassuring heart rate pattern which appears on a fetal monitor.

A key point to remember is that stabilizing your condition is always the primary goal. This doesn't mean that the baby is being ignored, just the opposite. If you can be stabilized, the baby's condition will also stabilize. The baby's body is simply responding to its environment, and the goal is to fix the environment.

How can I best care for myself and my baby?

Prenatal care continues to be the best way to identify and treat bladder infections early in order to prevent them from becoming kidney infections. The best way for you to be an integral part of this process is to keep getting good prenatal care, to take all of your antibiotic medication if it is prescribed for you, and to be aware of the signs and symptoms of a UTI and kidney infection.

At every routine prenatal visit you will be asked to obtain a clean catch urine sample. A urine dipstick is used to check for glucose and protein in the urine. In addition, your sample is evaluated for signs of a bladder infection including leukocytes and nitrites in the urine which are by-products in the urine indicating an infectious process. If leukocytes and nitrites are present, the urine sample will be sent to a laboratory for analysis and culture.

Some care providers may treat you with antibiotics at the time of the positive urine dipstick, especially if you have a history of bladder infections in the past. Others may wait until receiving the results from the culture and then treat the specifically identified organism with specific antibiotics. Regardless of your care provider's philosophy, bladder infections must be treated early.

If antibiotics are prescribed, be sure to take *all* of your medication to avoid the growth of resistant strains of bacteria. Sometimes, if you have a strong history for recurrent bladder infections or a history for kidney infection, you may be put on prophylactic antibiotic therapy. This is often a one-pill-a-day regimen to prevent bladder infections. Also, your urine may be cultured every trimester of your pregnancy, depending on your history and your care provider's philosophy of care.

In the event that a kidney infection develops, you will truly feel like you are sick. Your care provider will collect a clean catch urine sample, and will also assess how you are feeling. If it is determined that you do have a kidney infection, you will most likely be admitted to the hospital for intravenous antibiotics and close monitoring of both you and your baby. Kidney infections, particularly during pregnancy, are very serious and may require hospitalization for several days.

As a reminder, the signs and symptoms for a UTI are *urgency, frequency,* and *painful urination.* But, remember that in pregnancy, women may *never* have any of these problems, complaints, or discomforts. The signs and symptoms for a kidney infection are *fever, chills, back pain at the lower border of your ribs, nausea,* and *vomiting.* These are "classic" signs of a kidney infection, but you don't need to have all of them before calling your prenatal care provider with any concerns.

Also, if you're feeling well enough to pay attention, you may notice a decrease in the amount of overall movement and kicking of the baby. Much like when you are sick and don't feel like getting out of bed, the baby responds in the same manner to your illness. The baby tends to have little energy, with little reserve, so it conserves what is available, resting quietly and moving very little. Decreased fetal movement should *always* be considered a sign that something may be wrong until proven otherwise. If your baby moves less than six times in an hour after you've had something to eat and a large glass of water or juice, call your prenatal care provider right away.

Labor, delivery, and postpartum

In cases of recurrent bladder infections, labor and delivery should progress normally without any problems or concerns. Those times in which a simple UTI becomes a full blown kidney infection, the primary goal will be to treat the infection aggressively and send mom home from the hospital undelivered. Some complex kidney infections, such as those that progress to generalized infection (sepsis) or result in lung and respiratory complications can be more difficult to manage.

The goal will be to stabilize mom, thereby stabilizing the baby. If mom is very ill, her body will probably begin laboring on its own. At that time, all of the care providers, in consultation with mom and her family, will need to make some important decisions regarding delivery. There are many variables that will be evaluated prior to making any decision. The important point is to ask lots of questions about what is happening, what your options are, and what the outcomes are of each option.

After delivery, most mothers do very well with antibiotics and good follow-up care. Even some of the very sickest mothers tend to pull through because they generally begin pregnancy as healthy young women.

Chronic and Acute Kidney Failure

Kidneys require an excellent blood supply in order to do their many complex jobs. Kidney, or renal, failure is an inability of the kidneys to do their job. Chronic kidney failure is a progressive loss of kidney function. This long-term kidney failure can be the result of autoimmune diseases (such as systemic lupus erythematous), drug toxicity, disorders of the blood vessels, or metabolic diseases (such as diabetes mellitus).

It is in the glomerulus, or the many specialized small blood vessels of the kidney, where the filtration of blood and body fluids occur. In fact, glomerular filtration rate (GFR) is a term used to describe the amount of blood plasma being filtered through the kidneys. In pregnancy, the GFR is increased because of the increased blood volume. If the glomeruli are damaged and enough of them are unable to do their job, the GFR decreases, indicating a worsening of kidney disease or failure.

Acute kidney failure is an abrupt decrease in renal function with sudden increases of urea and creatinine in the blood. Causes of acute kidney failure include infections (such as septic abortion or untreated respiratory streptococcal infections), trauma, obstruction of the renal (kidney) artery which diminishes blood flow to the kidney, and preeclampsia. The concern with acute kidney failure is that severe damage can occur in a very short amount of time.

Who tends to have kidney disease and kidney failure?

People who struggle with some of the chronic diseases listed below tend to be at significantly greater risk for kidney disease and subsequent failure. The most common causes are:

- diabetes—a chronic disease that causes damage to blood vessels, including those of the renal system;

103

- hypertension—continued high blood pressure damages all blood vessels, including those of the kidneys;
- glomerulonephritis—an infection of the glomeruli or of the working blood vessels of the kidneys; and
- polycystic kidney disease—a less common disorder of the kidneys resulting in kidney failure.

Often, it is necessary for a nephrologist (kidney specialist) to take a biopsy, or sample of the kidney cells and tissue, to determine the exact cause of kidney disease. If someone is known to have a chronic medical condition known to cause kidney disease, a biopsy may not be necessary.

Why is kidney disease in pregnancy so risky and concerning?

In normal pregnancy the kidneys work hard to deal with the extra amount of fluid in the circulation. The enlargement, or dilation, of the kidneys and blood vessels enable the kidneys to do this increased work. However, there is a fine balance between meeting the needs of the pregnant woman and her baby and being pushed to the point of being unable to keep up with the increased demands.

The pregnant woman with chronic kidney failure may have a worsening of her kidney status and kidney function. Some of the signs that kidney function is declining include progressively worsening high blood pressure (hypertension) and increases in the blood of some waste products generally excreted by the kidneys (such as potassium, urea, and creatinine).

Anytime a mother has signs of worsening kidney disease, her baby is also experiencing the consequences of those same problems. If your blood pressure increases or stays high throughout pregnancy, the baby gets less blood supply through the placenta, resulting in poor fetal growth. The circulating waste products can also have an effect on the baby's metabolic balance and result in a sick fetus which is not tolerating its environment well.

In circumstances of acute kidney failure, the mother will often decompensate, or become very ill, in a short period of time. If mom is sick enough to progress into acute kidney failure and is extremely ill, the physician's goal will be to stabilize her rapidly and aggressively. Unfortunately, the baby becomes a secondary priority in such critical situations. Often, a baby whose mother is in acute kidney failure is well grown and well developed because the problem with its mom occurred suddenly. In the midst of a crisis, however, the baby will not do well until the mother is stabilized.

How can I best care for myself and my baby?

Chronic kidney failure

Chronic kidney failure is the only type of kidney failure which is known ahead of time. Thus, its complications with pregnancy can be anticipated. If you have a known kidney disease, the ideal situation is to have preconception counseling with both you and the father of your baby. This is a time when a high-risk obstetrician (often called a perinatologist or maternal-fetal medicine specialist) can sit down with you and your family prior to pregnancy and discuss potential pregnancy risks and outcomes.

If you are already pregnant, the very best thing you can do for you and your baby is to get early, comprehensive prenatal care. Your care during this time is critical in determining your health status and degree of kidney function in order to more accurately determine if your kidney status is changing or worsening. Management of your care will most likely include a perinatologist, nephrologist (kidney specialist), and neonatologist (high-risk newborn specialist).

Your first prenatal visit will include a thorough history and physical along with routine prenatal laboratory blood work and kidney function blood work. You will also be asked to obtain a twenty-four hour urine sample to be brought back to the laboratory for evaluation of the total amount of protein and creatinine in your urine. Early in pregnancy, an ultrasound will be done to confirm or establish an accurate gestational age for your baby.

Routine prenatal visits will occur every two weeks until thirty-two weeks gestation, as long as there are no complications. Each visit will include: obtaining a urine sample to dip for protein, glucose, and signs of UTI; taking your blood pressure; obtaining your weight; and generally assessing how things are going. For those with kidney disease, monthly twenty-four hour urine tests will be done and compared to previous tests. If tests show a trend of increasing protein in the urine, this is a sign of worsening kidney disease. Frequent blood tests to assess for any increase in blood urea nitrogen (BUN, for short) and creatinine will also be done. These two substances will increase in your blood if kidney function is diminishing.

At approximately twenty weeks gestation, the baby will be looked at closely, from head to toe, assessing its size, its organ development, and its growth. Beyond twenty-four weeks gestation, you will begin having serial ultrasounds, meaning that the baby will be frequently assessed by ultrasound for growth. During these ultrasounds, the amniotic fluid volume is assessed to see if it is too low, and the placenta will be assessed for signs of premature aging. Both of these can help identify problems of worsening maternal disease and, subsequently, how well or poorly the baby is tolerating the changes.

High blood pressure (hypertension) in chronic kidney disease is very common. One of the major goals throughout your pregnancy will be to keep your blood pressure under control. If you've had kidney disease for any length of time, you usually have high blood pressure also. (Please refer to the next part of this chapter for specific information regarding the control and management of chronic high blood pressure.)

The pregnant woman with underlying kidney disease or chronic high blood pressure is at significantly greater risk for preeclampsia. Briefly, preeclampsia is a disease of pregnancy which can cause very high blood pressure, worsening kidney disease, liver disease, seizures, and stroke. Additionally, it can cause severe growth restriction and a potentially poor outcome for the baby, including severe prematurity and death. (See Chapter XII regarding preeclampsia.) In a woman with kidney disease, preeclampsia can occur earlier in pregnancy than with other women, and it can be much more severe. Termination of the pregnancy is recommended in cases in which preeclampsia occurs at less than twenty-four weeks gestation. This may seem like a harsh solution, but in these circumstances, the mother is at risk for dying as a result of her high blood pressure and preeclampsia, and the baby, having lived in a uterus with minimal blood flow due to the high blood pressure and other problems with its placenta, will be very small for its age and will most likely not survive.

The first goal is to treat the underlying problem, but in chronic disease resulting in kidney failure, that strategy is not effective because the disease has already progressed to the point of causing permanent damage. So, the next step is to treat the symptoms. High blood pressure is a big problem and must be controlled for the safety and well-being of both mother and baby. If evidence of worsening disease such as high levels of protein in the urine; high levels of BUN and creatinine in the blood; clinical signs of mental confusion, muscle and bone pain; or uncoordinated movements appear, then it is time for renal dialysis.

Kidney (renal) dialysis is a process of taking blood out of a person's body, through special intravenous tubes or catheters, sending the blood into a dialysis machine, moving it across several thin membranes in the dialysis machine in order to purify the blood of waste products and toxins, and then returning it to the person's circulation. In order for a person with kidney failure to survive, this must be done three to five times each week, every week of the year, for the rest of their lives. Women on dialysis can carry a successful pregnancy. However, all pregnant women who require dialysis will need to increase their weekly hours on dialysis by as much as 50 percent. Additionally, nearly all women on dialysis will deliver prematurely. In severe cases of kidney failure, kidney transplant is often an option though not during pregnancy.

Acute kidney failure

In circumstances of acute kidney failure, the mother is often critically ill. The effect on the kidneys is usually only one manifestation of a traumatic event, or disease process, that affects all other organ systems. The primary goal will be to correct the underlying problem.

There are three phases of acute kidney failure, all with distinct problems which must be dealt with in critical care settings. Often, a pregnant woman in acute kidney failure will be placed in an intensive or critical care unit, and will be closely monitored and on many medications to help stabilize her condition.

Sometimes, the cause of kidney failure can be obstetrical, or caused by a problem of the pregnancy. For example, placental abruption (in which the placenta partially or completely pulls away from the uterine wall) or hemorrhage during or after delivery can cause severe bleeding and subsequent kidney failure. In these cases, the baby is delivered urgently, and the mother is then cared for in a critical care unit.

In those circumstances of acute kidney failure caused by trauma (excessive bleeding) or drug toxicity, for example, there will be an attempt to stabilize the mother, thereby stabilizing the baby. If she can be moved beyond the critical phases of acute kidney failure and remain pregnant with a viable fetus, she will begin dialysis as soon as possible.

Acute kidney failure is very difficult to anticipate. Even when your care provider recognizes the signs, the time frame from which to plan or intervene is usually only a few hours and maybe a day. You can continue maximizing your chances for a positive outcome for you and your baby by beginning prenatal care early and seeing your care provider often.

Chronic High Blood Pressure, or Hypertension

Chronic high blood pressure in pregnancy is defined as persistent elevation of blood pressure, greater than 140/90, prior to pregnancy or prior to the twentieth week of gestation. High blood pressure can be the result of kidney damage and kidney disease, resulting in an inappropriate response by renin in the kidneys, which can then cause high blood pressure. Or, the high blood pressure itself can be the offending agent, causing a decrease in blood flow to the kidneys, resulting in kidney damage, making the high blood pressure even more severe. Regardless of the initial triggering factor, high blood pressure in pregnancy puts mom and baby at risk for complications.

If chronic high blood pressure is a problem in your pregnancy, *please* refer to Chapter III on cardiac disease in pregnancy before continuing on with this section. It is important to understand how blood vessels work normally before understanding how they might play a role in high blood pressure.

Who tends to have high blood pressure?

People who are at risk for kidney disease are also at risk for high blood pressure. As discussed earlier, it is sometimes difficult to know which comes first, high blood pressure or kidney disease. We do know that high blood pressure is a significant problem for many Americans.

High blood pressure quite often is related to lifestyle choices: poor dietary habits (high fat, high sodium diets) and obesity, a sedentary lifestyle, stresses, smoking, alcohol use, and drug use. Many people are also at risk because of their genetic makeup.

Why is high blood pressure in pregnancy a concern?

Pregnancy is a time of great changes in the cardiovascular, or heart and blood vessel, system. In the circumstance of high blood pressure, the hormones of pregnancy work to relax the walls of the blood vessels, but this generally isn't enough to accommodate the increased fluid. The result is an overall higher resting blood pressure, with little tolerance in the system for stress or increased workload. Consistently high pressure can begin to damage the smaller blood vessels that actually transport blood to and from the cells and tissues. This includes the tissues of the heart, lungs, brain, kidneys, liver, and the ever important uterus.

The potential for a good pregnancy outcome is directly related to the severity of your hypertension *before* pregnancy. If your hypertension has been well controlled and is generally considered mild to moderate in severity, your chances for a positive outcome are pretty good. If, however, you come into pregnancy with severe hypertension, meaning consistent blood pressure of greater than 160/100, your chances of developing preeclampsia are great. The potential outcome can be quite serious for both you and your baby, including the risk for seizures and stroke in mom, and severe growth restriction and prematurity of the baby. If you have a history of severe hypertension prior to pregnancy, you may be advised to avoid pregnancy or to terminate a pregnancy early in gestation if your blood pressure is uncontrolled.

The concerns are many. First, you want to keep healthy throughout pregnancy if you are starting out with high blood pressure. Not only do you want to keep your blood pressure under control, but to prevent any damage to your vital organs, such as your heart, lungs, brain, and kidneys. Second, beginning a pregnancy with high blood pressure puts you at greater risk for preeclampsia (see Chapter XII on preeclampsia). Last, you want to maximize the chances for growing a healthy, normally grown baby.

What will happen?
How can I best care for my baby and myself?

The single greatest thing you can do for you and your baby is to get early, comprehensive prenatal care—a point I stress continually throughout this book. The first visit will include a thorough medical and family history, as well as a physical exam. A fair bit of time will be spent reviewing your current medications, particularly those to treat your high blood pressure, and any others which may impact or affect your blood pressure. The rest of your first prenatal visit will proceed much like the one outlined previously in this chapter.

One of the primary goals of your care will be to maintain a medication regimen that controls your blood pressure and yet sustains adequate blood flow and oxygenation of your uterus, placenta, and baby. If you already have underlying hypertension, you may already be on these same medications that have worked well for you prior to pregnancy.

A common type of medication is an ACE inhibitor (short for

angiotensin converting enzyme inhibitor). Lotensin and Vasotec are examples of ACE inhibitors. These drugs keep your blood pressure within acceptable limits, and they have the added advantage of minimizing further kidney damage due to high blood pressure. However, ACE inhibitors can have significant, adverse effects for developing babies, so they are never used in pregnancy.

Another group of anti-hypertensive medications that are often used in nonpregnant women are diuretics. These types of drugs help eliminate excess fluid in the circulation, thereby reducing overall pressure in the circulatory system. These are generally not used in pregnancy because they can significantly decrease the amount of blood and oxygen being delivered to the baby via the placenta and uterus.

Some common medications used to control blood pressure in pregnancy include Aldomet, labetalol (goes by many trade names), and Procardia. The goal is to find the lowest dose of any one medication, or combination of medications, to keep your blood pressure within an acceptable range. You may ask yourself, "What is an acceptable range?" That may differ from individual to individual. A very general range may be 130–140/70–80. Throughout pregnancy you will be monitored closely for signs that your blood pressure medication is doing its job. In fact, you may be asked to keep a daily log of when you take your medications, your daily routines, and your blood pressure, taken two to three times each day. These will help determine how things are going throughout your day and not just when you are in the doctor's office.

An important point to remember is that your baby has been dependent on a certain baseline blood pressure which may be as high as 140/90 on a regular basis. This means that much care needs to be taken as your medications are adjusted. Too great of a drop in your blood pressure could significantly compromise your baby since her circulatory system, primarily the placenta, is highly dependent on a fairly high baseline pressure.

So, in addition to your log of daily routines and blood pressure, it is strongly encouraged that you begin a log of fetal movement starting sometime between twenty-four and twenty-eight weeks of pregnancy two to three times daily. Simply take time, preferably after a snack or meal and a glass of juice or water, to count the number of times your baby moves in one hour. Lay down on your side (either side, it doesn't matter which), put your hand on your belly, and count how many times your baby moves, kicks, or punches. She should move at least six times during that hour. If the baby doesn't move, give your care provider a call to let him know what's happening.

In addition to closely monitoring your blood pressure throughout your prenatal care, you will continually be assessed for signs of preeclampsia. At every prenatal visit your healthcare providers will ask you, "Do you have a headache, changes in your vision like spots or blurriness, or any right upper abdominal pain?" You may get tired of these questions, but the purpose is to help make you aware of how preeclampsia may sneak up on you. So, if you do have a headache, particularly a pounding one that doesn't go away with Tylenol or increased fluid intake, call your care provider immediately. You should also call if any blurry vision or spots appear in front of your eyes and don't go away with rest, or if they get worse. And you should call with any upper abdominal pain—not the kind of pain you get when the baby rolls, or stretches, or kicks, but the kind of pain that is nagging, aching, and sometimes goes around to the right side of your back and doesn't go away, no matter what you do. These are classic signs of preeclampsia that *should not* wait until your next prenatal visit.

Labor, delivery, and postpartum

Kidney failure and high blood pressure pose many similar dilemmas when considering labor, delivery, and postpartum. In all of these conditions, the health of the mother and the health of the baby are being continually weighed against one another. Your care providers walk a fine line between trying to keep a baby in its mother's uterus as long as possible and protecting the mother from the complications of worsening kidney disease or high blood pressure.

Sometimes, the uterus and placenta can be a hostile environment if the mother has high blood pressure and the placenta isn't getting enough blood; or if excessive amounts of waste products are present in the mother's and baby's circulation, poisoning them both; or if the mother's body is struggling to stay alive, sometimes at the expense of the fetus. On the other hand, if blood pressure stays within acceptable ranges, minimizing further kidney deterioration, and growing a decent sized baby, mother and baby should fare well. It is a constant balancing act between what is best for the baby versus what is best for mom. Labor and delivery timing will vary from individual to individual, depending on mom's health status, the baby's tolerance, and the risk for making either of them sicker by waiting or choosing to deliver immediately. Some precautions and procedures you might anticipate include:

- hospitalization, prior to delivery, to closely monitor both mother and baby for signs of worsening kidney disease or high blood pressure;
- close monitoring of your blood pressure, either by a standard blood pressure cuff, or sometimes by a special catheter placed into the artery of your wrist to directly and constantly measure your blood pressure;
- close monitoring of the baby, either by an external fetal monitor (those kind with belts) or (during labor) by use of

an internal fetal monitor and pressure catheter, to directly monitor the baby's heart rate and the strength of contractions, respectively;

- frequent ultrasounds of the baby, measuring its growth, amniotic fluid, and placenta, as well as measuring its blood pressure through the umbilical blood vessels via Doppler ultrasound;

- an intravenous catheter to administer fluids as well as medications (these will very often be on an "IV pump" to absolutely control the amount of fluids being given);

- the possibility of taking several twenty-four hour urine specimens over the course of many days in order to see if the amount of protein being excreted is increasing (a sign of worsening kidney disease or preeclampsia);

- having blood drawn several times a week to assess for signs of worsening kidney disease or preeclampsia;

- probably being given medications (some as injections, some through an IV) to help mature the baby's lungs in anticipation of an early (preterm) delivery; and

- the possibility of a specialized intravenous catheter, called a Swan-Ganz catheter, to directly measure fluid volume and resistance, or pressure, in the circulatory system (this can also be used to administer fluids, like an IV, and medications).

The above list addresses many potential procedures to which you may be exposed in anticipation of this delivery. Remember, the goal is to keep that baby inside as long as it is safe for both you and the baby. The only way to determine "safe" is to keep a very close eye on your condition and that of the baby. Some of the items listed won't apply to you if you have only mild to moderate kidney disease or high blood pressure. However, because you are still at increased risk for preeclampsia, much of it may still apply.

If you have moderate to severe kidney disease and/or high blood pressure, nearly all of the procedures listed above will apply to your care and may be overwhelming, but know that this can occur over a period of several days or weeks, depending on your particular situation. The timing of your delivery will be made according to how well you and your baby are tolerating your given disease process. If either of you begins to become increasingly symptomatic, it is then time to talk with your family and care providers to make some decisions about how and when delivery will occur.

In Conclusion

Congratulations on taking the time to be informed and knowledgeable about your particular condition and the prospects for a healthy pregnancy. You covered a lot of material on kidney disease and pregnancy. However, I've only scratched the surface. So, remember to ask lots of questions, especially with regard to your particular health status and your particular history. Your health care provider will be able to point you in the direction of other texts or other healthcare personnel who will help you find answers to any additional questions you may have.

V

Rh Disease

Overview

Most people have heard of the terms "Rh positive" and "Rh negative" in discussions regarding blood type. Many people are aware of their particular blood type, such as A-positive or O-negative. General blood types exist in many different combinations as well as in less common combinations with less common blood cell characteristics. None are better or worse than another, they are simply different.

Blood groups and blood types have specific characteristics of an individual's red blood cells. All people have red blood cells, or RBCs, which are responsible for transporting oxygen and carbon dioxide around in the body. However, RBCs vary among different individuals. The work they do is the same, but they can have different groups of proteins on and in the cells themselves. These characteristics are inherited from our parents, much like our facial features and hair color.

Blood types

The A, B, and O blood group characteristics are indicated by specific types of proteins found on the surface of the RBCs, as well as inside the cell and in other body fluids like semen and saliva. Blood types A and B indicate two different proteins which exist on and in the RBC. Blood type O indicates the absence of either A or B proteins. It is also possible to have both A and B proteins present in a single individual. Thus, individuals can have type A blood, type B blood, type AB blood, or type O blood. ABO blood type is the most important RBC characteristic when discussing blood transfusions, but the *Rh factor* is the most important when discussing pregnancy and Rh disease.

The Rh factor is a group of proteins that occur only on the surface of the red blood cell. Simply put, if you have the Rh factor present in your RBCs, you are termed "Rh positive." If the Rh factor is absent then you are termed "Rh negative." So there are generally two parts to blood typing: the ABO part and the Rh part, and people are typed as A-positive, A-negative, B-positive, B-negative, AB-positive, AB-negative, O-positive, or O-negative.

Immune response

The immune system plays a key role in Rh disease and pregnancy because it is that part of our bodies responsible for fighting off disease and illness. It does this job by first recognizing foreign cells that have invaded the body and then by setting out to destroy these invading "non-self" organisms. It also forms antibodies against specific invading organisms that can be called on in the future to fight invasion by the exact same organism. Antibodies are made to recognize specific cells. For example, many of us have antibodies to the measles, mumps, some flu strains, hepatitis, chicken pox, and so on. These antibodies protect us from getting sick again if we come in contact with these specific invading organisms. It is this same immune response that is responsible for the problems associated with pregnancy when a mother is Rh negative and the baby she is carrying in her uterus is Rh positive.

What is Rh Disease?

Rh disease occurs when an Rh-negative mother and her husband conceive an Rh positive child. When a few of the baby's Rh positive red blood cells cross into the mother's system via the placenta, either through a fall or accident, an amniocentesis, during a miscarriage, elective abortion, or ectopic (tubular) pregnancy, or after delivery when the placenta is removed, the mother's immune system identifies these Rh positive fetal RBCs as foreign and sets out to immediately destroy them, as well as form long-term antibodies to fight them off at a later time.

If you are an Rh negative woman and you are carrying an Rh positive child during your first pregnancy, the chance of becoming sensitized and causing a problem for the baby is small. If the baby's RBCs pass into the mother's system, her body responds by producing antibodies and she becomes "Rh sensitized." As a result, she will *always* carry these antibodies in her immune system.

If you carry an Rh-positive child in a subsequent pregnancy, the antibodies created by the immune system during the first exposure respond more quickly to the foreign red blood cells from the baby. These antibodies attack and destroy the baby's RBCs in the mother's circulation, but more importantly, they also cross the placenta and begin destroying the baby's red blood cells circulating in the baby's body. Remember, we all need functioning red blood cells to carry oxygen and carbon dioxide, even a baby in its mother's uterus. There are no complications for the mother in

119

these circumstances, but there may be minor to serious complications for the baby. This is called hemolytic disease of the newborn.

Prevention: A very important point

There are very few places in health care where a problem has been so clearly identified and a method of prevention has been so effective. Rh disease is one of those rare opportunities to really make a difference for many mothers and their babies. If you are an Rh negative woman who is considering pregnancy, or you are currently pregnant for the first time, or you are pregnant for the second or third time, you may still benefit from the following method of preventing Rh disease during pregnancy.

Early in pregnancy a standard group of routine prenatal blood tests are done on nearly all pregnant women. Included in this panel of tests is a blood test to determine your blood type (A, B, or O), your Rh status (positive or negative), and your antibody status. In this simple test, the laboratory is looking for a reaction by specific antibodies that might be present in your blood, specifically, if you have an Rh antibody, and if you do, what is the antibody exactly. If the antibody screen is negative then you are considered "unsensitized." If it is positive, the lab goes on to identify the exact antibody. The risks for potential problems with this pregnancy are then addressed. Prevention is only necessary and effective if you are Rh negative with an antibody screen that is negative.

In this circumstance, sensitization can be prevented by giving the Rh negative woman an injection of Rh immunoglobulin (RhoGAM™) during and after pregnancy. Rh immunoglobulin is an antibody derived from human blood products, which is injected into one of your muscles, usually an arm or buttock. With this specific antibody, your immune system is fooled into thinking it has already made these antibodies and blocks your immune system from producing any more.

So if you are Rh negative with a negative antibody screen, it is considered standard prenatal care to give you injections of RhoGAM™ to prevent Rh sensitization. You will receive two shots, one at twenty-eight weeks gestation and then again within seventy-two hours after the birth of your baby, if your baby is Rh positive. This method of prevention seems to block sensitization for a period of about twelve weeks, which is why you need two injections during the course of your pregnancy. For this reason, it is important that RhoGAM™ be given with *all* of your pregnancies, even those which may result in miscarriage, elective termination, or an ectopic pregnancy.

RhoGAM™ is given any time the placenta is disturbed due to an accident or blow to the stomach, which could cause the placenta to pull away from the wall of the uterus. It should also be given after an amniocentesis and after an episode of vaginal bleeding (see Chapter XIII regarding these problems).

Hemolytic disease of the newborn

Hemolytic disease of the newborn, or HDN for short, can actually be one or a group of symptoms exhibited by the baby. HDN is also termed erythroblastosis fetalis. The most severe symptom, which can be seen on ultrasound examination, is an accumulation of fluid throughout the baby's body, also called hydrops. After delivery, other symptoms may include severe newborn jaundice (yellowing of the body and skin), and a low red blood cell count (anemia).

These symptoms develop as a direct result of a mother's antibodies attaching to and destroying the baby's red blood cells, or hemolysis. Thus the name hemolytic disease of the newborn. Each subsequent pregnancy can result in more severe disease in the baby. The baby begins to compensate for the decreased number of RBCs by attempting to make lots more RBCs in a short period of time. But in the baby's bodily efforts to fix the problem it creates more problems, primarily in the liver. The baby's liver becomes enlarged and unable to handle the increased work of making new RBCs and cleaning away the debris of all the dead blood cells. At this time the baby begins to accumulate fluid in its belly, lungs, and around its heart, which can be seen easily on ultrasound. The dead red blood cells form bilirubin and result in moderate to severe jaundice in the newborn. Additionally, the baby will be anemic because the mother's antibodies have broken up so many of the red blood cells.

Rh sensitized, now what?

The very first thing your care provider will do is take a thorough history. This will specifically include questions about previous pregnancies, how severely the babies were affected, and whether or not this father is the same father of your previous children. In addition, a physical exam will be done as in all first prenatal visits. You may also have an early ultrasound, not necessarily to evaluate for problems, but rather to confirm your baby's due date as it is important to accurately know when this baby is due.

Also, the prenatal lab work will be drawn early in your prenatal care. It may also be necessary to test for the father's blood type and Rh status. If this is your first pregnancy with this man, and he is also Rh negative, there is no reason for concern because the baby will also be Rh negative like his parents. Even if the father is positive, there is still a chance that you and he could conceive an Rh negative child, again eliminating any concern for the baby's health due to Rh disease.

If you are already known to be Rh sensitized, your antibody screen will be positive. The laboratory will specifically identify the antibody and then measure the amount of antibody present in your system. This measure, or titer, determines how early to begin watching and/or treating the baby for problems. The higher the titer, the sooner the baby will begin to have symptoms of hemolytic disease and the sooner it will require intervention.

What Should I Expect Throughout Pregnancy?

Antibody titers are expressed in ratios. For example, an Rh negative woman with a positive antibody screen and a titer of 1:4 is considered sensitized. Starting very early in pregnancy your care provider will draw blood frequently in order to assess your antibody titer. If the titer begins to rise, reaching the level of 1:8 or 1:16, then closer evaluation of the baby through ultrasound and amniocentesis will be necessary. Titers are valuable in determining when to begin fetal testing, but they are not very good at determining the severity of disease in a given baby. This means that even if a mother's titer is only 1:8 her baby can be very sick. On the other hand, a baby may have only moderate disease when his mother's titers are significantly higher at 1:16 or 1:32.

If you have a previous history of moderate to severe Rh disease in past pregnancies, assessment and management will begin as early as eighteen to twenty-two weeks. The high-risk pregnancy specialist will use ultrasound examination to look for any signs of fluid accumulation in the baby's belly, head, chest, or heart.

Amniotic fluid is removed from around the baby via amniocentesis in which a needle is guided through the abdomen and into the uterus using ultrasound. Its purpose is to draw fluid from around the baby which will then be evaluated in the laboratory for levels of bilirubin, a by-product of red blood cell breakdown which results in newborn jaundice. Bilirubin will be present in the amniotic fluid of a fetus with worsening Rh disease. Using a method called the delta-OD 450, the fluid is tested in a lab and is assigned a number value. Values vary according to gestational age so there is no list of absolute numbers which can tell you how well your baby is doing. There is however a graph, called the Liley graph, which can plot the delta-OD 450 according to gestational age.

Table 3. Care Plan for Rh Disease in Pregnancy

	ZONE 1 mild	ZONE II moderate	UPPER ZONE II moderate to severe	ZONE III severe
SEVERITY				
MANAGEMENT	amnio for delta-OD 450 every 4–5 weeks	amnio for delta-OD 450 every 1–2 weeks	amnio for delta-OD 450 every 1–2 weeks	fetal blood transfusion
DELIVERY	at term	37 weeks	34–36 weeks if fetal lungs are mature	deliver at once if fetal lungs are mature

The graph divides risk categories into zones, referred to as Zone I, Zone II, and Zone III. Zone I is the lower limit, indicating mild or minimal disease. Zone II is the middle or marginal zone, indicating a range of severity from moderate in the lower part of Zone II, to more severe disease in the higher ranges of Zone II. And Zone III is the upper or critical limit, indicating of severe disease. The delta-OD 450 method entails more than looking at the numbers; it also looks at the trend that develops over time. This means that several amniocenteses may be necessary throughout a sensitized pregnancy with the average time between amniocentesis of ten days to three weeks.

Another test, called cordocentesis or percutaneous umbilical blood sampling (PUBS), obtains some of the baby's blood in order to directly assess how severely affected this baby might be. This is performed much like an amniocentesis by injecting a needle into the uterus through the abdomen, but instead of taking out amniotic fluid, a small amount of fetal blood from the baby's umbilical cord is removed for evaluation. Fetal blood analysis allows for direct measurement of antibodies in the baby's circulation, assessment of the severity of the baby's anemia, assessment of actual bilirubin levels, chromosome studies, and direct evaluation of how the baby is compensating for the destruction of its red blood cells.

The need for amniocentesis versus cordocentesis varies, depending on the severity of disease in the baby. Cordocentesis carries a somewhat increased risk for complications during and after the procedure. But in a tertiary care center, which is a hospital specializing in high-risk pregnancy, the risk is about equal to amniocentesis.

What if the baby starts to get sicker?

Perhaps a better question would be: How will we know if the baby is getting sicker? And then ask the question: What do we do? Indicators that the baby is getting sicker, or severely anemic, are:
1. delta-OD 450s that move from Zone I or lower Zone II up into high Zone II or Zone III;
2. fetal blood sampling that indicates severe anemia; or
3. ultrasound evaluation that indicates significant fluid accumulation in parts of the baby such as the belly, chest, head, and heart. An important point to remember is that

any sign of fluid accumulation (or hydrops) is an indication of severe anemia.

The definitive treatment for severe anemia due to Rh disease is an intrauterine fetal transfusion. This is a very specialized procedure in which specially prepared blood is given directly to the baby through the baby's umbilical vein while the baby is still in the uterus. This is only done by a highly-skilled, high-risk pregnancy specialist (perinatologist). Its goal is to provide the baby with fresh red blood cells to carry oxygen.

Intrauterine fetal transfusion (IUFT) is a complex procedure that takes place in an operating room in the event that an immediate cesarean section must be performed. This is a rare but potential risk of fetal transfusion. When the transfusion is complete, the mother is placed on a machine to monitor the baby's heart rate. For the next two to six hours she will be watched closely for signs of uterine contractions and any signs of distress in the baby's heart rate.

The goal of the transfusion is to raise your baby's red blood cells to a level high enough to keep her healthy as long as possible. There is also a possibility that she will need repeated transfusions prior to her birth.

What are the risks and benefits of intrauterine fetal transfusion?

Risks associated with intrauterine fetal transfusion include bleeding from the needle site on the umbilical vein; development of a blood clot at the site of injection which can block any blood flow through the vessel to the baby; infection of the uterus and subsequently the baby; possibility of rupturing the bag of water or amniotic sac; and possibly, further movement of the baby's RBCs across to the mother, creating more antibodies in her immune system. During the procedure, there is also a risk that the baby will not tolerate the procedure well and drop its heart rate significantly enough to require immediate delivery. If this happens, a cesarean section is performed on the spot as all the appropriate personnel are on standby. The baby is then delivered and resuscitated in the operating room and will most likely be transferred to the neonatal intensive care unit for evaluation and treatment.

Given all of these risks, you may ask yourself why you would even consider putting your baby through this procedure. Over the past thirty to forty years, dramatically improved detection and treatment of moderately affected babies have improved survival rates from 34 to 57 percent in the 1960s and 70s, to nearly 89 percent today, with very good outcomes for the babies. The alternative is to have a baby whose condition continues to worsen, developing complications both in the uterus and after delivery. Intrauterine fetal transfusion is not performed on mildly affected fetuses, only on those who have become seriously ill. Without transfusion, these babies would either be born very early, suffering the consequences of both Rh disease and prematurity, or die in the uterus before birth or shortly after birth.

The goal of IUFT is to help the baby survive in a hostile environment — the uterus. Although the uterus is a hostile place, with the mother's antibodies destroying oxygen-carrying red blood cells, it is a better place to grow babies than a neonatal intensive care unit. The hope is to provide a place where baby can continue to grow until a time when it is more likely to tolerate life on the outside. The general timeframe we strive for is about thirty-two to thirty-four weeks gestation, depending on the severity of the disease. This may mean that you will need several amniocenteses to evaluate how your baby is doing and possibly several intrauterine fetal transfusions to get your baby closer to its due date.

127

How can I best care for my baby and myself?

As I've said before, the single most important thing you can do is to get early, comprehensive prenatal care. This is especially true if you already know you are Rh negative or if you know that you are Rh sensitized. Always keep your doctor and ultrasound appointments which for some of you may mean traveling great distances to get to a high-risk pregnancy center, but it is really the key to managing Rh disease in your pregnancy. If you are Rh negative but not sensitized, the most important thing you can do is to get your RhoGAM™ injections at twenty-eight weeks and within seventy-two hours after delivery. This will protect any future children you may have from the complications of Rh disease.

Second, you can be well informed by reading about Rh disease. Bookstores and libraries provide numerous resources, as well as medical and nursing professionals who can help you find other sources of information for you and your partner.

Finally, ask lots of questions. There are no dumb questions when it comes to your health and the health of your baby. If you don't understand something, ask for clarification. Medical terminology uses lots of acronyms and abbreviations when referring to tests and conditions, so much so that care providers often forget how to talk in normal, nonmedical terms and assume patients automatically understand them. Don't let anyone get away with this. You and your family need clear, concise answers, but you'll only get clarification if you ask for it.

Labor, delivery, and postpartum

In a baby with significant hemolytic disease, or a lot of fluid accumulation and severe anemia, intrauterine fetal blood transfusion is the appropriate treatment. If IUFT is successful in stabilizing a moderately or severely affected baby, vaginal delivery can be induced at thirty-two or thirty-four weeks, if the baby's lungs are mature enough.

Labor and delivery generally progress with minimal problems. The condition of the baby at the time of active labor is the greatest concern. If the baby is moderately to severely compromised, even with successful fetal transfusions, the baby may not tolerate labor well as labor and contractions can be stressful to a baby and is indicated on a fetal monitor tracing as fetal distress. In circumstances where the baby comes into labor already stressed, it may have minimal energy reserves for labor. This may put you at increased risk for cesarean section as the means of delivery. During labor, this will mean that you will have an intravenous line, an external fetal monitor, and probably an internal fetal heart rate monitor, as well as an internal uterine contraction monitor. These will be used to more closely assess the progression of labor and the baby's tolerance of labor itself. And, because your pregnancy will be a known preterm delivery of a potentially compromised baby, neonatal specialists will be present at the delivery, whether it is a vaginal or surgical delivery.

The postpartum period is generally uneventful for you, certainly with regard to being Rh sensitized. You will not be a candidate for RhoGAM™ after delivery because you are already sensitized and antibodies already exist in your system. The baby will most likely be observed in the neonatal intensive care unit (NICU) because it is still at risk for newborn anemia (too few circulating red blood cells) and potentially severe newborn jaundice. Your baby may not be out of the woods at this point and may require further transfusions in the NICU, but she has a much better chance at survival as a thirty-two or thirty-four week newborn rather than as a very ill twenty-four or twenty-six week newborn. Because your baby will most likely be preterm, she will require close observation for other problems related to prematurity.

Some Parting Thoughts

Rh disease in pregnancy can be a scary thing, especially if it's happening to you and your family. Prevention is the number one solution for those women who are Rh negative, but remain unsensitized. In other cases in which sensitization has already occurred, the best strategy is early prenatal care with frequent and appropriate management by well trained high-risk pregnancy specialists. We are fortunate to live in a time when management of this potentially catastrophic disease of pregnancy can be diagnosed early and treated appropriately and aggressively. The outcome is more often than not a live newborn.

Congratulations for taking the time and energy to be informed about the implications of Rh disease and pregnancy. It takes courage to face such a thing head on, but it is the only way to make truly informed choices about your care and the care of your unborn baby.

VI

Diabetes

Overview

This disease was discovered by the Egyptians around 1500 B.C., but no treatment was available until the early 1900s. Diabetes occurs when the body does not produce any or enough insulin. Insulin is needed to transport the sugar or glucose in your blood to tissues and organs that need the glucose (sugar) for energy. Without enough insulin, your blood sugar level remains high while your tissues and organs starve for fuel as the pancreas, the organ responsible for producing insulin in your body, stops functioning properly. Insulin, medication available since 1922, is used to treat diabetes.

There are three different types of diabetes. Gestational diabetes is a condition that occurs only during pregnancy. After delivery, the diabetes is usually no longer present. Gestational diabetes will be discussed in Part III. However, women who have gestational diabetes are at risk for developing Type II diabetes later in life. Type I diabetes, also known as insulin-dependent diabetes, affects approximately half a million people and occurs at any age, but is most often discovered between the ages of eleven and fourteen. Type II diabetes, also known as noninsulin-dependent diabetes, or adult-onset diabetes, affects more than 5 million people. The average age of onset for Type II diabetes is between fifty-one and fifty-five years old.

Pregnancy changes the way your body produces and reacts to insulin. Early in pregnancy your body increases insulin production and your tissues are very receptive to insulin. This is believed to be an attempt to provide more fuel stores for later use in pregnancy. As pregnancy continues, the placenta produces hormones that oppose the actions of insulin and some that increase the conversion of stored fuel back into sugar. When all this works properly, the body quickly converts food to stored fuel when eating, and when not eating quickly converts the stored fuel to glucose thus providing your baby with the needed fuel for growth.

Diabetes Mellitus Type I

Diabetes mellitus occurs when the islet of Langerhans cells in the pancreas either stops producing insulin or produces insufficient amounts. The symptoms of Type I diabetes are rapid weight loss, excessive thirst, excessive hunger, and frequent urination. Laboratory findings include ketones in the urine and high blood glucose levels.

Diabetes can affect many of your body's systems. The vascular system becomes affected and may cause damage to other parts of your body including your eyes, renal system (your kidneys), heart, and skin. The medical community has adopted a classification system for diabetics during pregnancy called White's Classification which uses letters.

Table 4. Diabetes in pregnancy: White's Classification

Class	(yr) Age of Onset	(yr) Duration	Presence of Vascular Disease	Therapy
A	any	any	0	modified diet or insulin
B	older than 20 yrs	less than 10 yrs	0	insulin
C	10–19	10–19	0	insulin
D	10 or 20	10 or 20	slight eye damage	insulin
F	any	any	kidney damage	insulin
R	any	any	severe eye damage	insulin
H	any	any	heart disease	insulin

Adapted from the American College of Obstetricians and Gynecologists: Technical Bulletin 92, May 1996.

Classifications B–D are assigned according to number of years you have had diabetes, age of onset, and amount of vascular involvement. Class F is when there is renal damage present. Class T is for renal transplantation. Class H is when heart disease is present. Class R is when there is eye damage known as retinopathy.

What are the main concerns for my baby and myself?

Diabetes does not affect fertility, so becoming pregnant is generally not a problem. Maintaining good diabetic control prior to becoming pregnant is very important. There is already a 6 to 8 percent risk for babies of diabetic mothers to be born with deformities, but this risk can increase to around 20 percent if blood sugars were high during the early period when the baby was forming. Tight glucose control decreases this risk. If high blood sugar levels continue during the pregnancy, the baby is at risk for being macrosomic, or very large. If your diabetes includes vascular disease, your baby may not grow well even if your blood sugars are high.

Babies of diabetic mothers are at risk for delayed development of lung maturity. This can cause the baby to have difficulty breathing if born early. An amniocentesis test should be done if your care provider plans to induce your labor early. The amniocentesis procedure involves guiding a needle using an ultrasound machine to visualize it into the uterus and removing some amniotic fluid from around the baby. Although the thought of this is scary, it is not painful. As the needle enters the uterus, most women notice a "cramp." Amniotic fluid is then quickly removed, and the procedure is over in a matter of minutes. This fluid is then analyzed in a laboratory to determine the maturity of your baby's lungs. If the lungs are not mature, waiting and repeating the test in one to two weeks may be indicated.

After the birth, your baby's blood sugar will be monitored closely. Problems with blood sugar control are common in babies of diabetic mothers for a period of time after birth. Blood sugar control is more difficult for large, heavy babies who have had more sugar or glucose available during the pregnancy and have produced more insulin as a result. After delivery, the high glucose levels are no longer present, but high insulin levels are still present. Therefore, the baby may have problems with low blood sugar, as well as difficulties with low calcium levels and jaundice.

Pregnant diabetic mothers can have problems with *low* blood sugar, especially during the first trimester. The baby is utilizing your glucose to grow, leaving less available glucose for your body. This can lead to times of hypoglycemia, or low blood sugar. Discuss with your care provider how best to control this problem.

It may take time and frequent adjustment of your insulin to regulate your glucose levels.

Extremely high blood sugar leads to a problem called ketoacidosis. This can be very detrimental to your baby. When ketoacidosis occurs, the risk for pregnancy loss increases tremendously. If it occurs very early in the pregnancy, the presence of large amounts of ketones have been linked with an increase in malformations. This reinforces the need for good diabetic control prior to and during your pregnancy.

You may be at risk for worsening eye problems during your pregnancy. Retinal changes may occur or worsen during pregnancy. An eye exam before pregnancy is very important since proliferative retinopathy, if present, may become progressive during your pregnancy and could cause permanent changes in your vision. Treatment should be undertaken prior to pregnancy when possible. Benign retinopathy may also worsen during the pregnancy but usually returns to the prepregnant state after delivery.

The combination of diabetes and pregnancy increases your chances for urinary tract infections and kidney infections known as pyelonephritis. These infections (or any type of infection) can cause problems with blood sugar control. Any infection needs to be treated. If you are a Class F diabetic, your renal problems may worsen as the pregnancy advances. Hypertension may worsen, and you are at increased risk for developing preeclampsia. Preeclampsia or kidney problems may force your care providers to deliver your baby prematurely. After delivery, during the postpartum period, the kidney problems generally return to the prepregnant state. Please refer to Chapter IV on kidney disease in pregnancy and Chapter XII on preeclampsia.

If your diabetic classification is H, you have heart disease with your diabetes and are at an increased risk to not survive the pregnancy. Therefore, serious consideration should be undertaken prior to deciding on becoming pregnant or continuing the pregnancy. Discussions with your cardiologist, the doctor managing your diabetes, and a specialist in high-risk pregnancies may be helpful in obtaining all the information needed to make this decision.

How can I best care for my baby and myself?

The following precautions will help reduce risk for complications:
- Maintain normal blood glucose levels at the time of conception and throughout pregnancy.
- Preconception prenatal care is crucial.
- Talk with your care provider before becoming pregnant.
- Discuss blood sugar levels and tests that need to be done.
- Have regular eye exams and evaluations of your kidneys.
- Discuss how often you should be testing your blood sugars once you are pregnant.
- You may need to increase insulin injections to three times a day.
- Keep an accurate record of your blood sugar and bring this record to your office visit.

Prenatal care should include an ultrasound during the first twelve weeks to ensure an accurate due date. The next ultrasound should be at approximately twenty weeks. This will be a review of systems or a targeted ultrasound. The ultrasound will involve measuring the baby and looking carefully for problems and malformations. You may also have a special ultrasound looking at the baby's heart called a fetal echocardiogram. In addition, you will have serial ultrasounds throughout your pregnancy to assess the size of your baby and to look for excessive amniotic fluid.

Around twenty-eight weeks, your care provider will begin weekly testing for your baby's well-being with a nonstress test (NST). Diabetic babies are at increased risk for stillbirth. This testing helps to detect babies that are having problems. A fetal monitor watches the baby's heart rate, any contractions, and your perception of fetal movement which is tracked by pressing a button. The fetal monitor strip is then evaluated.

A biophysical profile is another test that may be done. This thirty-minute test uses ultrasound to watch for movement, tone, fetal breathing motion, level of amniotic fluid, and placental grading, and includes an NST evaluation. It is also important for you to keep track of the baby's movements and to contact your care provider if there is a decrease in movement. After thirty-two weeks, you will have this testing done twice a week.

Labor, delivery, and postpartum

As a diabetic, you have a slightly higher risk for delivery by cesarean section. This may be in part due to the number of elective cesarean sections done for extremely large babies. A large head may also increase the need for a cesarean birth. When labor occurs naturally, or is induced, you will receive a continuous infusion of insulin and sugar water to control your blood sugar. You will also have your blood sugar tested very frequently during labor, and the insulin dosage will be adjusted as needed. Labor usually progresses normally.

Delivery of a large baby places you at an increased risk for an episiotomy and tearing since the baby's shoulders are also too large for the birth canal. A difficult delivery of the shoulders in severe cases may cause damage to the baby's shoulder nerve causing a condition known as a brachial plexus injury. Facial palsy, a drooping of a portion of the face, can also occur. These conditions are usually temporary and heal with time. The baby's clavicle, or shoulder bone, may also be broken during a difficult shoulder delivery, and in extreme cases, a prolonged period of time between delivery of the head and the rest of the body can lead to brain damage.

After delivery, your insulin needs will often drop significantly once you are able to eat. Low blood sugars are sometimes common in the first week after delivery. Breast-feeding women are encouraged to increase their diet by 500 calories. As your milk production increases, your insulin requirements may fall.

Finally, taking good care of yourself is the first step to a long, happy life together with your baby.

VII

Neurological Problems

The neurological system, or nervous system, in your body is the system in charge of all of the nerves. Every part of your body is affected by some type of nerve. At the very base of every nerve is a cell called a neuron which is responsible for every response that your body makes to any change in its environment. Because these neurons are everywhere in your body, some will be affected when there is a problem, while others will not. Imagine, for example, breaking your leg. Your leg may not work well, but your arm should work as usual. This is why problems with the nervous system can range from being relatively mild to very serious. It all depends on the area and the amount of injury or damage.

Although it is common to notice some numbness in your fingers or in your pelvis during different times of your pregnancy, these type of nervous system problems do not qualify as high risk. This chapter will address the type of nervous system problems that are considered high risk: seizure disorders, spinal cord injuries, and multiple sclerosis. Review the chapter on normal pregnancy for further information on common symptoms of numbness or tingling as well as all normal changes of pregnancy.

Seizures

Overview

Seizures, or convulsions, are an abnormal condition that affects the nervous system and especially the brain. When a seizure occurs, a sudden disorderly "explosion" of sorts in the neurons is responsible for sending messages to one another. Sometimes the cause for a seizure is known. For example, an injury to the brain may be temporary, yet still causes seizures. When there is no correctable cause for a seizure, this disorder is referred to as epilepsy.

Seizures affect less than 1 percent of the population. Seventy-five percent of the time the reasons are unknown. The other 25 percent are due to brain injury from accidents or tumor growth. There also appears to be an inherited or familial aspect to seizures. For example, if your mother had seizures, you have a one in thirty chance of developing seizures yourself.

What are the main concerns for my baby and myself?

If you suffer from epilepsy or past seizures, the most important concern during pregnancy is the prevention of seizures. Seizures can harm you and your baby. If you are planning on becoming pregnant, inform your neurologist and obstetrical care provider of your history. Your care providers will most likely continue all your medications though they may try to decrease or change your medication dosages to the least harmful medications for pregnancy. Phenobarbital is the medication of choice. The next safest medications are primidone or carbamazepine. If you are already pregnant, do *not* stop taking your medication as this could be very harmful. Remember, preventing seizures is extremely important during pregnancy.

There is a current controversy regarding antiseizure medication and the effects they may or may not have on babies. The medical community is unsure if it is the medications or the epilepsy itself that places the baby at an increased risk for malformations. The good news is that women on antiseizure medications still have an 85 to 90 percent chance of having a healthy baby. Discuss this concern with your care providers. If at all possible, valproate and trimethadione should be avoided or stopped altogether. Valproate increases the risk for malformations of the spine and spinal cord known as neural tube defects such as spina bifida. Trimethadione causes various forms of malformations in the majority of the babies exposed. Many people with seizure disorders are treated with the medication Dilantin™. Dilantin™ is very effective in the control of seizures but has been associated with abnormalities such as cleft palate and defects in the baby's fingers and toes. Your care provider will help you decide on the best anticonvulsant medication for you and your baby.

In approximately 40 percent of women during pregnancy, seizures may increase. This high percentage may be due in part to the increased blood volume and increased kidney function. Testing blood levels of your medication frequently may be needed during pregnancy.

Your baby is at risk for neonatal coagulopathy which causes the baby to have problems with blood clotting. Vitamin K, starting at thirty-four weeks, can help prevent this problem. Vitamin K is routinely given to every baby after delivery to help with clotting.

How can I best care for my baby and myself?

Prior to conception, your care provider in collaboration with your neurologist will discuss your medications and seizure activity. If you have not had seizures for several years, they may attempt weaning your medication. While your medication is being weaned, driving is not recommended. If seizure activity resumes, the medications will be restarted. If you are currently on valproate or the rarely used trimethadione, an attempt will be made to find other medications that work well for you.

Prenatal vitamins and 1 mg of folic acid daily will be an important routine. These medications have been shown to decrease the risk of neural tube defects, correct any vitamin D deficiency, and help prevent anemia during the pregnancy. Blood levels of your anticonvulsant medications should be followed every two to four weeks when starting folic acid. Your medications will be adjusted as needed. The best time to attempt conception is after your blood levels have stabilized.

Once pregnant, the most important aspect of your care is to limit or prevent seizures. Taking your medication is important even if it means taking other medications to calm nausea. Have your blood levels drawn regularly as recommended by your care provider. Increase your medications as recommended by your care provider. You may feel like this is too much medication, but remember pregnancy can decrease blood levels of these medications. Switching medications is not recommended since this can cause seizures to occur. Getting plenty of sleep is also important. People deprived of sleep have been shown to have more seizure activity. The pregnancy increases your risk for aspiration during a seizure. Aspiration is inhaling some of the contents of your stomach into your lungs, and this can lead to pneumonia and death.

The frequency of your prenatal visits will remain the same unless seizures are a problem or the baby's growth is lagging. A review of systems ultrasound or targeted ultrasound should be done at eighteen to twenty weeks. These ultrasounds focus on all of your baby's visible systems. It will help determine the presence of most birth defects such as neural tube defects, abnormalities of the limbs, and cleft palate. Your care provider may then decide to have a closer look at your baby's heart with a special ultrasound called a fetal echocardiogram, an ultrasound that looks specifically for heart defects. Ultrasounds for growth and the amount of amniotic fluid may be done every four to six weeks.

Labor, delivery, and postpartum

The process of labor usually proceeds normally. Some of your medications may be given through an IV. This is helpful for additional hydration if your labor is long or if you are vomiting and unable to keep your pills down. Blood levels may be checked during labor, and during postpartum, blood levels will need to be checked frequently. Your medications often need to be decreased.

Breast-feeding while on your medications is not a problem. Only insignificant amounts pass into the breast milk. These levels are usually much lower than what the baby was exposed to during the pregnancy.

Spinal Cord Injury

Overview

Spinal cord trauma is most often due to accidents and usually involve the cervical and thoracic spine. Spinal cord injuries do not prevent conception, but they do increase the risk of other conditions that can have a huge impact on pregnancy. The degree of impact is dependent on the level of injury to the spinal cord.

What are the main concerns for my baby and myself?

Fertility is not impaired by the spinal cord injury, and the baby is not affected by your problem and should grow normally. However, pregnancy can further increase the risk of urinary tract or kidney infections (UTIs), which can lead to preterm labor. Your urine should be checked for infection at each office visit or at any time you suspect an infection. If you are already prone to get UTIs, medication may be started to prevent urinary tract infection. If you intermittently catheterize yourself, you may need to do this more frequently due to the enlarging uterus, increased blood volume, and increased urine production. Self-catheterization will also become more difficult as the uterus grows and your reach is limited. Urinary incontinence (uncontrolled urinating) may become a problem and could be confused with the rupturing of your water. If you are unsure about the source of wetness, have this checked by your care provider. Constipation and problems with bowel evacuation programs may occur.

Autonomic dysreflexia is a neurologic response characterized by a rise in blood pressure, a drop in heart rate, becoming flush above the area of the spinal cord injury, and very pale below it. This can lead to convulsions and an enlarged heart. Autonomic dysreflexia can be triggered by labor, an over-distended bladder, or a urinary tract infection. This problem occurs in women with a spinal cord injury at or above the seventh thoracic vertebra of the spine. The classic symptoms are profuse sweating, pounding headache, blotchy skin, and the small hairs on the skin standing erect. Other symptoms include feelings of anxiety, tremors, nausea, chest pain, shortness of breath, or nasal congestion. Your blood pressure is often elevated, and your heart can race or slow with autonomic dysreflexia. In labor, an epidural can help control autonomic dysreflexia if it becomes a problem. Treating a urinary tract infection or a distended bladder will usually resolve autonomic dysreflexia if they are the cause. High blood pressure medications such as Procardia or nifedipine (generic) may be the first line of treatment for elevated blood pressure.

How can I best care for my baby and myself?

Pregnancy should not add any additional restrictions to your lifestyle. Transfers in and out of a wheelchair may become more difficult as the pregnancy advances. As stated before, intermittent catheterization becomes more difficult as your uterus enlarges. You may not be able to feel the baby move if your level of injury is too high, but movement can be felt with your hands once the baby is large enough.

You may or may not feel contractions, depending again on the level of your spinal cord injury. This can make it difficult to diagnose term or preterm labor. If you feel your belly tightening or "balling up" more than four to six times per hour, contact your care provider. You may be required to go to the hospital or office to be monitored for contractions.

Labor, delivery, and postpartum

Since labor can begin without your perception, your care provider may decide to induce labor. Spinal cord injury does not affect the muscles used in labor, but the muscles used during the pushing stage may not be functional. The good news is that these muscles are not always needed. Your body may be able to deliver your baby without assistance. Forceps or suction assisted deliveries are also options. Your risk of cesarean section delivery is not increased by your spinal cord injury.

145

Remind your nurses that autonomic dysreflexia can be a problem during labor. Explain to them that frequent position changes and keeping your bladder from overfilling can help prevent this problem, and let them know your previous symptoms.

Multiple Sclerosis

Overview

Multiple sclerosis (MS) is a neurological disease that affects 10 to 50 people per 100,000. There is no known genetic predisposition to multiple sclerosis. Interestingly though, the geographical region in which you live influences your risk for developing the disease. People who live 40 degrees north in latitude tend to be among those who have the 50 in 100,000 chance for developing MS. In general, communities and regions will have pockets or clusters where MS activity is high.

Symptoms of MS usually begin between twenty and forty years of age. These symptoms are caused by damage to the white matter in your brain and central nervous system. The damage is caused by the loss of the myelination layer coating your nerves called demyelination. Multiple sclerosis is a disease of remission and flares. Loss of coordination, disturbances of vision, and weakness of the arms and legs are common symptoms.

What are the main concerns for my baby and myself?

Your ability to become pregnant is not affected by MS. The medical community is unsure if pregnancy increases the risk of flare, but they do believe that the long term course of MS is not affected by having children.

How can I best care for my baby and myself?

Your pregnancy is not at risk from multiple sclerosis. The baby grows normally and the pregnancy usually progresses uncomplicated. The best thing you can do is to keep yourself healthy through proper nutrition, exercise, rest, and prenatal care. Follow the guidelines established by your neurologist and obstetrical care provider.

Labor, delivery, and postpartum

Labor will proceed normally, but weakness from multiple sclerosis may prevent adequate pushing during the birth of your baby. This may necessitate the need for the use of forceps or suction assistance during delivery. If you are confined to a wheelchair due to paraplegia from multiple sclerosis, read the previous section on spinal cord injury.

It is safe for women with multiple sclerosis to breast-feed their newborn baby. Refer to Chapter I on normal pregnancy, labor, and delivery and Chapter XIV on breast-feeding.

Congratulations for taking the time to learn about your type of neurologic disease, how it can affect your pregnancy, and how pregnancy will impact your condition. While we await a cure for many neurologic diseases, we now realize that women can overcome limitations set by their disease and experience a happy, healthy pregnancy.

VIII

Autoimmune
Diseases

Autoimmune diseases occur when the body fights against itself. Depending on the disease, certain parts of the body are seen as foreign, or not part of the self. The body's immune system is designed to destroy anything inside of it that is foreign. Think of a disease such as chicken pox. Once you've had chicken pox, your body recognizes the disease and fights it each time you are exposed. Hence, you don't get chicken pox again. However, with an autoimmune disease, the body interprets what is normal, or nonforeign, as foreign and fights to destroy it. Why this occurs is unknown.

Diseases classified as autoimmune include systemic lupus erythematosus (SLE), antiphospholipid antibody syndrome, idiopathic thrombocytopenia purpura (ITP), myasthenia gravis, rheumatoid arthritis, and certain thyroid diseases. These problems will be discussed in this chapter.

Systemic Lupus Erythematosus

Overview

Systemic lupus erythematosus is often referred to as simply lupus. Lupus is a chronic inflammatory disease that affects many systems of the body. It is diagnosed by the presence of at least four of the following eleven criteria:

- skin problems that might include a butterfly-like rash on the cheeks and circular reddened areas of skin;
- mouth ulcers;
- sensitivity to the sun;
- the presence of arthritis in two or more joints;
- an inflammatory process in the lungs called pleurisy or in the heart called pericarditis;
- neurologic disorder such as seizures or psychosis;
- problems with kidney function;
- blood disorders;
- immunologic disorders identified through blood tests; and
- the presence of antinuclear antibody in your blood.

Who gets this disease?

Lupus and most autoimmune diseases occur more frequently in women of childbearing age. Your general chance of having Lupus is 1 in 700. If you are African-American, your chance of having this disease increases to approximately 1 in 250. Pregnancy does not increase your chances of developing lupus.

The exact cause of Lupus has not yet been found. Lupus is a chronic disease with periods of active disease and periods of remission. The periods of active disease are often referred to as a lupus flare. During this time, patients experience one or many of the symptoms described above. The symptoms or ways in which the disease manifests vary from person to person. The most common symptoms patients report are joint pain or arthritis-type pain. Other symptoms might include mouth ulcers, skin rashes, fever, kidney problems, and high blood pressure. These symptoms are caused by the body producing antibodies which cause inflammation and damage body tissue and try to destroy the part of your body seen as foreign. Remission is the period when your body is not producing as many of the antibodies that produce the symptoms of lupus. The vagueness of complaints and the multiple ways the disease presents makes the diagnosis of lupus difficult and sometimes easy to overlook.

Should I be worried?

The ability to become pregnant remains normal with lupus, but sometimes the problem is in staying pregnant. With lupus, your risk for early and late pregnancy loss is increased. The actual risk for miscarriage is between 15 to 40 percent. If your body is producing those antibodies and damaging tissues, your risk for miscarriage and poor pregnancy outcome are increased.

Many care providers recommend becoming pregnant during a remission that has lasted five to seven months. It is unknown whether pregnancy increases your risk of flare. Unless your particular symptoms are kidney problems, pregnancy does not seem to accelerate the disease. Women with kidney involvement known as lupus nephritis have a small risk for significant permanent damage to their kidneys. If you do have active kidney involvement with your lupus and your kidneys are unable to function properly, your chances of developing preeclampsia are increased (refer to Chapter XII on preeclampsia).

Your pregnancy is considered high risk because of the many problems associated with lupus and pregnancy. Oftentimes the placenta does not function as well as it should, and babies can be very small. The baby may also be born with rashes on the face, scalp, and upper chest but these will normally disappear during the first year. Premature delivery and the possibility of the baby dying before birth are other complications.

The baby has a very small risk for developing a serious complication with the heart. Congenital heart block causes the baby's heart rate to beat around 60 times a minute instead of the normal 110 to 160. A formal cardiac ultrasound known as a fetal echocardiogram should be done after diagnosis of congenital heart block to look for other cardiac defects or malformations. Your care provider will work closely with a specialist in monitoring your baby before birth. These infants should be watched closely by ultrasound every one to two weeks and usually have no problems.

Occasionally, the baby develops swelling known as hydrops, or anasarca. This is a sign that the baby is having a problem known as congestive heart failure and must be watched closely in the hospital and often delivered prematurely. If your body is producing specific antibodies, known as SSA and SSB antibodies, your risk of having a baby with heart problems is greater.

How can I best care for my baby and myself?

When preparing for pregnancy, it is best to talk with your care provider about the management of your lupus prior to pregnancy. The discussion should also include timing the conception. As discussed previously, conception after a five to seven month period of remission may improve the chances of a good pregnancy outcome.

If you are planning a pregnancy you should be tested for the lupus anticoagulant, anticardiolipin antibodies, anti-SSA and anti-

SSB antibodies. A twenty-four hour urine collection should be tested for total protein and creatine clearance. You and your care provider should then discuss these results and the impact they may have on pregnancy, as well as current medication use. If you are on steroid therapy, you may need to continue this during the pregnancy. You may also be started on steroids, baby aspirin, or heparin during the pregnancy. Some medications for the treatment of lupus have been shown to potentially harm the baby so it is very important to discuss all medication options with your care provider. Drugs, given individually or in combination, may improve pregnancy outcome, but this has not been proven conclusively.

Prenatal care should include an ultrasound during the first twelve weeks for dating or as soon as you realize you are pregnant if this is after twelve weeks. This early ultrasound will be helpful to your care provider if your baby's growth is poor. The next ultrasound should be at approximately twenty weeks. This will be a review of systems or a targeted ultrasound to measure the baby and look carefully for visible problems and malformations. Since poor growth is a potential problem, your baby should have an ultrasound approximately every four to six weeks after the targeted scan to check for growth and the level of amniotic fluid.

The frequency of your office visits will increase and more lab tests will be done. Your blood pressure and weight gain will be monitored closely. Monthly twenty-four hour urine tests may be done to monitor kidney function. Bedrest is not common unless the baby is undergrown or preeclampsia occurs. Around twenty-eight weeks, your care provider may begin weekly testing for your baby's well-being.

The test most frequently used is a nonstress test (NST). A fetal monitor watches the baby's heart rate and any contractions, and your perception of your baby's movement is tracked by pressing a button. This information is documented electronically on a strip of paper and then evaluated. A biophysical profile is another test which may be done. This thirty-minute test uses ultrasound to watch the baby's movement, muscle tone or flexion, breathing movements, amount of amniotic fluid, and the condition of the placenta; the NST strip may be evaluated at this same time.

Labor, delivery, and postpartum

There is no increased risk of surgical delivery by cesarean section unless the baby is undergrown or you develop preeclampsia. The process of labor is normal. If you have been on steroids you will need extra doses through an IV since labor places extra stress on your body and increases your need for steroids.

Antiphospholipid Antibody Syndrome (Lupus-Like Syndrome)

Overview

Antiphospholipid antibody syndrome, also known as lupus-like syndrome, occurs in women with or without autoimmune disease. Women with this disorder have certain positive markers in the blood known as lupus anticoagulant and anticardiolipid antibodies and have frequent pregnancy loss or fetal death as a result. Common past medical problems may also include problems with blood clots or low platelet count. If you have a history of recurrent pregnancy loss, your chances of having antiphospholipid antibody syndrome is 5 to 10 percent. The risk increases to 30 to 40 percent if you have lupus. The cause of antiphospholipid antibody syndrome is still unknown.

What are the main concerns for my baby and myself?

Pregnancy loss is the main problem with this syndrome. Fetal death or stillbirth can occur during early or late pregnancy. The baby can be undergrown and the placenta may be small. Treatment improves the baby's survival rate to 75 to 90 percent, although the pregnancy is still at risk.

Women who have this problem are at risk for preeclampsia and blood clots called deep vein thrombosis. These clots can travel to the brain or lungs, and when severe or untreated, can be deadly. Treatment options include baby aspirin, heparin, and intravenous immunoglobulin known as IVIG. These drugs can be used separately or in combination. Clots also tend to occur when women with antiphospholipid antibody syndrome are on oral birth control pills. After delivery there is a small risk for developing fever, heart, and respiratory problems.

How can I best care for my baby and myself?

Prenatal visits are more frequent. You may be seen every one to two weeks starting from week sixteen until delivery. As with lupus, an early ultrasound is important for knowledge of correct dating. Frequent ultrasounds will begin at approximately sixteen weeks and continue every three to four weeks until delivery. At each ultrasound visit, the baby will be measured, the fluid level checked, and dopplers, which check the blood flow through the placenta, may be done. If the placenta is not functioning properly, the dopplers will indicate how serious the problem is. If the studies indicate a severe problem with the placenta, your care provider will begin to prepare you and your baby for delivery.

Problems with placental function cannot be cured, but there are certain proven things you can do to help, including keeping your blood volume high by drinking plenty of water to provide more blood flow to the placenta; bedrest; lying down on either your right or left side to increase blood flow to the baby; and soaking in a swimming pool or your bathtub a couple of times a day so that the slight pressure of the water pushes extra fluid from your body into your blood vessels increasing blood flow to the placenta.

Preeclampsia is another risk of lupus. Read Chapter XII on preeclampsia so that you can be aware of the warning signs.

Labor, delivery, and postpartum

Labor is not affected by antiphospholipid antibody syndrome but your chances of having labor induced at term or earlier are greatly increased. If you're carrying a small baby or develop preeclampsia, your risk for a cesarean section delivery is increased. These problems may cause the placenta to not work effectively thus decreasing the available blood flow to the baby. Your care provider will monitor the baby very closely during labor, and if there is any concern at all for your baby's health and safety, a cesarean will be performed.

Idiopathic/Autoimmune Thrombocytopenia Purpura (ITP)

Overview

Thrombocytopenia is a condition in which your blood platelets are very low. Platelets are essential for clotting. Idiopathic/autoimmune thrombocytopenia purpura (ITP) is an autoimmune disease that causes the body to interpret the platelets as foreign and then sets out to destroy them. This destruction and removal results in low levels of platelets in your body. Luckily the body needs relatively few platelets to clot effectively. The number of platelets left circulating in the blood varies from person to person. Women develop this problem more frequently than men. As with the other autoimmune problems, the cause of ITP is unknown.

What are the main concerns for my baby and myself?

Your baby is at risk for also having low platelets. The antibody you have crosses the placenta placing the baby at risk. The danger to the baby is minimal while the baby is inside you because the uterus and amniotic fluid act as a cushion preventing most trauma from ever reaching your baby. As long as there is no injury, clotting is not necessary. The baby's platelet count at the time of delivery and the method of delivery are more important problems which will be discussed in the labor and delivery section.

You are also at risk for bleeding problems. Low platelets often do not cause serious problems but can lead to excessive bruising and bleeding. When your platelets drop to a concerning level, your care provider may start medications such as steroids, high-dose intravenous immumoglobulin (IVIG), or immunosuppressive drugs. In severe cases, medical or surgical treatments may include a blood transfusion of platelets or possibly removing your spleen. If your spleen has been removed your platelet count may be normal, but your baby is still at risk for problems. The antibodies are still present in your body and will pass to the baby. Because your baby has a working spleen, it will destroy any platelets with the foreign antibody marker on them.

Your baby is also at risk for developing neonatal thrombocytopenia after delivery which means she will have very low platelets after birth. Your pediatrician should be informed of your condition even if your platelet count has been normal during the pregnancy. The baby should have lab work monitored for a minimum of one week as the baby's platelet count usually reaches the lowest between day four and six. The remaining antibodies that the baby received from you are gone from the baby's system within a few weeks to three months. If your baby has bleeding problems, she may be given the medications discussed above.

Now what?

The frequency of your office visits will remain the same even if your platelet count remains reasonable. Blood work will be checked more frequently, at least once a trimester, if not more often. If you are started on medications you will be seeing your care provider more frequently and having blood drawn more often. If you start bruising or bleeding contact your care provider right away.

When low platelets are found during the pregnancy, the reason needs to be determined since other disease processes can cause low platelets. Certain laboratory tests may be done to determine the cause. Your blood can specifically be tested for the presence of antiplatelet antibodies and a complete blood count and coagulation testing should also be done. If there is any suspicion of preeclampsia, liver functions should be tested for a problem called HELLP syndrome (refer to Chapter XII on preeclampsia for further information).

Your care provider may want to remove a small amount of bone marrow to rule out other problems as the cause of the low platelets. Your care provider should also ask about exposure to noxious substances and medications since certain medications and substances can cause platelet counts to drop.

If you do have a tendency to bruise or bleed easily, it will be important to keep yourself safe from anything that could cause you injury. Avoid activities that present a high chance of falling. Dress with protective clothing such as long sleeves and pants. Check your house and repair any loose areas that could potentially scratch you. Use extreme caution when getting in and out of the tub. Most of all, use common sense and keep yourself safe.

Labor, delivery, and postpartum

Delivery is the riskiest time for you and your baby if platelet counts are low. A low platelet count can lead to excessive bleeding during or after delivery, increased risk for tissue damage, and extensive bruising. Your care provider will only do an episiotomy if absolutely necessary and will be very careful when stitching you back together. If a cesarean section is done, care will be taken to minimize tissue damage and control bleeding. Platelets may be given if your platelet count is less than 50,000. If you have been receiving steroids you will need extra doses during labor.

Knowledge of the baby's platelet count is very helpful for making the decision regarding surgical or vaginal delivery. There are a couple of methods used to determine the baby's platelet count. During labor when your cervix is dilated your care provider may perform a procedure called a fetal scalp blood sample. A very small cut is made on the baby's head, and the blood is sent to the laboratory for a platelet count. The other method is to obtain a blood sample from the baby's umbilical cord. Prior to labor your care provider will most likely send you to a perinatologist or maternal fetal medicine specialist who performs this specialized procedure. A small needle is placed through your belly and into the uterus. It is carefully guided into the baby's umbilical cord, and blood is removed and sent to the laboratory for platelet count. The test results are good for twenty-one days. Labor and vaginal delivery will be planned or continue if the platelet count is greater than 50,000. If the platelet count is less, a cesarean section will be scheduled. New literature suggests that neither is needed, so discuss this with your care provider.

During the postpartum period, you are at risk for an early or late postpartum hemorrhage. If you are saturating more than one pad an hour call your care provider. Consult your care provider or a lactation specialist regarding the medications you are taking and the transference of antibodies through breast milk.

Myasthenia Gravis

Overview

Myasthenia gravis is an autoimmune disorder that affects the muscles and skeletal system. Muscle weakness and extreme lethargy or fatigue are the classic symptoms of this autoimmune disorder. Symptoms include drooping eyelids, double vision, difficulty speaking, swallowing, and clearing mouth, and lung secretions. As with the other autoimmune diseases, twice the number of women compared with men have this problem. Women have a 1 in 12,500 chance of developing myasthenia gravis and this often develops when women are in their twenties and thirties.

The cause of myasthenia gravis is unknown, but it is believed that antibodies against acetylcholine receptors responsible for nerve impulses cause the weakness and fatigue. Again, the body is seeing a part of itself as foreign and tries to destroy it. These antibodies have been found in 80 to 90 percent of people with myasthenia gravis.

160

What are the main concerns for my baby and myself?

Pregnancy does not appear to change the long-term prognosis of myasthenia gravis. During pregnancy, the disease could become worse, remain the same, or go into remission. No predictors have been found to identify the women who will become worse. Medications need to be closely monitored and adjusted during the pregnancy. If a severe crisis occurs and medications are not helping, a procedure called plasmapheresis may be used. This procedure removes the blood from the body, filters out the high level of antibodies, then returns the blood to the body. Plasmapheresis may need to be repeated every three to six weeks.

The risk of a preterm delivery may be increased, though the reason is unknown. The medications used to treat myasthenia gravis have an action similar to that of the contraction-stimulating medication oxytocin. It has been theorized that this action increases preterm labor rate. Another reason may be that one of the medications used to stop preterm labor, magnesium sulfate, is absolutely contraindicated in myasthenia gravis.

There is less than a 25 percent chance of your baby having neonatal myasthenia gravis. This problem develops within the first few days after birth. Neonatal myasthenia gravis is self limiting, lasting from a few weeks to approximately fifteen weeks—the time it takes the baby's body to remove your antibodies. Infants with this problem have poor sucking efforts, a weak cry, and in rare cases, difficulty breathing. You should inform your baby's pediatrician that you have myasthenia gravis and ask how he will follow your baby's condition after birth.

How can I best care for my baby and myself?

A team approach should be taken during your pregnancy. The care provider you have chosen for your pregnancy should work closely with your neurologist and rheumatologist. Consultation about the use of medications and dosage changes are important. Most medications for myasthenia gravis can be continued during the pregnancy. Pyridostigmine, the most commonly used medication, does not cross the placenta. Your baby, therefore, does not receive any of the medication. Avoid extreme fatigue and stress during the pregnancy and delivery to prevent crisis.

Pregnancy can be a frustrating time because your medication dosage may need to be adjusted multiple times when symptoms flare. You also may need to see your neurologist or rheumatologist more frequently.

Since preterm labor can be a problem, be aware of the signs and symptoms of labor. If you are having more than four to six contractions an hour call your care provider. Refer to Chapter X on premature labor for a complete understanding of contractions.

Labor, delivery, and postpartum

During labor you have an increased chance of a myasthenic crisis. This results because labor decreases your stomach's ability to digest, and the medications used to control the myasthenia gravis may sit undigested in your stomach during labor. Intravenous medications will be administered if a myasthenic crisis occurs.

Your body is very sensitive to narcotic medications, and if you receive them you must be monitored very closely. An epidural is the best form of pain control during labor and necessary if you deliver surgically. General anesthesia should be avoided if at all possible. If you do need general anesthesia you may need to be placed on a ventilator for a while after the surgery.

The muscles involved in the process of labor are not affected by myasthenia gravis, but the muscles used for pushing are. So the first part of labor proceeds normally, but the pushing stage may be prolonged or require some assistance with vacuum suction or forceps, if absolutely necessary.

If you develop an infection after delivery, have your OB/Gyn consult your neurologist or rheumatologist about the antibiotics that are safe, since some can cause myasthenic crisis. Breast-feeding is not recommended because antibodies are found in the breast milk and may increase the risk of neonatal myasthenia gravis.

Rheumatoid Arthritis

Overview

Rheumatoid arthritis is a chronic, destructive, and sometimes deforming autoimmune disorder. It is an inflammatory disease that affects the connective tissue in the joints. Once again, the body interprets something in itself as foreign and tries to destroy it by causing a painful inflammatory response.

Rheumatoid arthritis affects 2 percent of the entire population. Women are affected two to three times more often than men and are usually diagnosed between the ages of twenty and sixty. There seems to be a genetic predisposition toward the development of rheumatoid arthritis as rheumatoid arthritis appears to run in families. Classic symptoms are warm, swollen, reddened, and painful joints. The finger joints are most commonly affected, but any joint may become involved. The body produces antibodies, rheumatoid factor, and sometimes antinuclear antibodies.

What are the main concerns for my baby and myself?

Fertility is normal in women with rheumatoid arthritis. The disease may go into remission in as many as 75 percent of women while they are pregnant. During the postpartum period the majority of women experience a flare in the disease. Otherwise, women with rheumatoid arthritis have normal pregnancies. One concern is that many of the medications used to treat rheumatoid arthritis are not recommended for routine use during pregnancy. The risks and benefits of each medication should be discussed with your rheumatologist and OB/Gyn care providers.

How can I best care for my baby and myself?

There are no anticipated restrictions or limitations since the pregnancy is usually normal. Pain may not even be a problem if the disease goes into remission. If pain is a problem, contact your care provider and try nonmedicinal therapies to relieve pain such as warm baths, massage, ice, as well as any other measures you have found helpful. Whirlpool hot tubs can also be used as long as the temperature is not excessive. If you start sweating it is time to get out and cool down.

Labor, delivery, and postpartum

The labor and delivery process should proceed normally. Be sure to remind your care provider and nurses of any joint limitations you have. Comfortable positions and those that prevent potential trauma or joint inflammation should be used. It is during the postpartum period that rheumatoid arthritis flares. Contact your rheumatologist if this occurs. Your medications may need to be changed.

Thyroid Disease

Overview

Thyroid disorders affect 0.2 percent of all pregnancies. There are two types of thyroid problems that are autoimmune in origin: Hashimoto's thyroiditis and Graves' disease.

Diseases due to an underactive thyroid are called hypothyroidism. They can be caused by Hashimoto's disease, irradiation, surgery, or less often, by failure of the pituitary or hypothalamic glands. If you have untreated hypothyroidism, you may notice a tendency toward dry skin, extreme tiredness, constipation, weight gain, and hair loss. You may complain of being cold or prefer warm weather, and you may have a goiter in which the enlarged thyroid is visible on your neck.

Graves' disease is a condition in which your thyroid works overtime and is known as hyperthyroidism. Because the job of your thyroid is to regulate metabolism, if your thyroid works too much, then your metabolism also works too fast. You may notice an intolerance to heat, weight loss (but are always hungry), diarrhea, slightly faster heart rate, sense of nervousness, and even tremors. You may have a goiter, and your eyes may bulge a little; a condition called exophthalmos. Hyperthyroid diseases that are not associated with the autoimmune system include multinodular goiter and subacute and chronic thyroiditis.

What are the main concerns for my baby and myself?

Hypothyroid

Women who have untreated hypothyroid diseases often are infertile and have difficulty becoming pregnant. Once the imbalance is corrected women often regain their ability to have children. If you become pregnant with untreated hypothyroidism, you are more likely to develop a problem with pregnancy, and your chances for miscarriage, stillbirth, or undergrown or malformed babies are increased. You may also experience more problems with anemia, postpartum bleeding, or preeclampsia. These complications do not occur as frequently when hypothyroidism is treated. If your thyroid levels are normal, you have a very good chance of having a normal pregnancy and a normal baby. Synthroid is the medication used to treat hypothyroidism in pregnant women. This medication has been found to be safe for use during pregnancy.

Hyperthyroid

Hyperthyroidism does not affect the ability to become pregnant. If you have a mild to moderate form of the disease and have not been treated, your pregnancy may still be very uneventful, but severe or uncontrolled hyperthyroidism is associated with poor pregnancy outcome with an increase in the occurrence of undergrown babies and preterm birth. Preeclampsia may also be more common. With treatment, the pregnancy usually progresses normally. When diagnosis occurs during pregnancy the most common treatment is the medication Propylthiouracil (PTU) which has been found to be safe during pregnancy. Methimazole is the other medication used to treat hyperthyroidism. This medication has been associated with some adverse effects on the baby, but recent studies have shown this association to be trace. Other treatment methods for hyperthyroidism are reserved for after delivery. Radioactive iodine can damage the baby's thyroid so it is not used during pregnancy. Surgery is only used as a last resort.

Once treatment has begun, it may take up to four weeks before your symptoms subside. When this occurs the dose of medication may be reduced. Your care provider may follow the levels of thyroid in your blood as frequently as every two weeks.

If you have ever been treated for Graves' disease with surgical removal of your thyroid or have had radioactive iodine it is very important to inform your care provider of this. Your body can still produce antibodies that will cross the placenta and possibly affect your baby. The baby will then need to be watched for signs of hyperthyroidism while growing inside of you and after birth. If your hypothyroidism was not caused by treated Graves' disease, you need not worry about this problem. Most of the time this problem is temporary, disappearing after the maternal antibodies have cleared the baby's system. Your pediatrician will monitor the baby closely for signs that it has been affected. These signs and symptoms include failure to gain weight, irritability, feeding difficulties, elevated heart rate, irregular heart rate, or rapid breathing. The baby could also go into heart failure, so your baby should be closely watched for this complication during the first two weeks after delivery.

Thyroid storm is an uncommon life-threatening complication that can occur with hyperthyroidism. It is a condition that requires you to be in the hospital and probably in the intensive care unit. The stress of labor or infection can stimulate a thyroid storm. Symptoms include extremely high fever (greater than 103), extremely high heart rate, agitation, tremors, anxiety, nausea, vomiting, or diarrhea. A medication called propranolol is used to regulate and slow your heart rate. Propylthiouracil (PTU) is used to control the high levels of thyroid, iodine is used in small amounts, and steroids can also be used. Intravenous fluids, heart rate monitoring, and cooling measures (Tylenol, cooling blankets, and cool baths) will be implemented.

167

How can I best care for my baby and myself?

If your disease is being treated appropriately, pregnancy should proceed normally. Continue your synthroid, PTU, or methimazole as directed by your care provider.

Labor, delivery, and postpartum

Labor and delivery usually proceed normally since thyroid problems do not affect the process. Thyroid storm can occur during labor so be aware of the symptoms, and let your nurse know if you are experiencing any symptoms. Undiagnosed Graves' disease can flare during the postpartum period.

Breast-feeding is safe when Propylthiouracil (PTU) is used because this medication does not pass into the breast milk. Methimazole freely passes into breast milk without adverse effects as long as the dosage is below 15 mg. Synthroid is also safe to use during breast-feeding.

IX

Twins, Triplets, and More

Overview

Greek mythology and the Bible give early examples of multiple births. Romulus and Remus were twins raised by the mother wolf. Esau and Jacob were the twin boys of Rebekah and Isaac. The overall spontaneous twinning rate is 1.2 per 100 live births, the rate varies depending on the type of twins. Triplets occur 1 per 6,889 and quadruplets 1 per 575,000 births. These statistics do not include pregnancies that have an early loss of one baby. Home pregnancy tests and the use of ultrasound have demonstrated a greater number of multiple pregnancies than quoted. So, if you are diagnosed with a multiple pregnancy early on (four to six weeks) be aware of the possibility of loss. Once a normal heartbeat and normal growth or size have been confirmed, your chances for this type of loss decrease considerably.

Your chance for having a multiple birth varies depending on whether the babies are from one egg that splits or from separate eggs, if you've taken infertility drugs, or if multiple embryos were implanted. Identical twins develop from the fertilization of a single egg which later divides into two babies. These children look identical because they have the same genetic makeup. The rate of having identical twins has remained fairly constant at one twin birth per 85 live births. Your chance of having identical twins is the same no matter your age, the number of babies you have had, your race, if you took infertility medications, or if you were a twin yourself.

Fraternal multiples develop when the mother releases more than one egg, and these eggs are then fertilized by different sperm. You are more likely to have a multiple pregnancy as you become older until the age of thirty-five when your chances decrease. The following also increase your chances of a multiple birth: if you have had three or more pregnancies, if you are a twin yourself, if you are tall and large, if your race is African-American, if you are using infertility drugs, or if you are having multiple embryos implanted. Interestingly, Nigeria has the highest rate of twin births, and Japan has the lowest rate.

The use of the fertility drug Clomid increases your chance of having twins to 8 per 100, triplets to approximately 0.5 per 100, and quadruplets to 0.3 per 100. Pergonal, another fertility drug, increases your chance even further. The twinning rate jumps to 18 per 100, triplets 3 per 100, and quadruplets to 1.2 per 100. Assisted reproductive technology (ART) is a term used to describe procedures like in vitro fertilization (IVF), gamete intrafallopian transfer (GIFT), zygote intrafallopian transfer (ZIFT), and similar infertility procedures. Years ago, children born as a result of ART were called "test-tube babies." When ART involves multiple eggs or fertilized ovum, your chances of having multiples increase slightly above Pergonal use: 22 per 100 for twins, 4 per 100 for triplets, and 1.2 per 100 for quadruplets.

In pregnancies with triplets or more, the babies can all be identical, fraternal, or have a mixture of both. This mixture of fraternal and identical occurs when multiple eggs are released and fertilized and one or more of these fertilized eggs divides into two or more separate babies.

What are the main concerns for my babies and myself?

Whenever you carry more than one baby, your pregnancy is considered high risk since the chances for having a problem during the pregnancy are increased. Of course, your pregnancy may proceed smoothly without complications. Maintaining a positive mental attitude is important. If you have problems, remember: You did not do, say, or think anything that could have caused your problem. Feeling guilty or beating yourself up does not help you or your babies so try focusing on what you can do to help your babies.

During early pregnancy you may have more problems with nausea and vomiting than a "singleton" pregnancy. You are also at risk for hyperemesis gravidarum, a condition in which you experience so much vomiting that you become dehydrated and may need intravenous fluid replacement by your care provider or at the hospital. Medications can help this condition. In severe cases, a mother may need her whole dietary intake through IV if she is unable to keep any foods or fluids down for an extended period of time.

Anemia is a condition in which you lack enough blood cells to carry oxygen. Iron supplementation is used to combat this problem. Heavy or excessive bleeding with delivery can be a cause of anemia. The uterus has grown larger than usual, making the action of contracting and becoming firm after delivery more difficult. This may lead to more blood loss. The risk of needing a blood transfusion is low but present.

A multiple pregnancy puts you at risk for an early delivery. Prematurity is defined as delivery before the thirty-seventh week of pregnancy. Twin pregnancies have a 25 to 35 percent chance of delivering prematurely. The risk for triplets is higher, and quadruplets are guaranteed an early delivery.

Reasons for early delivery are numerous. One or more of your babies may be small and undergrown. The medical terminology for this problem is intrauterine growth retardation (IUGR), which does not mean your baby has any mental retardation, only that he or she is small. Multiple pregnancies have a 10 to 15 percent risk for IUGR. After your babies are delivered, the nursery personnel will call an undergrown baby "small for gestational age" (SGA). (Gestational age is determined by how many weeks pregnant you were when you delivered.) Babies grow poorly due to a number of problems.

Pregnancies that develop from one egg can share some placental vessels causing a problem called twin-to-twin transfusion syndrome (TTTS). Whether your babies share vessels depends on the time when the egg divides. Your care provider may call this the babies' placentation, or chorionicity.

Eggs dividing from the time of ovulation to day three after ovulation are completely separate and share nothing other than common genetic material. They are known as diamniotic-dichorionic (Di-Di). The amnion and chorion are the two layers of your bag of water that fuse together. Diamniotic dichorionic means each baby has its own amnion and chorion. (They are each in separate sacs.) Since there are two babies, the pregnancy contains two amnions and two chorions; thus, the term *di*, or two, is placed in front of the words *amnion* and *chorion*. These twins do not share any vessels and do not develop twin-to-twin transfusion syndrome.

Eggs that split three to eight days after ovulation create diamniotic-monochorionic twins. Two-thirds of twins developed from a single egg are this type. In this case, each baby has its own amnion (diamnionic) but share a single chorion (monochorionic) meaning that each baby has its own placenta but share some vessels. These twins are at risk for twin-to-twin transfusion syndrome.

Eggs that divide day eight to thirteen after ovulation live in the same bag of water, have one placenta, and share a single amnion and a single chorion, and are called monoamnionic-monochorionic (Mo-Mo) twins. Since they share the same swimming area, these babies have a very high risk for dying due to cord entanglement. These babies have a low risk for twin-to-twin transfusion syndrome. Less than 2 percent of twin pregnancies from a single egg are monoamnionic-monochorionic.

Eggs that split day thirteen to eighteen result in conjoined twins (Siamese twins). This problem is extremely rare: 1 in 50,000 to 80,000 deliveries. Whether the twins can be separated after birth depends on the organs and body parts that are shared. These children often need to be delivered by cesarean section.

Twin-to-twin transfusion syndrome occurs only in diamniotic-monochorionic twins, and only about 15 percent of diamniotic-monochorionic twins develop this problem. TTTS occurs when one baby gives the other baby part of his or her blood volume and does not receive enough in return. Mothers may experience a very large amount of uterine growth to the point of having difficulty breathing. Most women describe the growth as happening almost overnight. An ultrasound is used to determine if the problem is twin-to-twin transfusion syndrome. The baby donating the blood has less circulating blood. He urinates very little; therefore, the amniotic fluid is low to near absent, a condition known as oligohydramnios. The baby is usually undergrown and may be referred to as the donor baby or the stuck twin. Because the baby's location in the uterus does not change, he is called the stuck twin, not because the baby does not move. The baby receiving the blood is called the recipient. Because the baby has too much blood volume, he urinates often, causing excessive amniotic fluid. This condition is known as polyhydramnios.

Twin-to-twin transfusion syndrome can be mild, moderate, or severe. The mild form rarely needs treatment and may only be found after delivery. The moderate form occurs in the late second or early third trimester. These babies will often be born early. The treatment includes removal of the excessive amniotic fluid from around the baby with polyhydramnios. The procedure is repeated when the fluid becomes excessive. The severe form develops during the second trimester. In addition to removal of excessive fluid, mothers who meet certain criteria have the option of experimental laser surgery available before twenty-two weeks. The laser clots off the shared vessels. Success rates with laser surgery are around 75 to 80 percent.

There are other reasons why one of your babies could be smaller than the other. One baby's placenta may have implanted in an area with less blood supply from you. The placenta may not have developed properly or be working well; therefore, it has difficulty providing adequate nutrition for the baby. If one of your babies is small and the placenta is not working properly, an ultrasound will help your care provider to find out what the problem is. You may be sent to a perinatologist, a doctor specializing in high-risk obstetrics and obstetrical ultrasound. The ultrasound will include an in-depth look at your babies and possibly dopplers, which are a way to check how easily the blood flows through the placenta. Problems with placental location and functioning cannot be cured, but certain things such as keeping your blood volume high by drinking plenty will provide more blood flow to the placenta. Bedrest may be recommended. Reclining, positioned on either your right or left side also increases blood flow to the babies. Soaking in a pool, or your bathtub if no pool is available, is relaxing as well as beneficial as the slight pressure of the water pushes extra fluid from your body into your blood vessels thus increasing blood flow to the placenta.

A baby may also be small because of a genetic abnormality or birth defect. Genetic abnormalities can only be determined by obtaining chromosomes. These can be obtained by amniocentesis or percutaneous umbilical blood sampling (PUBS), depending on the urgency of the information. Results take twenty-four to forty-eight hours with blood sampling, and amniotic fluid takes approximately ten to fourteen days. If both or all your babies are being tested, blue dye may be placed into the amniotic fluid so the care provider will know they are in a different sac each time they remove fluid. This dye is filtered out by the placenta, and your urine may turn green or blue in a few hours.

If one of your babies dies, the influence this death has on the pregnancy depends on the gestational age of the baby at the time death occurs and the type of placentation or chorionicity of the babies. Early losses, less than eight weeks, do not impact the pregnancy; the baby is flattened and reabsorbed as the uterus grows. These babies may have had a chromosomal abnormality or a problem with the placenta. Babies that die at a later gestation may cause problems for the mother or the surviving baby. If the baby was a twin of a diamniotic-monochorionic type, the surviving twin may have suffered some brain trauma when the baby died as blood flow and volume changes may have injured the surviving twin's brain. Twins that do not share placental vessels are not at risk for this problem. The loss *does* increase your risk of early rupture of membranes, preterm labor, and bleeding during the pregnancy. You need to be tested for a rare complication called disseminated intravascular coagulation (DIC), a blood clotting problem that can occur if one of your babies dies. The test is a simple blood draw every few weeks.

Preeclampsia, also known as toxemia or pregnancy-induced hypertension (PIH), happens more frequently in multiple pregnancy. The more babies you are carrying, the greater your risk of developing preeclampsia. Preeclampsia is three to five times more common in twins, and it is often the reason why pregnancies with three or more babies get delivered early. Read Chapter XII on preeclampsia for more information. Research studies have repeatedly shown that taking one baby aspirin per day significantly decreases the frequency and severity of preeclampsia.

How can I best care for my babies and myself?

Having more than one baby at a time makes your pregnancy high risk. You will have more office visits and more ultrasounds. Most care providers will see you every two weeks until twenty-four to twenty-eight weeks, when you will be seen weekly. An early ultrasound is very helpful in determining the type of pregnancy you have. Looking carefully or measuring the membrane during the early part of the pregnancy can determine if the pregnancy is at risk for twin-to-twin transfusion. If you are at risk, you will be scheduled for an ultrasound every two weeks starting at twenty weeks to look for TTTS. You should also have a complete review of systems around twenty weeks.

Your care provider may feel it is necessary to ultrasound your cervix to measure the length. This is done with an ultrasound transducer specially shaped to fit inside the vagina. This measurement may be repeated during your pregnancy if there are any concerns about preterm labor or an incompetent cervix. A cervix is considered incompetent when it shortens considerably without contractions. Cervical lengths of 30 mm to 40 mm are normal. If your cervix is less then 20 mm, it bears close watching, bedrest, possible placement of a stitch known as a cerclage, and/or hospitalization.

The majority of mothers of multiples end up on bedrest at some point during the pregnancy. Bedrest can mean anything from stopping work and limiting your housework, to a quick shower a day and up to the bathroom only. This is called strict bedrest. Suggestions for easing the trial of bedrest are numerous. Articles and books have been written on this topic alone. Here are a few suggestions:

- Borrow or rent a small refrigerator and place it next to the couch.
- Keep your juice, meals, and snacks for the day in here.
- Have friends and family prepare meals, rent videos, or clean for you and your family. (Remember how good it feels when you help other people, allow others to feel just as good.)
- Try to keep your days and nights separate by sleeping in one room and spending your day in another.
- Change into comfortable day clothes every morning.
- Organize your picture album; take up a hobby you can do in bed; read; watch videos; call old friends you may have lost touch with; and try to remain positive.
- If you become hospitalized, you may want to designate a friend or family member to answer questions about your health or medical condition since answering the same questions may become irritating.
- Have friends tell you all about what is going on in their lives.

You will usually remain fairly comfortable until the early to mid second trimester. You might not even find out you are having more than one baby until this time if an ultrasound has not been done. The babies' growth increases in the second trimester and escalates even more in the third trimester. Some women have found a pregnancy support girdle helpful. Support for your back and growing belly can be accomplished with multiple pillows or a body length pillow while in bed. Placement of a pillow between your knees has been found to be comforting. Tub baths, or resting in a pool, may free you of that heavy feeling, but remember to drink while in the tub or pool to avoid dehydration. A backrub or massage by your husband, a friend, or a professional may relieve some discomfort. In extreme cases of discomfort, your care provider may send you to a physical therapist. If you feel like you have grown excessively over a short period of time, contact your care provider. One or more of the babies may have too much amniotic fluid.

Increasing your calories by eating more is a must for mothers of multiples. You should gain 40 to 45 pounds if you are expecting twins. Triplets increase the needed weight gain to approximately 55 to 60 pounds. Mothers carrying four or more babies may gain as much as 60 to 70 pounds. Gaining the necessary weight may not be easy. Initially, you may experience nausea and vomiting. Later, your stomach will be crowded by the growing babies, so small frequent meals, high in protein, are recommended. Your prenatal vitamin is essential for your iron and mineral needs.

Labor, delivery, and postpartum

Vaginal delivery is still an option if you are having twins. If you are having three or more babies, in most cases you will be delivered by cesarean section. Labor and a vaginal delivery will be permitted with twins when the first baby or both babies are positioned with their heads down. If the body part in your pelvis is not a head prior to labor a cesarean section is usually recommended. You will labor in a hospital room and most oftentimes deliver in the operating room for safety reasons. If you are near term, the babies will be monitored initially until both babies are considered healthy. You may then be encouraged to walk, shower, or sit in a tub or jacuzzi during a portion of the labor. Having an IV during labor and delivery is a standard precaution, and blood work can be drawn when the IV is placed. Remember you are at risk for postpartum bleeding and for a cesarean delivery of your second baby. Often, your care provider will recommend an epidural for delivery in case you need surgery. If you are laboring prematurely, your care provider will most likely want the babies monitored during the entire labor, which means you will be in bed during the labor. Delivery of twins is most safely accomplished in the room where cesarean sections are done. When your cervix is close to or fully dilated, you will be moved to the operating room. This may occur before or after you start pushing.

After your first baby is born, an ultrasound may be used to find the position of your second baby. The delivery method of your second child depends on a number of things. If the baby is head down, you will be able to push. However, the second baby's head is not deep in your pelvis as the first baby's was, and the umbilical cord may be in front of the head. When this happens the second baby will need to be delivered by a cesarean section. If the second baby is breech, your care provider can deliver the baby three different ways: 1) You can push this baby out as a vaginal breech. 2) Your care provider can perform a breech extraction—a method in which the care provider reaches up and grabs the baby's feet, pulling him or her out gently. 3) Your care provider may also decide that a surgical birth by cesarean section is the safest method of delivery.

A cesarean section is most often done while you are awake and under epidural or spinal anesthesia. One or two family members are often allowed in surgery with you, and many people will be present in the room providing care for you and your babies.

When you are admitted for a scheduled cesarean section, blood work will be taken and you will be given IV fluids to hydrate you. (Your care provider will have told you to not eat or drink anything for at least six to eight hours before surgery.) You will sign a consent for the surgery. The babies' heart rates will then be monitored. A foley catheter, which is a small, soft, rubber tube, is placed into your bladder to keep it empty during the surgery. Your belly is usually shaved from your belly button down to an inch or so into your pubic hair. (These two procedures may be done in the operating room or while you are still in your room.) You will then be moved to the operating room where an anesthesiologist will place your epidural or spinal block. Your belly will be scrubbed with a solution to kill germs, and a drape will be placed in front of you to block your view of the surgery. This drape is part of the sterile field that helps prevent infection. In about thirty to forty minutes your babies will be born. Afterward, you will be moved to the recovery room where you will remain for around an hour.

Breast-feeding your many babies is an exhaustive but rewarding challenge. As with single pregnancies, breast-feeding does not always come naturally and a newborn must learn to suck, swallow, and breathe, all at the same time. A person who specializes in working with breast-feeding mothers (lactation specialist) is a must for the mother of multiple babies.

Breast-feeding takes practice, and timing is crucial. It is best to establish a feeding schedule for your babies rather than feeding on demand. Feeding on demand often leads to exhaustion, frustration, and crankiness. You can start a schedule, for example, by feeding baby "A" on one breast. When he is done and baby "B" is still sleeping, awaken baby "B," stimulate him, and feed him on the other breast. Then crawl back into bed for a couple more hours. There are many good breast-feeding resources out there, including *The Breastfeeding Sourcebook* by M. Sara Rosenthal.

It is recommended that you rent a hospital grade electrical pump. Refer to Chapter XIV on breast-feeding and your high-risk pregnancy. If your babies must be placed in the intensive care nursery, you will want to pump to establish your milk supply. If they are not in the intensive care, you may still want to pump in order to have a supply of milk for bottle-feeding helpers such as dad and other family members.

You worked very hard to get these babies home. You deserve to enjoy them. When breast-feeding or pumping is no longer enjoyable or you are resenting it, then it is time to stop. You have come too far to have something such as feeding your babies be a dreaded task. Some mothers of multiples simply find they "don't like" nursing so many babies. If this is true for you, let go of the guilt and buy formula.

Your postpartum course should be similar to that of any newly delivered mom. Your new freedom of increased activity often results in a large amount of swelling for the first couple weeks after the birth of your babies. This is largely due to your restricted activity during pregnancy as the large fluid volume accumulated during pregnancy tries to find its way out.

Giving birth is an extraordinary experience, and to have this same experience duplicated, triplicated, quadruplicated, or quintuplicated is indeed a blessing. But the feeling of being overwhelmed with one baby is also multiplied by each additional baby. Be kind to yourself and realize that it will take time to establish a routine and bond with these babies. Bonding is a process, not an event. Take each day, one at a time. Teamwork is the key to sanity. Allow your partner, family, friends, and community to help you. The saying goes, "It takes a village to raise a child," so follow this recommendation and allow other people to help. Trust yourself and your ability to mother these babies on the outside as well as you did when they were inside, and be proud of this amazing accomplishment!

The mother of multiples has special needs that continue long after the postpartum period. The following are national resources for mothers of multiples.

Sidelines National Support Network
Candace Hurley, Executive Director
P.O. Box 1808
Laguna Beach, CA 92652
(714) 497-2265

Triplets Connection
P.O. Box 99571
Stockton, CA 95209
(209) 474-3073

National Organization Mothers of Twins Club
12404 Princess Jeane N.E.
Albuquerque, NM 87112-4640

Parents of Twins with Disabilities
2129 Clinton Ave.
Alameda, CA 94501

Twins Magazine
5350 S. Roslyn, Suite #400
Englewood, CO 80111-2125
(303) 290-8500

M.O.S.T. Mothers of Supertwins
Maureen Boyle
P.O. Box 951
Brentwood, NY 11717
(516) 434-6678

PART THREE

Diseases of Pregnancy

X

Premature Labor

Overview

The uterus is a strong muscular organ, and like any muscle, it must work to stay in shape. When a muscle works, it is said to contract. When a muscle is not working, or is at rest, it is relaxed. It makes sense then that the uterus would need to contract to stay in shape and be able to stretch with a growing baby. As with all types of exercise, too much of a good thing can be not-so-good. Too much contracting of the uterus can lead to the cervix shortening (effacement) or opening (dilation). When your uterus contracts and starts to shorten or open your cervix before you are full term, it is called *premature,* or *preterm,* labor. Preterm labor occurs prior to thirty-seven weeks of your pregnancy. Preterm labor is most serious when it leads to preterm delivery.

The only way your care provider can determine whether your cervix has changed is to do a vaginal exam and feel your cervix or to use a special ultrasound device that gently slips into the vagina and produces an ultrasound picture of your cervix onto a screen. This picture is "frozen" on the screen and your cervix can then be measured. This type of ultrasound measurement is highly technical, but it gives a very accurate measurement of your cervix.

In most cases, the cause of preterm labor is unknown, but there are many things that contribute to a cervix shortening and opening.

Who Gets Preterm Labor?

Many women in general will fall into the category of "at risk" for preterm labor, and some women will be at "high risk" for preterm labor. This range will depend on the number of risk factors as well as the severity of the factors that put them at risk. As you review this list of things that lead to preterm labor, check off those that apply to you.

Factors that make a mother at risk for preterm labor:
- previous preterm labor or birth
- infections such as urinary tract or vaginal
- multiple babies: twins, triplets, or quads
- an abnormally shaped uterus or defects in the uterus such as fibroids
- previous surgery on the uterus
- previous surgery on the cervix such as cone, LEEP, or laser
- cervical incompetence (the cervix shortens and opens without contractions)
- exposure to Diethylstilbestrol (DES)
- if the mother is younger than eighteen or older than thirty-five years of age
- if the mother weighs less than 100 pounds
- too much or too little amniotic fluid
- abnormalities of the baby such as birth defects
- problems with the placenta working properly (caused by high blood pressure, high MSAFP, chronic diseases, etc.)

- bleeding during pregnancy
- placenta previa
- late or no prenatal care
- chronic illness
- premature rupture of membranes (your "water breaks")
- abdominal surgery during pregnancy
- smoking and drug use

There are quite a few things that can trigger preterm labor. What this means is that during your pregnancy there will be times when you are at more risk for contractions that will change your cervix, and times when you are at less risk.

Some women have a condition known as incompetent cervix. With incompetent cervix, the cervix dilates or effaces without any contractions. Second trimester losses are often due to incompetent cervix because the cervix is just not strong enough to hold up against the pressure of the growing baby. Unfortunately, the cause of incompetent cervix is not completely understood. However, daughters of mothers who took a medication called diethylstilbestrol (DES) during their pregnancy are at greater risk for incompetent cervix. Other potential causes may be due to any kind of damage to the cervix from surgical procedures, infection, or trauma. When a women is diagnosed with incompetent cervix, a special procedure called a cerclage becomes an option for a successful pregnancy.

A cerclage is a surgical procedure to place a suture into your cervix. Picture a purse string pulled tight to keep the contents closed inside. A cerclage is similar; however, it supports the cervix and keeps it tightly closed. A cerclage can help protect the placenta with placenta previa so that it may be left undisturbed. Your care provider would determine whether you are an appropriate candidate for such a procedure.

What are the symptoms of preterm labor?

Your uterus is a muscle. When it contracts, it hardens. When the contraction stops, your uterus softens. As previously discussed, it is normal and necessary for your uterus to contract a little. Two or three contractions an hour is normal. It is also normal to contract after sexual intercourse, after vaginal exams, when you change positions, or from walking up or down the stairs.

You may notice a cramping sensation in your lower back or belly. This cramping can either be painful or virtually painless. When this cramping occurs, you will feel a tightening or "balling up" of your belly if you put your hand on it. This is actually your uterus contracting.

Your cramps may feel similar to menstrual cramps. These may also be accompanied by diarrhea. Although diarrhea alone does not cause preterm labor, it does start a cramping rhythm of your belly. It can also lead to dehydration which can be quite serious and require replacement of fluids through an IV. Remember: Dehydration is never, ever, a good thing in pregnancy, so drink those fluids!

Often with preterm labor there is a feeling of pressure in the lower part of your belly. This sense of pelvic pressure or fullness can extend to the back or legs. A heavy pressure in your vagina or rectum can mean that the baby has dropped down into the lower part of your pelvic bones. When this occurs, a rapid change in your cervix at this time can lead to a preterm delivery of your baby.

Contractions are not necessarily painful. You may notice more of a dull ache in your back. A constant or rhythmic ache may be caused from the persistent contracting of your uterus and from the baby putting pressure on your pelvic bones.

It is important to pay attention to your vaginal discharge. The key to vaginal discharge is *change*. You may recall in Chapter II on normal changes in pregnancy, vaginal discharge normally increases in pregnancy due to the increase in hormones. You may notice your vaginal discharge increase, a change in the consistency of the discharge, or a slight change in the color or the odor.

Discharge can increase from the production of prostaglandins, which lead to contractions. It can also be due to the fact that the thick plug of mucus that serves to protect your amniotic sac and your baby from germs begins to loosen and may come out as your cervix begins to open. You would notice this on toilet paper after you go to the bathroom, on your panties, or it may just fall into the toilet. This thick, cervical mucous plug will be quite different than the normal, clearish white discharge you usually see.

The change in discharge may also be a mucous response to infection or germs. Infection can cause your discharge to change to a thick, curdy white, as seen with a yeast infection. It can be a grayish color and have a fishy odor as with bacterial vaginosis. Infection may be evident in a green or dark yellow vaginal discharge that is seen with many other vaginal infections and sexually transmitted diseases. Changes in vaginal discharge are important and should be discussed with your care provider. Infection is the primary cause of preterm labor and delivery. If it can be prevented or treated early, you can anticipate good health for you and your growing baby.

A major warning sign for preterm labor is leaking of water from your vagina. When the sac or membrane that surrounds your baby breaks, a leak occurs allowing the amniotic fluid to flow out. Amniotic fluid is normally clear and relatively odorless. It is different from vaginal discharge because it is truly *water*. If you notice that your panties are continually wet and it is more than typical perspiration, if you notice spurts of water coming from your vagina, or if you notice a large gush of fluid, your membranes have probably broken. It will be important to call your care provider and relay what has happened.

What things should I be concerned about with preterm labor?

The biggest worry with preterm labor is delivering your baby early. In the United States, 1 out of every 10 babies is born early. This statistic is higher in some countries and a little lower in others. The problems your early baby will face depends on how early the baby is and how much he weighs. A baby born at 24 weeks has about a 10 percent chance of survival. These chances increase significantly to about 55 percent by 26 weeks and 77 percent by 28 weeks. These babies may be faced with a variety of health problems. Common problems will involve breathing, vision, strokes, and hearing. Some of these very early babies can have learning disabilities or suffer from mild to severe cerebral palsy. After 28 weeks and when the baby is bigger than 3 pounds, survival increases. By 32 weeks, survival is greater than 96 percent and with proper care, the risk of serious health problems drops considerably.

Concerns for you will center around infection or bleeding. Refer to Chapter XIII on bleeding in pregnancy if your preterm labor is associated with bleeding problems. If your care provider has determined that you are infected inside your uterus, it will be important to deliver your baby. At this point, it is no longer healthy for you to remain pregnant.

How can I best care for my baby and myself?

If your care provider has told you that you have preterm labor due to contractions or more of a "silent" changing of your cervix, follow instructions carefully. Provided there is no sign of infection and the preterm labor is very early (your cervix has not changed much), your care provider will have you follow some instructions for home care. This might include decreasing your activity, eliminating sexual intercourse or sexual stimulation that could create contractions, taking a leave from work, and being on bedrest at home. Your care provider may order a special monitor for measuring contractions and your baby's heart rate at your home. This machine hooks up by phone to an office where nurses will assess the information from the monitor. Nurses may also visit you at home to check on your progress. The many changes in health care allow new ways for you to be safely cared for at home, provided that you are committed to the work it takes to be on bedrest.

Bedrest requires commitment. You will need to rely on help from family and friends. Sometimes it is helpful to just imagine the baby or babies you are carrying inside. Mothering your children does not start after they are born. Mothering begins when life begins. You have been a mother from the time of conception. Your commitment to helping this baby grow and be the strongest and healthiest she can be will be evident in your willingness to do what is necessary to hold off your preterm labor. In general, for every one day your baby safely lives inside of you, he will save three days in an intensive care nursery.

If you are at home on bedrest, find your "primary" place to rest and make it efficient. Have a nearby table for writing materials, a telephone, and books. Have extra pillows and blankets for fluffing nearby. Move a TV set where you can watch it. If possible, have a VCR available for movies and educational films such as childbirth education and parenting. If you usually work outside the home and your employer is willing to have you work a *few* hours at home while you are lying down, consider getting a laptop computer, FAX machine, and necessary files within reach. Bedrest at home can be creative, as long as the anxiety of working at home is not creating more labor. The key to bedrest is *rest*. Sitting up is still putting pressure on your cervix; therefore, a reclining position is necessary. As reviewed in the chapter on normal pregnancy, never lie flat on your back. When you do lie flat, it compresses the big vessels that provide blood and oxygen to you and your baby. A slight tilt of your hips one direction or the other is enough to open those vessels. A small pillow or a towel rolled up serves nicely to keep you from lying flat.

If you are home alone most of the time, a small refrigerator at the side of your bed or couch with juices, sandwiches, and fruit would be ideal. If this is not practical, a small cooler with ice works nicely. You will need to drink plenty of fluids, so plan on a continuous supply of water and juices. (Soda does not count in your daily fluids as it has a tendency to dehydrate you.) A good rule of thumb is to drink at least one 8-ounce glass of water an hour while you are awake.

You can best care for yourself and your baby by paying close attention to what is happening. If you are feeling cramping in your back or belly, put your hands on your belly to see if it is getting hard. Ask yourself if you have done anything physical to have created this particular contraction. Remember that physical activity, sexual stimulation, and dehydration can lead to contractions.

If your uterus has a tendency to contract quite a bit, your care provider may give you medication to control the contractions. Following is a list of the most common medications prescribed to stop contractions.

Brethine or terbutaline (generic)

This is often the first drug used in the control of contractions. Terbutaline acts to relax the muscle of the uterus, thus decreasing contractions. Terbutaline is used safely in pregnant women.

However, the Food and Drug Administration (FDA) has not officially approved terbutaline for the purpose of stopping contractions. (It is approved for relaxing bronchial spasms and ironically it relaxes the uterus as well.) Some common side effects of terbutaline include rapid heart rate or palpitations, headache, tremors, anxiousness, and dry mouth. Be sure and take your medications as prescribed by your care provider. If the side effects are extreme, call your care provider immediately so you may get a different medication.

Yutopar or ritodrine (generic)

This is an FDA-approved medication for treating preterm labor. It seems to be as effective as terbutaline but is much more expensive and therefore not as widely used. Ritodrine also relaxes the uterus, and the side effects are similar to terbutaline.

Procardia or nifedipine (generic)

This medication has recently been found to also decrease contractions by blocking the muscle's communication system. Women who are unable to take terbutaline may be prescribed nifedipine. If preterm labor is very difficult to control, this medication may be used in addition to terbutaline. Common side effects of nifedipine include headache, dizziness, heartburn, and low blood pressure. Nifedipine works best if you crunch the capsule in your teeth before you swallow it.

Magnesium sulfate

This is the same medication that would be used if you were hospitalized and needed very aggressive treatment to stop your contractions. Magnesium sulfate is also discussed in Chapter XII on preeclampsia as a medication to prevent seizures. In a similar fashion to nifedipine, magnesium sulfate disrupts the communication that allows muscles to contract. This medication is usually given through an IV infusion directly into your vein.

Indocin or indomethacin is a medication sometimes used effectively to stop premature labor. It works by inhibiting prostaglandins which are a part of the final nerve pathway for a contraction. Indomethacin is only used when the baby's lungs are immature and before thirty-four weeks gestation. Because prolonged treatment with indomethacin can result in a decrease in amniotic fluid and *potentially* cause heart, lung, digestive, and kidney problems in the newborn, it is only used for less than forty-eight hours at a time, then stopped for about one week. After that, these oral capsules can be used again to stop contractions should they begin.

A monitor connecting your belly to a machine gives a continual printout of your baby's heart rate as well as the frequency of your contractions. Magnesium sulfate is very effective in stopping contractions but the side effects are quite miserable. The first thing most women notice is a warm flushing feeling that goes through their body, followed by a generalized hot sensation everywhere. Once the medication reaches levels that are high enough to stop contractions, there is an overall sense of weakness and fatigue. Remember, magnesium sulfate is keeping the muscles in your uterus from contracting, but it also keeps all of your other muscles relaxed as well. If you are put on magnesium sulfate, you will feel very tired, somewhat disoriented, have a very dry mouth, congestion, and may be very sensitive to light. Your nurses will know how to care for you so that you are as comfortable as possible through this difficult time.

What happens if my preterm labor is bad enough that I need to stay in the hospital?

When your care provider has determined that it is necessary for you to be in the hospital, you can anticipate a few things. Upon admission to the hospital, you will find that it is impossible to do many things at once. This works for a hospital staff, but it can be very overwhelming for a mother who is scared for her baby as well as for herself (not to mention poor dad and any other family members). Unfortunately, if your situation is quite emergent, it is in the best interest of your baby to do your best to participate in the decision making, recognizing that there is little time to ponder your options. If you or your family question the decision-making process or the care you are receiving, you have the right to ask for another opinion or to be referred to a perinatologist, an obstetrician who specializes in high-risk pregnancies.

The first thing your care provider will want to do is to make sure your baby is okay. This is done in a variety of ways. A monitor used to graph the baby's heart rate and your contractions will be at your bedside. A two-part device will be placed on your belly: First a monitor that picks up the soundwaves of your baby's heart will be positioned so that you can hear the beating heart. Next a monitor that senses the tightening of your belly will be placed near the upper part of your uterus. This will track the contractions. Oftentimes your baby's tolerance of contractions, rather than the presence of contractions, will determine the next action taken. If your baby's heart pattern indicates that she is in distress, it may be necessary to deliver you immediately. More often, however, the biggest problem is stopping the contractions.

The next way to evaluate your baby is by ultrasound. Ultrasound is reviewed in detail in the chapter on normal pregnancy. In brief, it is a method of visualizing soft tissues, bones, and fluid inside the body. The person evaluating the ultrasound will be able to determine if your baby is in immediate danger, the baby's position and size, the amount of amniotic fluid, and the general position of your placenta. He or she will then determine if an amniocentesis is indicated.

Briefly, an amniocentesis is a procedure that involves guiding a needle into the uterus and removing some amniotic fluid from around the baby. This fluid is then analyzed in the laboratory for presence of infection and to determine the maturity of your baby's lungs. If infection is present, it will not matter whether your baby's lungs are mature as she will need to be delivered because it is no longer safe for her to be inside. If no infection is present and your baby's lungs are not mature (she is unable to breathe on her own), your care provider may then decide to give you some medications to speed up the process of lung maturity.

Betamethasone is a steroid given to pregnant women to help stimulate the baby's lungs so he can breathe on his own outside the uterus. It also helps decrease the chance of bleeding inside the brain as well as help with the functioning of the intestines. Betamethasone works best if the birth of the baby can be delayed for forty-eight hours. Two days does not seem like very long, but when you are trying desperately to keep a baby inside, it can feel like a lifetime.

Another controversial medication used in some hospitals around the world is *thyroid releasing hormone*. This medication, when given in divided doses over a twenty-four hour period, has been found to decrease respiratory disease in the premature newborn. If your care provider is not familiar with the use of this medication, you might ask if it is a possibility for you. It will probably be several years before the benefits of this medication are fully recognized.

During the critical first forty-eight hours of labor, you may be placed on magnesium sulfate. After this period of time, you will be weaned to terbutaline shots or pills. Once your uterus has settled down, you will probably relax in your new "home away from home." With medications every few hours, nurses checking on you, monitoring your baby's heart rate and the contractions, it may seem like the hospital is the very last place to possibly get any rest. Before you know it, you will establish a routine that works for you. If you are to be in the hospital for an extended period of time, arrange your hospital room so that it is comfortable for you. Pictures, blankets, and pillows from home add a nice touch and a sense of comfort. Participate in the decision of when *you* want to shower, what you would like to eat for meals as well as snacks (many women actually lose weight in the hospital), and if you prefer to stay up late and sleep in the mornings or vice versa. You will be less frustrated if you have some control over your environment. Keep a journal or diary of your pregnancy. Log specific milestones of your pregnancy and changes with your baby. Later, you'll appreciate the opportunity to remember these important events.

Labor, delivery, and postpartum

Let's first review the warning signs of preterm labor:
- contractions—painful or *painless* tightening or "balling up" of your belly
- abdominal or menstrual cramps, with or without diarrhea
- pelvic pressure or fullness in lower belly, pelvic area, back, or thighs
- constant or rhythmic dull ache in the lower back

- a change in type or amount of vaginal discharge
- ruptured membranes (your water breaks)

The warning signs indicate that something is *not* normal. These signs are often experienced as rhythmic tightening, pressure, or pain, four, or more times an hour that is different pressure than what you experience from a growing baby on your back or pelvis. Any of these warning signs along with the sense that something is just not right should be a trigger to call your care provider right away.

If your labor is leading to a preterm birth, ideally the delivery will be well controlled, with all the necessary people present to attend to you and your baby. Unfortunately, preterm births happen very quickly with little time for anyone, including you, to prepare. A premature labor and delivery may only take a couple of hours compared to the average ten to fifteen hour labors of full-term pregnancies.

Review Chapter II on normal pregnancy for a detailed explanation of the process of labor. As your labor progresses and your cervix opens, you may find your contractions are stronger and longer lasting. They may occur more frequently. You may also notice that a bloody mucous plug from the cervix and your membranes break.

Your labor may be short, but that does not mean you will be free from pain. It is unlikely you will have completed childbirth classes before your delivery. Because this may be the only section of this book you'll have time to read, I will repeat the basics of labor and delivery here. In early labor, you probably won't *need* to breathe through your contractions in a focused way. However, you may want to try some relaxation breathing techniques before the pain becomes too strong. Begin and end every contraction with a deep, cleansing breath. When you breathe during a contraction, try to use your belly muscles. Practice by putting your hand on your belly and letting it rise and fall with your breaths. This forces the muscles that instinctively tense with a contraction to relax. Some women find this method of breathing helpful throughout their entire labor. You may want to establish a visualization meditation during your contractions.

A visualization/relaxation technique

- Begin with a deep cleansing breath.
- Close your eyes.
- Relax every part of your body: head and neck, shoulders, arms, hands, fingers, chest, back, belly, hips, bottom, legs, feet, and toes.
- Picture a place in your mind where you feel warm and safe (this may be in your home; a place where you went as a little girl; or a warm sandy beach on an island, the breeze blowing and the rhythmic sound of the water in the background). Formulate the details in your mind, so that when the contraction gets closer, you can call on this image and have all the details in place.
- Slowly breathe with your contraction.
- When the contraction ends, take a deep cleansing breath and return to reality.
- Open your eyes.

Focused breathing will make a tremendous difference in your ability to deal with contractions. If you feel that you would like medication or an epidural, be sure to communicate your wishes to your nurses and care providers. It is everyone's goal to help you get through this labor. You are not alone and medication or an epidural may actually help your labor. Listen to your body, it will tell you what it needs in the way of breathing, pain relief, and rest.

Transition is the last phase of labor before you begin to push out your baby. The uterus is working extremely hard, and it is very difficult to relax. You may feel nauseated, cold, trembly, restless, discouraged, and scared. You will notice an increase in bleeding from your vagina and an almost unbearable pressure in your rectum. You may find that you want to stop breathing during your contraction and grunt or bear down as with a bowel movement. Let your nurse know what you are feeling. Try to stay focused with your contractions; keep breathing. Think of one contraction at a time. Each contraction is one less than you will ever feel again. If you feel the urge to bear down and push, try blowing quick breaths as if you are blowing out a candle.

When your cervix is completely dilated or your premature baby is squeezing out of your cervix, your care provider will tell you to go ahead and push. Rest between the contractions, but when a contraction begins, take a couple of deep, cleansing breaths. Keep your face relaxed and your eyes open during pushing. All energy should be focused on your bottom. A wrinkled up face, eyes squeezed tightly shut, a mouth losing air through screams, take precious energy that should be reserved to push out your baby. Small, premature babies are under much stress at this point so it isn't a good idea to prolong the pushing phase. If you need to cry or scream, it is better to cry or scream between contractions. As the contraction grows in strength, take a breath and hold it. Now, while holding your breath, bear down straight into your bottom with all of your might. Hold that push long and strong. It may be helpful to count in your head, to ten if possible. Quickly grab some more air, hold it, now bear down again, long and strong. Try to repeat this one more time during your contraction. Now let this contraction go, letting your whole body sink into the bed. Take a deep cleansing breath. You may want an ice chip and will want to rest, even sleep, in between contractions. As your baby's head is crowning, bulging on your perineum, you may want to reach down and touch your baby's head for the first time. If a mirror is available, it may be motivational for you to see your baby's head and even watch it move as you push.

If the skin and muscle around your vaginal opening does not stretch enough to allow the baby's head to come out, your care provider may feel it is necessary to make the opening larger by cutting an episiotomy. This small incision and any tears that occur are repaired with stitches after the birth of your baby, and they generally heal quickly.

After the baby's head is out, your care provider will tell you *not* to push while the baby's mouth and nose are being cleaned out. This is done to prevent your baby from breathing in anything left in his mouth when he takes his first breath. You will give one final push before you open your eyes and see your baby enter this world. The baby will be quickly dried off and handed to the specialized nursery staff who will care for this precious miracle. You will be unable to accompany your baby to the intensive care nursery immediately after delivery; therefore, you may want your partner or another family member to stay by your baby's side and ask questions.

The remainder of your recovery and postpartum period will be similar to that of a mother who gave birth to a full term infant. The biggest difference you may experience involves being separated from your newborn and breast-feeding. Refer to Chapter XIV on breast-feeding as well as *The Breastfeeding Sourcebook* by M. Sara Rosenthal.

Preterm labor and delivery are a serious and frightening complication of pregnancy, so serious that the United States has designated it a national problem and is taking steps to decrease the number of preterm births through education, nutrition, and better health care during pregnancy. Prevention is the key to decreasing preterm births. By recognizing how important your role is in mothering your baby while pregnant, you will better tolerate the inconveniences of treatment. Think about how your response to recommended treatments will impact your child's life forever. Our role as parents is one of sacrifice and unconditional love. There is no greater time to start practicing than the present. Trust yourself to be a great mother.

XI

Gestational Diabetes

Overview of Diabetes

Diabetes occurs when the body does not produce any or enough insulin which is necessary to transport the sugar, or glucose, in your blood to tissues and organs that utilize it for energy. This can also occur because of a resistance to insulin in tissues and organs. Without enough insulin your blood sugar level remains high while your tissues and organs starve for fuel. The pancreas, the organ responsible for producing insulin in your body, stops functioning properly. (See Chapter VI for more information.)

Gestational diabetes is one type of diabetes that occurs only during pregnancy and disappears after delivery. However, women who had gestational diabetes are at risk for developing diabetes later in life.

Pregnancy changes the way your body produces and reacts to insulin. Early in pregnancy, the body increases insulin production and the body's tissues are very receptive to insulin. This is believed to occur as an attempt to provide more fuel stores for later in pregnancy. As pregnancy continues, the placenta produces hormones that oppose the actions of insulin and some that increase the conversion of stored fuel back into sugar. When all this works properly, the body quickly converts food to stored fuel when eating, and when not eating quickly converts the stored fuel to glucose thus providing your baby with the needed fuel for growth.

Gestational Diabetes

Overview

During pregnancy, the hormones produced by the placenta that provide food for your growing baby may cause your blood sugar levels to rise. These hormones may cause the baby to grow too large, a condition known as macrosomia. The larger the baby, the greater the risk for a difficult delivery. Controlling the blood sugar level decreases the problem of macrosomia, and gestational diabetes may be controlled by diet alone or by a combination of diet and insulin.

Some care providers test all pregnant women for gestational diabetes. Other care providers will only test women who have any of the following risk factors: a previous large baby; a previous pregnancy with excessive amniotic fluid; an infant born with malformations; an unexplained stillborn; family history of diabetes; obesity; spilling sugar in your urine; excessive weight gain in the current pregnancy; or excessive amniotic fluid in the current pregnancy.

Testing is done at twenty-six to twenty-eight weeks. A one hour glucola, or glucose tolerance test, is done. You eat normally the day of the test. At the office or laboratory you are given a very sweet drink. One hour after finishing the drink, blood is drawn. The blood is sent to the laboratory and tested for a glucose level. If the blood glucose level is high, a three-hour glucose tolerance test is done. After not eating overnight, you will have an initial blood sugar level drawn. Again, you are given a very sweet drink. Blood is then drawn at one, two, and three hour intervals after the drink. When two or more of these levels are elevated you are diagnosed with gestational diabetes.

What are the main concerns for my baby and myself?

With proper treatment and control of your blood sugar, you and your baby will be healthy and the pregnancy will progress normally. Obviously, a large baby can complicate your delivery. This may mean increased trauma to your vaginal area, a cesarean section, or possible increased trauma to your baby during delivery. However, your risk for problems at delivery is normal if the baby is not large.

How can I best care for my baby and myself?

Follow your care provider's recommendations. Eat the diet recommended by your care provider or a nutritionist. This diet usually includes a 2,200 to 2,400 calorie diet. The diet is specifically divided up into 45 percent carbohydrates (breads, cereals, fruits, etc.), 25 percent proteins (meat, cheese, milk), and 30 percent fat. Some dietitians will further break down your fruits and milks into specific categories. You will be taught the best way to recognize these food sources and the quantity or number of servings from each food group. You can keep track of your servings on a daily log.

You may need to routinely check your blood sugar levels or your care provider may check them when you come in for your prenatal exams. In most areas, home blood glucose monitors are available for loan to women with gestational diabetes. Talk to your care provider about this option. Test your blood sugar level according to the method prescribed by your care provider. You will learn to prick your finger, obtain, and test your blood. Your care provider will adjust your diet or insulin to maintain blood sugars in the following parameters:

Fasting blood sugar (FBS): less than 100
Blood sugar 2 hours after eating a meal: less than 120

Keep an accurate record of your sugars. Bring this record to each office visit. You may also be taught to test your urine for ketones and/or glucose.

Keeping track of your baby's movement from twenty-eight weeks until delivery is always important. Call your care provider if your baby is not moving as much as usual. If you are on insulin, your care provider will start you on twice weekly testing of your baby's well-being. The test most frequently used is a nonstress test (NST). A fetal heart monitor watches for the baby's heart rate and any contractions, and your perception of your baby's movement is tracked by pressing a button. This information is documented electronically on a strip of paper and evaluated.

Another test that may be done is a biophysical profile. This is a thirty-minute test done by ultrasound. The baby is watched for movement, muscle tone or flexion, breathing movements, the amount of amniotic fluid, and the condition of the placenta, along with a possible NST.

Labor, delivery, and postpartum

As long as your baby is growing normally your labor and delivery should proceed normally. If your baby is large, your risks are increased for certain problems. The baby's head can be too large to move down the birth canal, and you may need to deliver by cesarean section. There may also be difficulty and delay in delivering the baby's shoulders. A delay in delivery, if prolonged, can lead to brain damage in severe cases. A difficult delivery of the shoulders may damage the baby's shoulder nerve causing a condition known as a brachial plexus injury. Facial palsy, a drooping of a portion of the face, can also occur. Both of these conditions are usually temporary and heal with time. The baby's shoulder bone, called the clavicle, may be broken during the delivery. This will also heal quickly.

During the postpartum period your blood sugars should return to normal. A few blood sugars will be checked for a day or so after delivery. If blood sugars do not return to normal, you may actually have undiagnosed Type I or Type II diabetes. Women with gestational diabetes are at a marked risk for developing Type II diabetes and have a 17 to 29 percent chance of developing Type I diabetes. Lifetime follow-up should include a yearly check for blood sugar elevations. If you are overweight, you should try to lose those extra pounds. Obese women with gestational diabetes are at increased risk to develop Type II diabetes later in life.

XII

Preeclampsia, Toxemia, and Pregnancy-Induced Hypertension

Overview

Preeclampsia is a disease that only occurs during pregnancy. Preeclampsia, pregnancy-induced hypertension (PIH), and toxemia are essentially interchangeable terms used by your care provider for this disease. This disease is characterized by swelling, high blood pressure, and the presence of protein in the urine. Preeclampsia occurs in 5 to 10 percent of all pregnancies. It can appear suddenly, without warning, any time throughout your pregnancy, labor, or in the early postpartum period. This disease can also be chronic, gradually becoming worse over a period of time. It may be mild or severe. But, no matter how ill you become with this disease, whether it's sudden or gradual, the only cure is delivery of the baby. There are medications and treatments to keep you from becoming more ill with the disease, but no medications will make the disease go away entirely.

Your care provider will begin to look for signs of preeclampsia during your second trimester and continue through your postpartum period. Sometimes, early treatment can prolong a pregnancy and lessen complications for both mother and baby.

If you are diagnosed with preeclampsia before your baby's due date, your care provider will occasionally want to prolong your pregnancy. If you are close to your due date, your care provider will most likely prepare you and the baby for delivery.

After delivery, the disease eventually goes away, and it is unlikely that you will suffer any long-term effects of the disease. Occasionally, there are complications that will require medical attention for a time after you deliver. This may include taking blood pressure medication and frequent follow-up visits with your care provider.

Could it happen to me?

Women who are at the greatest risk are those who are pregnant with their first baby. Women who are having another baby but with a new partner are also at a significant risk. If you have had preeclampsia during another pregnancy or if you have a family history of preeclampsia (for example, if your mother or sister had preeclampsia with a pregnancy), your risk also increases. African-American women and women who are financially challenged, underprivileged, under twenty, or over thirty-five are also at increased risk. Medical conditions such as lupus, diabetes, or high blood pressure (chronic hypertension) put you at risk for developing preeclampsia. If you are pregnant with more than one baby, such as twins or triplets, the risk increases. If there is something wrong with either your baby or your placenta, such as the presence of a chromosomal abnormality or an abnormal maternal serum alpha feto protein (MSAFP), you also are at an increased risk for preeclampsia.

What could happen to my body and to my baby?

Preeclampsia causes swelling (edema), high blood pressure (hypertension), and the spilling of protein in your urine (proteinuria). Death is a very rare occurrence. Obvious complications of preeclampsia are: swelling, high blood pressure, poor kidney function, poor liver function, pulmonary edema (fluid in the lungs), and possible seizure. A poor blood supply to the baby will decrease the baby's nutrients to grow and be healthy.

How does this happen?

This disease can resolve almost as quickly as it comes on. There are many theories about what causes preeclampsia, but to this day, despite extensive clinical research, the cause remains a mystery. Preeclampsia has become known as the disease of theories. However, the most current research has lead care providers to believe this disease is a type of immunological response to the products of conception (embryo, placenta, membranes, etc.). This means that perhaps the woman's body becomes "allergic" to the baby and placenta. It is possible that tiny protein molecules from the baby mix with the mother's blood causing a reaction which in turn causes a release of certain chemicals that damage the mother's blood, blood vessels, and major organs.

The blood and blood vessels

Preeclampsia causes vasospasm, a condition in which your blood vessels squeeze and then relax almost like a muscle spasm. This causes the smooth lining of the blood vessels to become damaged and rough. Once this damage occurs, the body will send out cells to repair the damage. The cells that arrive first are platelets, tiny saucer-shaped cells in the blood which are the foundation of blood

211

clots and essential to stop bleeding throughout the body. As platelets and other blood products try to repair the damage, they form little clots along the blood vessel wall causing the blood vessel to become even more narrow and further decreasing blood flow to the organs, almost like a clogged drain. The body continually makes new platelets; however, there is a limited supply of platelets in the body at any one time. Once they have become depleted, spontaneous bleeding can occur. For instance, a cut hand or a bloody nose may not stop bleeding.

Other cells passing by the damaged lining of the blood vessels break open, often spilling their toxic contents. These toxic waste products cause high blood pressure and even more damage to other organs. Vasospasm and the miniature blood clots cause further damage by decreasing blood flow and thus decreasing the oxygen supply to vital organs such as the brain, kidneys, and liver.

High blood pressure is one of the most common symptoms of preeclampsia. Think of it as a constant vasospasm, as though the blood vessels are squeezed tightly closed. If the blood pressure rises too high it can cause seizure. If you begin to have high blood pressure you may have a severe headache or see spots or floating stars before your eyes. Untreated severe high blood pressure may also result in a stroke (bleeding inside the brain).

The brain

The term preeclampsia refers to the disease state before a seizure. Once a woman has had a seizure with this disease it then becomes eclampsia. The word eclampsia roughly translates from Greek to mean flash of lightning, because this disease can strike without warning. A seizure does not make the disease go away, but further complicates it. Eclampsia is a very serious disease and requires urgent medical attention for both you and your baby.

The damage from the vasospasms can also become so bad that your blood vessels become "leaky" and lead to severe swelling. In actuality, the blood vessel can no longer keep the essential fluid the body needs inside the vessels. The fluid that has leaked out into your tissues is edema. This edema manifests as a swollen face, eyelids, hands, or very swollen legs and feet. Swelling can also occur inside the body. A collection of fluids can accumulate in the brain, a condition called cerebral edema. Cerebral edema can cause a pregnant woman to have a seizure. For a mother with severe preeclampsia, a seizure can occur up to three weeks after delivery. If a mother has a seizure from this disease, she may experience a loss of eyesight or violent or psychotic behavior, both of which are temporary. The chance of a seizure causing death to the mother ranges from 0 to 14 percent. However, risk of harm to the baby is much higher. If the mother has a seizure it could cause an early birth, a lack of oxygen to the baby, or a loss of blood supply to the placenta. Untreated high blood pressure can lead to a stroke in the brain. Any of these things can cause harm to your baby and require immediate medical attention.

The heart

Your heart has an increased work load when you become pregnant. Blood volume increases by 40 to 50 percent causing your blood to dilute during pregnancy. With this increased blood volume the blood vessels in your legs and the rest of your body *normally* relax making room for the extra blood. Picture a pair of pantyhose. They hold a small leg, but will stretch to hold a much larger one, too. If you have preeclampsia, the vasospasm squeezes the vessels causing very little room for the extra blood. This in turn causes the vessels to leak out the watery portion leaving your blood very concentrated, like sludge. If you have concentrated "sludge" in your vessels with a lot of pressure behind, it is like a kinked garden hose with the water turned on. The water source must work very hard to get past the kink. Similarly, your heart will work very hard at circulating your concentrated blood.

The kidneys

Vasospasm can also occur in the kidneys. The kidneys are a filtering system for the body. When vasospasm occurs in the kidney, the kidney does not receive enough blood and oxygen, resulting in kidney damage. This kind of damage causes the kidney to become "leaky" and is unable to keep certain products inside your body. The first thing it will leak is protein, the substance the body needs to maintain water balance. Losing a lot of protein causes the body to swell with water in your hands, face, and feet. The kidneys are also unable to make an adequate amount of urine when there is decreased blood flow. Essentially, the kidneys cannot do their job well. The kidneys are then unable to filter out the waste products, save the good things your body needs, and make urine. Think of a big dirty sponge that is being squeezed over and over without using clean rinse water. Eventually the sponge will be dry but with tiny dirt particles stuck inside. If this process goes untreated kidney damage can occur. This does not physically hurt, but will eventually harm other organs in the body.

The liver

Preeclampsia can vary in severity. If you have a severe form of this disease, the liver becomes affected. Mothers who have preeclampsia have a 4 to 12 percent chance of developing HELLP syndrome (*H*emolysis, *E*levated *L*iver enzymes and *L*ow *P*latelets). This syndrome is characterized by a combination of laboratory changes.

Hemolysis refers to those broken cells that were damaged when they traveled through the narrow, clogged vessels. Laboratory tests will show changes in your blood. The blood cells are damaged due to the hemolysis, liver functions tests rise, and your blood clotting ability decreases due to a lack of platelets.

As discussed at the beginning of this chapter, most changes occur because of vasospasm. HELLP syndrome is caused by vasospasm in the liver. The blood vessels in the liver experience the same kind of damage from vasospasm. Mini-clots decrease oxygen to the liver tissue, and the other normal cells traveling through the vessels break open, spilling their contents (hemolysis). This process progresses very rapidly and can quickly become severe or even deadly. Think of it as if this disease were strangling your liver. Inside the liver is swelling, with congestion and pressure. The liver tissue does not receive enough oxygen from the decreased circulation and it begins to suffocate.

When the liver tissue begins to die it will produce certain products called liver enzymes. Blood tests will indicate a rise in liver enzymes. This process in the liver can cause physical pain. To the pregnant mother it may feel like painful heartburn or as a radiating pain under the breastbone or to your right shoulder. You may experience great fatigue, nausea, vomiting, or difficulty in taking a deep breath.

It is possible for the liver to rupture. Because the liver is full of large blood vessels, and all your blood passes through the liver just as through your heart, liver rupture is fatal more than 50 percent of the time. Other serious complications of HELLP syndrome include excessive bleeding (DIC), placental abruption (the placenta coming away from the uterine wall too early), kidney failure, and fluid collection in your lungs (pulmonary edema). Death in mothers who have HELLP syndrome ranges from 0 to 24 percent.

The baby and placenta

Just as vasospasm damages the liver and the kidneys, it also causes damage to the baby's placenta. Vasospasm and mini-clots develop in the vessels of the placenta which supply the baby with blood, oxygen, and nutrients. With a decreased blood supply, the baby cannot grow well. Eventually this will result in a severely under-grown infant. For instance, a mother with preeclampsia may have a baby weighing 3 pounds instead of a baby who would have nor-mally weighed 7 pounds at birth.

The vasospasm not only affects the baby through poor oxy-genation, but it also can cause separation of the placenta from the wall of the uterus. This is called placental abruption, a devastating disorder (discussed in detail in Chapter XIII on bleeding during pregnancy).

Signs and Symptoms

Preeclampsia is known to care providers as the "Great Masquerader." Preeclampsia can look like many other conditions such as the flu, a kidney infection, or gallbladder disease. Pregnant women with this illness may have any or all of the signs and symptoms and be equally as ill. For instance, a woman with this disease may have high blood pressure and protein in her urine but not appear swollen. Or, she may have horribly high liver enzymes, very few platelets, and a normal blood pressure. Diagnosing it is like putting together a puzzle. Your care provider will need to gather information about how you are feeling, how you look, how the baby looks by ultrasound and fetal monitor, as well as evaluate your laboratory tests.

After you are approximately twenty weeks into your preg-nancy, your care provider will become especially interested in following your weight gain, your blood pressure, and your urine for protein. Other specific signs and symptoms can include swelling of your face, hands, and feet; headaches; blurred vision or seeing spots; persistent painful heartburn; or poor growth in the baby. All of these things can be discovered during a prenatal visit. If you think you have any of these signs or symptoms at home or at work call your care provider right away. Remember, there is no such thing as a dumb question. It is smart to ask if you think something is wrong with you or your baby.

How will I know if I have preeclampsia?

If you are considered high risk for getting preeclampsia during your pregnancy—for example, if you are diabetic or have twins—your care provider may see you more frequently in the office after you are approximately twenty-four to twenty-six weeks along in your pregnancy. Your care provider may also start you on one baby aspirin per day throughout your pregnancy. It is also possible that a visiting nurse will come to your home to check your weight, your blood pressure, your urine for protein, and to listen to the baby's heart rate. But you can also be trained to do all of these things for yourself at home with a scale, home blood pressure monitor, urine test strips, and an external fetal heart rate monitor.

If your care provider becomes concerned, blood will be drawn and tested while you are in the office to help identify preeclampsia. Testing your blood for worrisome changes can indicate poor kidney function, liver function abnormalities, and a decrease in platelets. Your care provider may even want to have you collect your urine for a twenty-four hour time period and bring it in for testing.

If your care provider becomes suspicious, you may be hospitalized for testing. This way the nurses in the hospital can follow your weight daily, check your blood pressure frequently, obtain laboratory tests, and monitor the baby's heart rate.

217

Following the baby's progress can also give your care provider a lot of information about whether or not you have this disease. An ultrasound of the baby for growth measurements and checking the blood flow in the umbilical cord (Doppler flow studies) are helpful in determining whether or not the baby is being affected. The external fetal monitor is also useful to determine the well being of the baby by tracing his fetal heart rate pattern.

Your care provider may send you to a perinatologist, an obstetrician specializing in high-risk pregnancies. Further investigation may require a repeat ultrasound of your baby or additional blood for analysis.

Essentially, you will be diagnosed with preeclampsia if your blood pressure is elevated, if you have significant swelling, and/or if there is protein in your urine. A high blood pressure would be considered 140/90, or if the top number (systolic pressure) is greater than 30 points or the bottom number (diastolic) is greater than 15 points from the blood pressure reading when you first became pregnant. For example, if you started with a blood pressure of 100/60, a high blood pressure for you would be 130/90. Normally, a large amount of protein is not found in a woman's urine so such a finding would be significant. Some swelling of your hands and feet is normal during pregnancy, but your care provider will be able to determine whether it is serious or not.

I have it, now what?

If you have preeclampsia you may need to be hospitalized. Bedrest at home is only a temporary treatment in the early stages of this disease. If you live in a small town or a city with a hospital that is not equipped or staffed for a premature baby, you may be transferred to a larger facility by ambulance, helicopter, or airplane with a team of medical professionals. If the larger facility is far away, your care provider will turn your care over to another doctor who can look after you there. A new set of doctors and nurses can sometimes be stressful, but most often, the staff at such hospitals will be prepared to make you feel comfortable and at ease by providing a peaceful and quiet environment. Although it is comforting to have your family nearby, this is a time when you need rest, quiet, and the elimination of undue stress. Complications of preeclampsia can be worsened by bright lights, loud or constant noises, and fatigue. Listening to soft music, dimming the lights, and very limited visiting hours are necessary to protect you from becoming even more ill.

Once diagnosed with preeclampsia, it is almost always necessary that you deliver immediately. After being admitted to the hospital, the doctors and nurses together with your care provider will gather your medical history and perform a physical exam. You will require an intravenous catheter in your arm and blood will be taken and sent to the laboratory for testing. Your baby's heart rate will be checked with the fetal monitor, and you may have an ultrasound to further evaluate the baby.

If you are delivering your baby before the due date, you may undergo an amniocentesis, a procedure that involves inserting a needle into the uterus and removing some amniotic fluid from around the baby. The amniotic fluid reveals whether your baby's lungs are mature enough to breathe air on the outside of your uterus. This procedure is not painful and is most often described as "a weird cramp" as the needle is inserted into the uterus. The entire procedure does not take more than a few minutes or as long as it takes to draw blood from your arm. If the fetal lungs are mature, delivery should follow. Whether you have an amniocentesis or not, your care provider will give you medication to help prepare your baby for premature delivery.

The medications

Betamethasone is a type of steroid that can be given to a pregnant mom. It crosses the placenta and helps stimulate the cells in the baby's lungs and prepares them to breathe air. Betamethasone can decrease the incidence of severe breathing problems in a premature baby. Steroids can also decrease the risk of brain hemorrhage and intestinal problems in your premature baby. Optimally, this medication needs forty-eight hours to work. However, sometimes preeclampsia is too severe to allow the necessary time for this medication to work, and delivery is done before the forty-eight hours are up.

Medications that help the baby's lungs and brain prepare for early birth vary widely in their use across the country. Your care provider will prescribe these medications accordingly. (See Chapter X on preterm labor.)

Magnesium sulfate is a standard medication used in treating women with preeclampsia. It is administered directly into your vein through IV tubing. Magnesium sulfate is an anticonvulsant that works to prevent you from having a seizure by depressing your central nervous system and relaxing the muscles in your body. Essentially, it blocks the nervous system at the muscle level and has direct action on your blood vessels. When given through your IV in an appropriate dose, the drug's effects will decrease your risk of having a seizure. Magnesium sulfate is well known for its side effects which include flushing, sweating, nasal congestion, extreme thirst, sleepiness, confusion, depressed reflexes, muscle weakness, decreased blood pressure, and low body temperature. Dangerous side effects are only seen with very high doses of magnesium sulfate. The staff will check your blood level for signs of too little or too much magnesium sulfate quite often, which means frequent needle sticks for you. You will probably remain on this medication for the next twenty-four to forty-eight hours after you deliver. This medication can temporarily affect the baby immediately after birth and may include a change in heart rate pattern tracing on the external fetal monitor.

Another medication that may be used to help treat your disease is dexamethasone. This drug is also used in the treatment of HELLP syndrome. It is thought to help tame the damage that occurs to the lining of the blood vessels and subsequently to the liver. It helps decrease the amount of cells damaged by the vasospasm. If this drug is used, it will also help mature the baby's lungs like the drug betamethasone.

Other drugs such as hydralazine, labetalol, and nifedipine may be used to help lower your blood pressure. These drugs can be administered in a pill or through your IV. How often and how much of a drug or combination of drugs you will need to keep your blood pressure under control will vary. If you had high blood pressure before pregnancy, you may already be taking one of these drugs or a similar drug to help control your blood pressure.

Delivery

Just because you have preeclampsia does not mean you will automatically require a cesarean section (c-section) to deliver your baby. A vaginal birth is optimal and recommended. Your care provider will consider many factors when determining whether or not you will be able to safely deliver your baby vaginally. Factors that may impact a decision to attempt a vaginal birth include whether your cervix is dilated or favorable for delivery, if your baby is well enough to tolerate labor and delivery, and if *you* are well enough to tolerate labor. If your placenta is severely damaged or separated from the wall of the uterus a c-section will be necessary.

It may be possible for you to have an epidural for pain control with a vaginal delivery or for a cesarean section. Of course, there are complications that could keep you from having an epidural, in which case you can receive pain medication through your IV or be put to sleep for a c-section. The person responsible for your anesthesia will determine if it is either safe or appropriate for you to have an epidural.

Can there be serious complications?

Complications can sometimes become so severe that you may require a team of specialists. This means that if your care provider is not a physician, for instance a midwife, your care will likely be transferred to a physician.

If your kidneys are not making enough urine, or your lungs are "leaky" and filling with fluid, or you have very *severe* swelling, your doctor may place a large IV in your neck vein or in the large vein next to your collarbone. Once this type of IV is placed, a small device can be placed inside the IV which will give the nurses and doctors very important information about what is going on inside of you. If your blood pressure is difficult to control, you may need an IV-like device placed in an artery similar to an IV but continually measuring your blood pressure through your artery. Both of these IVs require special machines and specially-trained nurses at your bedside, so you may be transferred to an intensive care unit where those things are available.

Another special treatment to help you get well is a type of dialysis called plasmaphoresis. This procedure is similar to kidney dialysis. Your blood is slowly taken out through a very large IV and processed through a special machine and then returned to your body. This machine washes out the bad toxins from your blood. All the while you will be monitored closely for changes by nurses and technicians.

Other treatments or tests that may be required are blood transfusions, x-rays, Cat scans, and ultrasounds. If you become seriously ill with complications from preeclampsia and need one or all of these things, your doctor should explain these treatments in detail to you and your family.

Preeclampsia is a serious illness during pregnancy and should never be taken lightly. A mild case can become severe in a matter of hours. The only cure at this time is delivery. Perhaps a future cure will be discovered, but for now, good prenatal care is the key. Recognizing this harmful disease early and quickly is the best treatment for both mother and baby. Your education is also very important. Obviously, aspects of this disease are part of an inevitable process you cannot control. However, knowing the risk factors and signs of preeclampsia will help you prepare for possible events during your pregnancy. Being prepared ahead of time sometimes can offer a degree of comfort and eliminate the fear of the unknown.

Of course, every woman and every pregnancy is unique and not always treated the same. Rely on your care provider to take care of you and your baby. If you are not completely at ease or receiving what you think is the best care, talk to your care provider. If you are still not completely satisfied, change to a new provider. You, too, have a responsibility in the care provider-patient relationship, so speak up and seek to understand and be understood. Preeclampsia should never be ignored. Your health and safety as well as the health and safety of your baby comes first.

XIII

Bleeding with Pregnancy

Overview

More than any other complication, hemorrhage, or bleeding, can be profound for the baby, the mother, her family, and care provider. Bleeding during pregnancy can mean a number of things, but it should always be taken seriously. Excessive bleeding can lead to other deadly complications such as kidney failure and difficulty with breathing.

Normal changes with pregnancy can magnify excessive bleeding. An extra two liters of blood will be circulating in your body by the time you are six months along in your pregnancy. Your blood volume increases to an impressive 45 percent by the time you reach your due date. With this much extra blood your heart naturally works harder and faster to keep up. These changes occur so that the baby will have plenty of blood, oxygen, and nutrients to grow and thrive. During the delivery of her baby and after the birth, a mother naturally loses a fair amount of blood, about a quart. Mother nature has designed it so that you lose the extra blood that was made during your pregnancy, and you are left with a normal blood supply after delivery and a better ability to take care of your baby than you might have been after a large loss of blood which would leave you very weak.

However, when you do experience abnormal bleeding, a large quantity of blood can be lost quickly with few changes in your vital signs. Because of a pregnant woman's natural ability to compensate for blood loss, the actual amount lost can be deceiving to a care provider causing an unnecessary delay of treatment. Early recognition of the problem and swift treatment is the best way to avoid a dangerous situation.

In early pregnancy (first trimester) a small amount of bleeding can be common and not particularly harmful. As long as you are *not* having a miscarriage a small amount of bleeding can be tolerated. It is always necessary for your care provider to know about *any* bleeding during your pregnancy. Bleeding in early pregnancy can mean a variety of things, but most often it is a warning flag for your care provider to be aware of possible complications that could arise later during your pregnancy.

The most life-threatening bleeding occurs later in pregnancy, usually after twenty-four weeks and then immediately following delivery. Placentia previa and placental abruption (abruptio placentae) are two common disorders that can cause a mother to hemorrhage during her pregnancy. Both disorders pertain to the placenta, so an understanding of the placenta is necessary to understand both of these disorders.

The placenta

The placenta, or the afterbirth, is a spongy, disc-shaped organ that develops with and for your baby at conception. The fertilized egg travels down the fallopian tube to the uterus and finds a place along the wall of the uterus to bury itself into the lining among little oxygen-rich blood vessels. As your pregnancy progresses, the placenta coordinates many different efforts enabling your baby to survive. Special cells working for the placenta invade the lining of your uterus. This invasion ultimately alters your blood vessels and allows them to accommodate for the increased blood volume needed to supply the placenta and the baby. The placenta is an amazing organ that transforms your uterus into a thriving place for your baby. A primitive placenta is formed and functioning by day seventeen. The placenta is fully developed and operational by the tenth week of pregnancy, and will continue to grow until it reaches its final form at around twenty weeks. When you reach your due date the placenta will weigh approximately one pound.

The many vessels created in the placenta are intertwined with the lining of your uterus. A complex web of vessels within the placenta supplies both the placenta and the baby with oxygen and nutrients. The mother's blood supply continuously keeps the placenta filled with oxygen rich blood. Oxygenated blood flows to the baby through a large blood vessel in the umbilical cord called the umbilical vein. The blood then returns to the placenta through two vessels called umbilical arteries. Besides filtering your blood to provide the baby with oxygen and healthy nutrients, the placenta, in return, empties waste products from the baby into your blood. The placenta is a busy organ that also produces many hormones to support the pregnancy. It truly functions as the gatekeeper for your baby.

Because the placenta has such an important role during your pregnancy it must remain undisturbed to do its job. The many blood vessels connecting it to you need to be on a healthy surface inside your uterus where it can be nurtured and protected. Once the baby is born, its job is complete and it releases itself from the uterus and is delivered.

Placenta Previa

One common reason for bleeding during pregnancy is placenta previa. Placenta previa happens 1 out of every 250 pregnancies and commonly recurs 4 to 8 percent of the time.

A placenta previa means that the baby's placenta is implanted on the uterine wall near or over the opening of the uterus, or the cervix. Normally the placenta should be located on one of the sides or on the roof of the uterus away from the cervix. Picture the cervix as the door to the uterus. The cervix is shaped like a neck, it is long and cylindrical, and is the opening to the birth canal. The cervix is the connection between the uterus and the vagina and is positioned at the end of the uterus. Both your menstrual blood and your baby escape the uterus through this opening. You could say that a placenta previa is "putting the cart before the horse."

A placenta previa can be complete, partial, marginal, or low-lying. A complete previa means that the entire opening of the cervix is covered with the placenta. A partial previa means that part of the placenta's surface is covering the cervical opening. A marginal previa means the placenta is resting at the opening of the cervix but does not cover it, and a low-lying placenta rests very near the opening.

Because the placenta is a vascular organ, any disruption by pulling on it, poking at it, or stretching it, causes the vessels connecting it to the uterine wall to break. When these blood vessels are broken bleeding occurs. As you may already know, labor causes the cervix to open and thin out with contractions. If the placenta is implanted over or near the surface of the cervix, large blood vessels will be ruptured as the cervix changes.

A placenta previa of any form means complications that are usually far greater for the baby than for the mother. Early delivery may be necessary to stop serious bleeding. The placenta must be removed to stop a life-threatening hemorrhage. A complete placenta previa carries the most risk and poorest outcome.

How does it happen?

A placenta previa is caused when the fertilized egg implants in the lower part of the uterus near the opening. Most of the time this is purely unfortunate luck. However, there are some existing factors that may put you more at risk, including a previous baby, smoking, being thirty-five or older, or having had a previous trauma to the lining of the uterus (endometrium). Previous trauma can cause scarring on the uterus, and scarring may occur from a D & C (dilation and curettage) which is sometimes done after a miscarriage or if you have had problems with a heavy, constant menstrual flow. Another type of trauma that could leave scarring on your uterus is an abortion or a previous cesarean section. It is also associated with twins, triplets, quadruplets, and being pregnant many times.

How will I know?

Oftentimes, a placenta previa will cause the baby to lie in the uterus sideways (transverse) or bottom first (breech). Placenta previa is often discovered during a routine ultrasound examination as the placenta's location can be seen during the ultrasound. However, 90 percent of the time when a placenta previa is discovered during an ultrasound in early pregnancy it will *not* be a previa at term. The lower segment of the uterus thins and stretches as the baby grows. This growth results in the placenta moving away from the cervix or the cervix actually grows away from the placenta. Essentially, growth of the uterus can clear a path for the delivery of the baby.

You may first discover a placenta previa if you experience painless, bright red vaginal bleeding. There is about a 25 percent chance that bleeding will be associated with contractions. Bleeding will sometimes begin for a mother after intercourse, douching, or a pelvic exam. Remember, douching is *never* okay during pregnancy. More often, however, the bleeding begins spontaneously. You may also pass reddish brown clots or bright red clots from your vagina. These clots may be very small, very large, or somewhere in between. This type of bleeding usually begins between thirty and thirty-four weeks if you have a placenta previa. The first episode of bleeding is not life threatening. However, any type of bleeding should be reported to your care provider. Your care provider will want to know the color and amount of bleeding when you call, so keep careful track of how many sanitary napkins you have soaked and bring them with you to either the office or the hospital. Sometimes, placenta previa is not discovered until you are actually in labor and you begin to have heavy, bright red vaginal bleeding that might be mistaken as heavy "bloody show."

What now?

If you are diagnosed with a placenta previa it is almost always necessary for you to be hospitalized at some point during your pregnancy. Bleeding can be provoked or be completely spontaneous. Contractions commonly cause bleeding for mothers with a placenta previa. Bedrest is the best treatment for preventing contractions as well as avoiding inserting anything into the vagina, including intercourse or a pelvic exam. Your care provider will determine whether it is safe for you to be at bedrest at home or in the hospital.

You may encounter a few other routine treatments if you are hospitalized for a placenta previa. Treatment includes having an IV placed in your arm in case you begin to bleed and your care providers need to treat you swiftly and safely. Other treatments include monitoring your baby's heart rate and periodically checking your blood count. Your blood will also be sent to the laboratory to determine your blood type. This way if you do have excessive bleeding, a blood transfusion can be prepared quickly to match your specific blood type.

Most importantly, treatment for a placenta previa safeguards the baby from an early birth. The ultimate treatment for excessive bleeding is delivery so it is of the utmost importance that you do not experience preterm labor. Contractions will only worsen your situation, and they are one of the more common triggers that cause bleeding. Contractions will pull on the lower part of your uterus where the placenta is implanted and cause disruption and bleeding. Medications to stop contractions (tocolytics) may help to avoid disrupting the placenta any further and decrease the risk of serious bleeding. The use of these medications can help delay a premature birth.

Medications may also help mature the baby's lungs (see Chapter X on preterm labor). Even if you do not experience preterm labor, accelerating your baby's lung maturity is essential, since it is next to impossible to predict when you may have a serious amount of bleeding that could necessitate delivery. So preparing your baby for an early birth is good planning.

Whether you experience a large amount of bleeding or a series of small episodes, you may need a blood transfusion. Donated blood is always carefully pretested for infectious diseases such as hepatitis and HIV and is prepared to be given to you through an IV, though many women choose to have family members with the same blood type donate blood early. This way their blood is ready in case of an emergency. Transfusions are reserved for when your blood count is terribly low. A terribly low blood count can harm you and your baby as your body needs to carry oxygen to all your vital organs and to the baby.

You may also receive several ultrasound exams to follow the status of your placenta, your baby's growth, and the amniotic fluid level. Serial ultrasounds help determine if your baby is growing as expected and feeling well. In addition, frequent ultrasounds can help your care provider determine whether or not the placenta has moved away from the cervix. This can be done safely with a special ultrasound tool called a vaginal probe, the same type of instrument used in ultrasound but shaped to fit just inside the vagina. This procedure is done carefully so as not to disturb the placenta resting over or near your cervix.

As you might expect, a vaginal delivery is usually not possible with this disorder. The delivery method will be highly dependent upon where the placenta is located. With a complete previa it is *always* necessary to deliver the baby by cesarean section. Most often, a partial previa is managed the same way. Your care provider will determine whether or not the opening of your cervix is free of the placenta so that the baby can be safely delivered.

Another approach to careful planning is an amniocentesis. Your care provider may want to test for fetal lung maturity with an amniocentesis. The amniotic fluid can be tested to determine whether or not your baby is ready to breathe air. This is done when you are near your due date around thirty-six weeks. If your baby's lungs are mature, a delivery can be scheduled and a catastrophic hemorrhage during your pregnancy can be avoided.

Can there be serious complications?

There are several complications that are associated with a placenta previa. Your care provider will first be concerned with excessive bleeding during delivery even with a cesarean section. A placenta previa is located low in the uterus, the same place the cesarean incision is made to deliver the baby. This means that the placenta is often cut at the same time causing rapid blood loss for both the mother and baby. A second complication is excessive bleeding after the delivery of the baby and placenta. This is called postpartum hemorrhage. Normally the uterus should clamp down upon itself with long, strong contractions. This normal response stops the large blood vessels that were once connected to the placenta from bleeding. With a placenta previa the lower part of your uterus may be less apt to contract down upon itself after delivery, leaving those large blood vessels unattended and open to bleed. The last worrisome complication associated with a placenta previa is an accreta, an abnormality of the placenta's bed of vessels. Sometimes the placenta will anchor itself further down into the muscle tissue of the uterus (myometrium) in order to secure a stable surface for growth. This type of placenta is able to function without problem during the pregnancy. However, when the placenta should release itself from the uterine wall after the delivery of the baby, it cannot. With accreta the placenta is entangled much too deeply into the lining of the uterus and often must be surgically removed resulting in a profuse blood loss. This complication can end with a hysterectomy. Certainly many other efforts would be made first to preserve the uterus prior to removing it, but when there is *persistent* life-threatening bleeding after delivery, the only alternative is a hysterectomy. Your care provider should determine what, if any, of these complications apply to you at the time of your delivery.

Placental Abruption

This disorder is the premature separation of the placenta from the uterine wall. Placental abruption affects 1 out of every 200 pregnancies. Harm to the baby is based on the severity of the abruption and whether or not the baby is delivered prematurely. With swift suitable treatment, maternal death is less than 1 percent. Abruption may reoccur 10 percent of the time with a subsequent pregnancy.

As you already know, the placenta implants on the uterine wall during pregnancy and is connected to you with many inter-twining blood vessels. These blood vessels maintain their working status until the baby is delivered. Once the baby is delivered the placenta will release itself, the connecting vessels will close and recede back into the uterine lining, and bleeding will taper off.

With a placental abruption the many large blood vessels are ruptured between the placenta and the uterine wall. Once this happens bleeding can occur quickly and in large amounts. A collection of blood accumulates between the placenta and the uterus and then forces the placenta to further separate from the wall of the uterus. This can be life threatening for both mother and baby.

A devastating form of abruption occurs when all of the placenta is separated before the birth of the baby. When this tragic event happens it is called a total abruption. Early separation of the placenta can also occur in small amounts on different areas of the placenta's surface, a condition called a chronic abruption. A partial abruption occurs when a large portion of the placenta separates from the uterine wall. This can have many different degrees of severity. An abruption will range in percentage according to the amount of placenta lost to early separation, and the only absolute way to determine this is through an examination after the delivery. More importantly, in order for the baby to survive, at least half of the placenta needs to be attached and functioning.

How does it happen?

The cause of abruption is truly unknown, but there are many conditions highly associated with placental abruption. Conditions that increase the risk of abruption include chronic hypertension, smoking, toxemia (see Chapter XII on preeclampsia), and having either twins or triplets. Other risk factors include having too much amniotic fluid (polyhydramnios), having a short umbilical cord, or using any form of cocaine. Experiencing trauma during pregnancy can also increase your risk of abruption. Examples of trauma can include a motor vehicle accident, a fall, or being a victim of physical abuse. Unfortunately, the belly is often a primary target for a batterer, and abruption may result from being hit, kicked, or stabbed in the abdomen.

How will I know?

Abruption is often discovered when bright red or dark clotted blood is discharged from the vagina. However, bleeding from the vagina is not always the case. An abruption can also be internal, or concealed, and vaginal bleeding may not occur. This happens when the collection of blood between the surface of the placenta and the uterus is trapped and does not escape through the cervix into the vagina. Sometimes, the blood forces its way into the bag of water around the baby. In this case, blood would not be seen until you break your bag of water. However, most of the time the blood makes its way down to the cervix between the bag of water and the uterine wall and is discharged into the vagina.

Pain associated with an abruption can vary from mild to severe. Contractions usually intensify the pain with an abruption. Other signs include tenderness across your belly or if your belly feels very hard. An obvious sudden increase in the size of your belly or the onset of labor may also be worrisome signs of an abruption. Labor is nature's way of trying to correct the problem. Obviously, if the placenta is coming away from the uterine wall it is not properly transporting blood and oxygen to the baby. Therefore, the baby will experience distress and even death. These will appear as abnormalities in the heart rate on an external fetal monitor.

What now?

If you experience any or all of the signs and symptoms described, your care provider will want to see you right away. A sudden, total abruption requires immediate medical attention. A rapid delivery would be necessary to save your life and your baby's life. This is usually done by c-section unless your baby is delivering immediately through your vagina.

If it is unclear whether you are having a total abruption, an ultrasound examination can help rule out a placenta previa since an abruption is difficult to diagnose with an ultrasound. Other helpful information for your care provider would include your health history, admission of any drug use, any possible trauma that you may have experienced prior to your symptoms, and a physical examination.

Laboratory tests can also be helpful in determining the significance of an abruption so that your care provider may want to draw blood from your arm. An IV will administer fluid to you and provides access to your veins in case you require a blood transfusion, which is reserved for a life-threatening situation. The only true treatment to control life-threatening bleeding is delivery of both the baby and the placenta.

Sometimes, a chronic abruption can be managed without immediate delivery. This is solely based on how the baby is doing. If an abruption occurs before your due date and the baby's heart rate is reassuring, there may be time to give you medications to help mature the baby's lungs. At this time, your pregnancy would last only as long as the baby could tolerate it. Medications to stop contractions (tocolytics) are controversial in the treatment of a chronic abruption, and your care provider will determine if they are appropriate for you. If you experience abruption on or near your due date, vaginal delivery is recommended as long as mother and baby are doing well.

Can there be serious complications?

Complications from a placental abruption stem from excessive bleeding. A very large quantity of blood can be lost during an abruption. This would require a c-section and thereby increasing blood loss from the surgery itself. Sometimes, when a mother has lost a significant amount of blood, a disorder called disseminated intravascular coagulation (DIC) can occur. DIC interferes with your blood's natural ability to clot, and this will result in further blood loss. Excessive bleeding and DIC often require a blood transfusion.

As discussed with treatment for placenta previa, a hysterectomy is reserved as a last resort to control bleeding. The removal of your uterus is only done when all other efforts have failed and it is obvious that the surgery is necessary to save your life.

The most devastating complication of placental abruption is death of the baby. The placenta is the baby's life support while inside the uterus. If the placenta does not readily supply the baby with oxygen and blood, it cannot survive.

Are there other causes of bleeding?

Other disorders that can cause bleeding during pregnancy include a cervical polyp (a tumor) or cervical cancer. An infection in either the cervix or the vagina can also cause vaginal bleeding. A vasa previa is when the baby's umbilical cord vessels are in the membranes overlying the cervical opening. The vessels of the cord can rupture causing bleeding. This disorder is rare but can be life threatening for the baby. "Bloody show" is the bleeding that occurs when you are in labor and your cervix is changing. This is normal and does not pose any threat to you or your baby.

In any case, all vaginal bleeding should be taken seriously and should be reported to your care provider immediately. Treatments may sound drastic, but they are necessary to preserve your life as well as the life of your baby.

PART FOUR

The Final Details

XIV

Breast-Feeding and Your High-Risk Pregnancy

Overview

In most cases, your high-risk pregnancy should not stop you from successfully breast-feeding your baby. The way you start out may certainly be different than you had envisioned, but your overall success is still a very real possibility. In rare cases, breast-feeding is not recommended or complications may arise, but your care provider can assist you with getting a good start. The purpose of this chapter is to let you know that breast-feeding is still a possibility with a high-risk pregnancy and to provide some important tips. If you have already decided to breast-feed or you are still undecided, seek additional information through your care provider or through available published material.

Lactation specialists are trained to help women with special breast-feeding needs as are support groups and organizations such as the La Leche League and the International Lactation Consultants Associations. All of these avenues of support can be found either in the hospital, through your care provider, or in the phone book.

There are many decisions to make during your pregnancy and after your baby is born. You may spend a great deal of time researching the safest car seat or finding the best stroller or the right crib for your baby. You may also make a great effort to eat well, take your prenatal vitamins, and avoid things that are harmful such as alcohol and drugs during your pregnancy. All of these things are providing your baby the very best environment to grow and thrive, and the choice to breast-feed is one of those important decisions.

This decision deserves as much of your undivided attention as your choice of a care provider, car seat, and color of the nursery. The decision of whether to breast-feed should be made before you give birth. There certainly will be instances when you cannot or you choose not to breast-feed your baby. Infant formulas today are designed to contain the same properties as breast milk, but nothing can replace *your* breast milk. Examine all the benefits of breast-feeding for you, your baby, and society before making your decision.

What Are the Benefits?

The woman's body is truly a magnificent work of art. During your pregnancy, the body designs breast milk to provide the right nutrition for your baby as well as protect him from disease. Your body will create breast milk that is the precise number of calories from proteins, sugars, fats, and enzymes that will be easily digested by your baby. If you have a premature baby, the breast milk that you produce will be especially designed to meet the special needs of your preemie. That milk will be distinctly different from the milk you would produce if your baby had been born full term. Breast milk can meet all the needs of your baby for good growth and development.

In addition to providing the perfect nutrition for your baby, your breast milk will include a special combination of the right vitamins and minerals needed for overall good health. Amazingly, the colostrum (the substance that your breasts make before your "milk comes in") is full of antibodies your baby needs for immunity against bacteria and viruses. Colostrum is a fabulous custom feature that your body possesses because it is designed specifically for your baby's environment. You build antibodies against bacteria and viruses that you are exposed to, and you pass these on to your baby to protect him in his new environment (the outside world). This feature cannot be replicated and is not found in any infant formulas.

There are many advantages of giving your baby breast milk. Breast-fed babies have less diarrhea, ear infections, lung infections, and bacterial meningitis (an infection in the spinal cord or brain). All of these things mean fewer visits to the pediatrician and less expense for you with office fees and prescriptions. Strong evidence also suggests that breast-feeding your baby may protect your child against sudden infant death syndrome and from diseases later in life such as diabetes, Crohn's disease, and ulcerative colitis. Breast-feeding also enhances your baby's mouth and face development because of the exercise it provides.

The physical benefits for your baby are many, but there are also physical benefits for you when you choose to breast-feed. These benefits include less bleeding after delivery when the baby is allowed to nurse immediately following delivery, and a speedier loss of the weight gained during pregnancy due to the calorie-burning milk production. You will also be at less risk of breast cancer before menopause.

Is there a downside?

The downside to nursing is that you cannot directly see the amount your baby is receiving each time she nurses. This may make you uneasy at first, but there are plenty of ways to tell if she is receiving enough breast milk. She will be satisfied after nursing, she will have moist eyes and mouth, and she will consistently gain weight. Since you are the sole provider of nutrition for your newborn, your partner and family will not be able to participate in feeding the baby at first. This can sometimes make for a tired mother but it is easily resolved after three to four weeks, once you have established your milk supply. Talk to your pediatrician or lactation specialist about giving the baby a bottle early during breast-feeding so as not to create nipple confusion for the baby or jeopardize your milk supply.

Remember, when you choose to breast-feed you will always have the baby's milk fresh, ready to go, and at the right temperature. There is no cleanup, no cost, and it comes in a handsome carrying case. If you do choose to breast-feed your baby, your success will be determined by your motivation, perseverance, and supportive friends, relatives, and care providers for you and your newborn.

What if I have a preemie?

It is not unusual for a premature baby to be unable to nurse directly from the breast right away. In this case you must begin pumping your breasts soon after you deliver to begin the production of breast milk. Importantly, if you deliver your baby prematurely, your success will be enhanced with the guidance of a lactation specialist who can look at your individual situation and design a plan to help get you started with pumping your breasts for your premature baby in the intensive care nursery. Stimulating your breasts with a breast pump will begin your milk production just as your newborn would with suckling. You must pump as frequently and as long as your baby would nurse at the breast in order to build and maintain your supply. Optimally, you will need to pump at least seven times in a twenty-four hour period. This will yield the best results and is done with the greatest ease if you use a hospital grade electric breast pump, which can be rented by the month from most hospital programs or through local organizations. This type of pump can also be purchased from such programs. Investigate the monthly rental cost and compare it to the cost of purchasing a pump that you could keep. If you become the owner of such a pump it certainly can be used for other pregnancies or shared with a sister or friend. Avoid store-bought pumps or hand-powered pumps.

You must follow specific instructions to properly handle and store your colostrum and breast milk. Once you begin to collect, first the colostrum and then your breast milk, you will keep it in the freezer until your baby is ready to be fed. It is vital to tell both the nurses and physicians caring for your baby in the intensive care unit that you are planning to breast-feed. By sharing this information, a coordinated effort can be planned for storing your milk as well as introducing your baby to the breast as soon as possible.

Once your baby is well enough and old enough, you will both need to learn how to breast-feed. Both you and your baby will not automatically know what to do. At this point your care provider, your baby's care provider, and your lactation consultant can help you learn how to be a successful breast-feeding duo.

What if I take medications?

Just as during your pregnancy, some medications cannot be taken while you are breast-feeding. Always discuss any medications with your care provider as well as your baby's care provider. They will help you determine whether or not it is safe to take certain medications. Common medications that are not compatible with breast-feeding include aspirin, cocaine, chloramphenicol, cimetidine, cyclosporine, doxorubicin, iodine, lithium, methotrexate, narcotics, and thiouracil. Obviously, it is best to avoid any over-the-counter drugs, alcohol, cigarettes, and street drugs while breast-feeding.

Can there be complications?

There can be complications with both pumping your breasts and breast-feeding. Many resources, including *The Breastfeeding Sourcebook* by M. Sara Rosenthal, are available to help explain common complications and how to avoid most of them. Educating yourself through books and classes can help you be successful with breast-feeding.

Women who have had complications during their pregnancies and deliveries such as preeclampsia, life-threatening bleeding, or a serious infection are at risk for being unable to produce an adequate supply of breast milk. Your care provider and lactation consultant can help you to identify whether this problem applies to you. Some conditions and diseases prohibit you from breast-feeding. Contagious diseases such as hepatitis B virus, CMV (cytomegalovirus), and HIV (the virus that causes AIDS) are contraindicated with breast-feeding. These viruses can be passed on to your baby through your breast milk. If you have breast cancer or have had surgery on your breasts such as implants or a reduction you may not be able to successfully breast-feed.

Ultimately, you will decide on how to choose to nourish your infant. Breast-feeding is a physical and emotional endeavor. Know that assistance is available if you choose to breast-feed your premature infant or after a term high-risk delivery. Seek assistance and support as you travel the road of lactation. Determination will get you started, and the emotional bond will perpetuate with nursing your baby. Any amount of breast milk is beneficial for your baby, whether it is two weeks' worth, or a year. A supportive environment can help you overcome perceived obstacles so carefully weigh the benefits before you decide.

You worked very hard to get your baby home. You deserve to enjoy him. When breast-feeding or pumping is no longer enjoyable or you are resenting it, it is time to stop. You have come too far to have something such as feeding your baby be a dreaded task. Some mothers simply find they "don't like" nursing. If this is true for you, let go of the guilt and buy the formula. Most importantly, believe in yourself and your decisions.

XV

Glossary of Pregnancy-Related Terms

Abortion Loss of a pregnancy, either accidentally or purposefully, before viability (twenty-four weeks).

Abruptio Placentae A condition in which the placenta has begun to separate from the inner wall of the uterus before the baby is born.

Afterpains Cramplike pains due to contractions of the uterus that occur after childbirth. They are more common in subsequent pregnancies, tend to be most severe during nursing, and last two to three days.

Albuminuria Albumin (a protein) in the urine is an abnormal finding and often associated with kidney disorders and with toxemia of pregnancy.

Alpha Fetoprotein (AFP) A protein produced by a growing fetus that is present in amniotic fluid and, in smaller amounts, in the mother's blood. Larger than normal amounts are found in the maternal bloodstream if neural-tube defects are present in the fetus.

Amniocentesis Removal of amniotic fluid by insertion of needle into the amniotic sac; amniotic fluid is often used to assess fetal health or maturity.

Amniotic Fluid Liquid surrounding the fetus, composed of secretions from the placenta, fetal urine and other minor constituents. It circulates constantly and is replaced every few hours.

Amniotic Sac The sac that surrounds the baby inside the uterus. It contains the baby, the placenta, and the amniotic fluid.

Analgesic A drug that relieves pain and does not cause unconsciousness.

Anemia Any condition in which the number of red blood cells is less than normal. This term usually applies to the concentration of the oxygen-transporting material in the blood, which is the red blood cell.

Anencephaly A type of neural tube defect that occurs when the fetus's head and brain do not develop normally.

Anesthesia Relief of pain by loss of sensation.

Anomaly A malformation; an organ or structure that is abnormal in position, structure, or form.

Antenatal Before birth.

Antepartum Time between conception and the onset of labor; usually used to describe the period when a woman is pregnant.

Antibiotics Drugs that treat infections.

Antibody A protein in the blood produced in reaction to foreign substances, such as bacteria and viruses that cause infections.

Antigen A substance or part of a substance (living or nonliving) that is recognized as foreign by the immune system, activates the immune system, and reacts with immune cells or their products.

Aorta The main vessel leading from the heart providing oxygenated blood to the body.

Apgar Score A scoring system used to evaluate newborns at one minute and five minutes after delivery. The total score is achieved by assessing five signs: heart rate, respiratory effort, muscle tone, reflex irritability, and color. Each of the signs is assigned a score of 0, 1, or 2. The highest possible score is 10.

Areola Pigmented or colored ring surrounding the nipple of the breast.

AROM Artificial rupture of amniotic membranes through the use of a device such as an amnihook.

Arrhythmia Irregular or missed heartbeat.

Aspiration Swallowing or sucking a foreign body or fluid, such as vomit, into an airway.

Autoantibodies Antibodies that attack parts of your body or your own tissues.

Baby Blues See *depression.*

Back Labor Pain or labor felt in the lower back.

Bacterial Vaginosis A bacterial infection of the vagina, formerly called *Gardnerella vaginalis* or *Hemophilus vaginalis,* characterized by a foul-smelling, grayish vaginal discharge that exhibits a characteristic fishy odor when 10 percent potassium hydroxide (KOH) is added.

Bag of Waters The membrane containing the amniotic fluid and the fetus.

Beta hCG A highly specific fragment of the human chorionic gonadotropin (hCG) complex which is very important in assessing (1) the presence of pregnancy, (2) the health of the fetus, and (3) the diagnosis of an ectopic pregnancy. (This is the hormone that is detected and measured in pregnancy tests.)

Bilirubin A substance present in blood. Levels are monitored closely in newborn babies. An excess of bilirubin is generally treated by exposure to light.

Biophysical Profile An assessment of fetal heart rate, fetal breathing, fetal body movement, fetal muscle tone, and the amount of amniotic fluid. Heartrate is determined by the nonstress test (NST). Ultrasound is used for the other four measurements.

Biopsy Removal of a small piece of tissue for microscopic study.

Birthing Room A room used for labor and delivery with a relaxed atmosphere.

Birth Stool A small wooden chair that a woman may sit on during labor and delivery.

Blastocyst Stage of early embryonic development; the product of cleavage.

Bloody Show Small amount of vaginal bleeding late in pregnancy; often precedes labor.

Board Certification Provides doctor with additional training and testing in a particular specialty. In the area of obstetrics, the American College of Obstetrician Gynecologist offers this distinction. Certification requires expertise in the care of a pregnant woman.

Bonding The psychological union of the mother, father, and child. It is most desirable immediately after birth, but there are some excellent alternatives if this is not possible.

Bradley Method Partner-coached natural childbirth.

Braxton-Hicks Contractions False labor pains.

Breech Presentation Abnormal position of the fetus. Buttocks or legs come into the birth canal before the head.

Candida Albicans The most common cause of yeast infections in the vagina; common in pregnancy.

Carrier A person who shows no signs of a particular disorder but could pass the gene on to his or her children.

Centimeter Unit of measurement used to describe cervical dilatation.

Cephalic Pertaining to the head.

Cephalopelvic Disproportion A condition in which the baby is too large to pass safely through the mother's pelvis during delivery.

Cervical Dilation Process in which the cervical os and the cervical canal widen from less than a centimeter to approximately 10 cm, allowing delivery of the fetus.

Cervical Os The small opening of the cervix that dilates during the first stage of labor.

Cervix The "neck" between the external os and the body of the uterus. The lower end of the cervix extends into the vagina.

Cesarean Delivery (C-section) Delivery of the fetus by means of an incision into the abdominal wall and the uterus; also called abdominal delivery.

Cesarean Hysterectomy Surgical removal of the uterus immediately after cesarean delivery.

Chancre An infectious sore caused by syphilis and appearing at the place of infection.

Chloasma The darkening of areas of skin on the face during pregnancy.

Chorioamnionitis Inflammation of the membrane surrounding the fetus.

Chorionic Villi Microscopic, fingerlike projections that make up the placenta.

Chorionic Villus Sampling (CVS) A procedure in which a small sample of cells is taken from the placenta and tested.

Chromosome Each cell has twenty-three pairs of chromosomes. They carry the genes, which carry all the inherited characteristics.

Circumcision Surgical removal of the prepuce (foreskin) of the penis.

Cleft Palate Deformity of the palate, the part of the upper jaw, or mouth.

Colostrum Thin, yellow fluid that is the first milk to come from the breast; most often seen toward the end of pregnancy. It is different in content from milk produced later during nursing and contains important antibodies that protect the baby from infection.

Condyloma Acuminatum Warts found on the vulva, vagina, or cervix.

Congenital Disorder A condition that affects a fetus before it is born.

Conjoined Twins Twins connected at the body; they may share vital organs. Also called Siamese twins.

Conjunctivitis Inflammation of the mucous membrane lining the eyelids.

Constipation Bowel movements that are infrequent or incomplete.

Contraction Tightening and shortening of the uterine muscles during labor, causing effacement and dilatation of the cervix; contributes to the downward and outward descent of the fetus.

Contraction Stress Test (CST) Response of fetus to uterine contractions to evaluate fetal well-being.

Corpus Luteum Area in the ovary where the egg is released at ovulation. A cyst that forms in this area after ovulation is called a corpus luteum cyst.

Cradle Cap An oily, yellowish crust that may appear on the newborn's scalp caused by excessive secretion of the sebaceous glands in the scalp; also called seborrhea dermatus.

Crowning Appearance of the presenting fetal part at the vaginal opening during labor.

Crown-rump Length Measurement from the top of the baby's head (crown) to the buttocks of the baby (rump).

CST See *contraction stress test.*

Cystitis An infection of the bladder.

Cytomegalovirus A rare virus that can cause certain problems related to infertility and birth defects.

D & C (Dilation and Curettage) Surgical procedure in which the cervix is dilated and the lining of the uterus is scraped.

Delivery Expulsion of the infant with placenta and membranes from the woman at birth.

Depression A feeling of helplessness and hopelessness that can involve anyone at any time. It may occur during early pregnancy and soon after delivery but is usually temporary unless there is an undercurrent of previous depression.

Diastasis Recti Separation of abdominal muscles.

Diethylstilbestrol (DES) Non-steroidal synthetic estrogen. Used in the past to try to prevent miscarriage.

Down Syndrome A genetic disorder caused by the presence of an extra chromosome and characterized by mental retardation, abnormal features of the face, and medical problems such as heart defects.

Dysplasia Abnormal changes in the cells of the cervix.

Eclampsia Convulsions and coma in a woman with preeclampsia; not related to epilepsy.

Ectopic Pregnancy A pregnancy in which the fertilized egg begins to grow in a place other than inside the uterus, usually in the fallopian tubes.

EDC (Estimated Date of Confinement) Anticipated due date for delivery of the baby. Calculated from the first day of the last period counting forward 280 days. Also referred to as EDD (Estimated Date of Delivery).

Edema Swelling of the tissues due to the retention of fluid.

Effacement Thinning and shortening of the cervix that occurs late in pregnancy or during labor.

Ejaculation Expulsion of the seminal fluids from the penis.

Electronic Fetal Monitoring A method in which electronic instruments are used to record the heartbeat of the fetus and contractions of the mother's uterus.

255

Embryo An organism in the early stages of development.

Endometriosis A condition in which tissue similar to that normally lining the uterus is found outside the uterus, usually on the ovaries, fallopian tubes, and other pelvic structures.

Endometrium The lining of the uterine wall.

Engorgement Vascular congestion or distention. In obstetrics, the swelling of breast tissue brought about by an increase in blood and lymph supply to the breast, preceding true lactation. Occurs as the milk supply increases.

Epidural Block Anesthesia that numbs the lower half of the body.

Episiotomy A surgical incision made into the perineum (the region between the vagina and the anus) to widen the vaginal opening for delivery.

Estimated Date of Confinement See *EDC*.

Estrogen A female hormone produced in the ovaries that stimulates the growth of the lining of the uterus.

Fallopian Tube Tube that leads from the cavity of the uterus to the area of the ovary.

False Labor Tightening of the uterus without dilation of the cervix.

Fasting Blood-Sugar Blood test to evaluate the amount of sugar in the blood following a time period of fasting.

Ferrous Gluconate Iron supplement.

Ferrous Sulfate Iron supplement.

Fertility The ability to reproduce.

Fertilization Joining of the sperm and egg.

Fetal Alcohol Syndrome (FAS) A pattern of physical, mental, and behavioral problems in the baby that is thought to be due to alcohol abuse by the mother during pregnancy.

Fetal Anomaly Fetal malformation or abnormal development.

Fetal Distress Evidence that the fetus is in jeopardy, such as a change in fetal activity or heart rate.

Fetal Goiter Enlargement of the thyroid in the fetus.

Fetal Growth Retardation (IUGR) Inadequate growth of the fetus during the last stages of pregnancy.

Fetal Monitor Device used before or during labor to listen to and record the fetal heartbeat. Can be *external* monitoring (through maternal abdomen) or *internal* monitoring (through maternal vagina) of the baby inside the uterus.

Fetus Refers to the unborn baby after twelve weeks of gestation until birth.

Fibroids Benign (noncancerous) growths that form on the inside of the uterus, on its outer surface, or within the uterine wall itself.

Fontanel In the fetus, an unossified space or soft spot consisting of a strong band of connective tissue lying between the cranial bones of the skull.

Footling A breech presentation in which one or both feet present.

Forceps Instrument used to help remove baby from the birth canal during delivery.

Foreskin Loose skin covering the end of the penis or clitoris; prepuce.

Frank Breech Baby presenting buttocks first during delivery. Legs are flexed and knees extended.

Fundus The upper portion of the uterus between the fallopian tubes.

Gene A DNA "blueprint" that codes for specific traits, such as hair and eye color.

Genital Herpes Simplex Herpes simplex infection involving the genital area. It can be significant during pregnancy because of the danger to a newborn fetus infected with herpes simplex.

German Measles (Rubella) A simple virus disease which is of little significance unless it occurs during pregnancy. In early pregnancy, in particular, it can cause marked birth defects.

Gestation Period of intrauterine development from conception through birth; pregnancy.

Gestational Diabetes The occurrence of diabetes during pregnancy (gestation).

Glucose A sugar that is present in the blood that is the body's main source of fuel.

Glucose-Tolerance Test Blood test done to evaluate the body's response to sugar. Blood is drawn at intervals following the ingestion of a sugary substance.

Glucosuria Glucose in the urine.

Gonorrhea Contagious venereal infection transmitted primarily by intercourse. Caused by the bacteria *Neisseria gonorrhea*.

Gravid Pregnant.

Group B Streptococcal Infection Bacteria sometimes found in the vagina that can lead to a serious complication in the newborn.

Heartburn Discomfort or pain that occurs in the chest. Often occurs after eating. It can sometimes be relieved or prevented by avoiding foods that make it worse, eating several, small meals a day, avoiding greasy or spicy foods, avoiding lying down after eating and sleep propped up, and eating a small amount of a fatty food about thirty minutes prior to eating a meal.

Hemorrhoids Varicose veins of the rectum; may be external or internal. To care for hemorrhoids, avoid getting constipated, increase fluids and fiber, strengthen the area with Kegel exercises, and apply an ice pack or witch hazel.

Heparin Medication used to prevent blood clots.

High Risk Having an increased possibility of suffering harm, damage, loss, or death.

Human Chorionic Gonadatropin Hormone produced in early pregnancy. Measured in a pregnancy test.

Hyaline Membrane Disease Respiratory disease of the newborn.

Hydramnios A condition in which there is an excess amount of amniotic fluid in the sac surrounding the fetus.

Hydrocephalus Excessive accumulation of fluid around the brain of the baby. Sometimes called "water on the brain."

Hyperemesis Gravidarum Severe nausea, dehydration, and vomiting during pregnancy. Occurs most frequently during the first trimester.

Hyperglycemia Increased blood sugar.

Hypertension, Pregnancy-induced High blood pressure that occurs during pregnancy. Defined by an increase in the diastolic and/or systolic blood pressure.

Hypotension Low blood pressure.

Hysterectomy Surgical removal of the uterus.

Immune Globulin Preparation Substance used to protect against infection with certain diseases, such as hepatitis or measles.

Incompetent Cervix Cervix that dilates painlessly, without contractions.

Incomplete Abortion A miscarriage in which part but not all of the uterine contents are expelled.

Induction of Labor The process of causing or initiating labor by use of medication or artificial rupture of membranes.

Infant Child under one year of age.

Infertility Diminished ability to conceive.

Informed Consent A legal concept that protects a person's rights to autonomy and self-determination by specifying that no action may be taken without that person's prior understanding and freely given consent.

Insulin A hormone that controls the levels of glucose (sugar) in the blood.

Intrapartum The time from the onset of true labor until the delivery of the infant and placenta.

In Utero Within the uterus.

Iron-Deficiency Anemia Anemia produced by lack of iron in the diet. Often seen in pregnancy.

Isoimmunization Development of specific antibody directed at the red blood cells of another individual, such as a baby in utero. Often occurs when an Rh-negative woman carries an Rh-positive baby or is given Rh-positive blood.

Jaundice A buildup of bilirubin that causes a yellowish appearance in the baby.

Kegel Exercises Perineal muscle tightening that strengthens the pubococcygeus muscle and increases its tone.

Labia External folds of skin on either side of the vulva.

Labor Productive uterine contractions which produce dilation of the cervix, descent of the baby, and its expulsion into the world.

La Leche League A national organization devoted to the encouragement of breast-feeding.

Lamaze Method A method of childbirth preparation, also known as psychoprophylaxis.

Lanugo The fine hair that sometimes grows on a baby's back and shoulders at birth; it goes away in one or two weeks.

Laparoscopy Surgical procedure performed for tubal ligation, diagnosis of pelvic pain, or diagnosis of ectopic pregnancy.

Last Menstrual Period (LMP) The last normal menstrual period experienced by the mother prior to pregnancy; sometimes used to calculate the infant's gestational age.

Leboyer Method A quiet, peaceful delivery experience designed to reduce birth trauma to infants.

Letdown Reflex Pattern of stimulation, hormone release, and resulting muscle contraction that forces milk into the milk ducts, making it available to the infant; milk ejection reflex.

Leukorrhea Vaginal discharge characterized by a white or yellowish color; primarily composed of mucus.

Lightening Change in the shape of the pregnant uterus a few weeks before labor. Often described as the baby "dropping."

Linea Nigra Line of increased pigmentation running down the abdomen from the belly button to the pubic area during pregnancy.

Lochia Maternal discharge of blood, mucus, and tissue from the uterus; may last for several weeks after birth.

Macrosomia A condition in which a fetus grows very large; this problem is sometimes found in babies of diabetic mothers.

Mammogram X-ray study of the breasts to identify normal or abnormal breast tissue.

Mask of Pregnancy Increased pigmentation over the area of the face under each eye. Commonly has the appearance of a butterfly. See *Chloasma.*

Mastitis Inflammation of the breast.

Maternal Serum Screening A group of blood tests that check for substances linked with certain birth defects.

McDonald Cerclage Surgical procedure performed on an incompetent cervix. A drawstring-type suture holds the cervical opening closed during pregnancy. See *Incompetent cervix.*

Meconium A greenish substance that builds up in the bowels of a growing fetus and is normally discharged shortly after birth.

Meconium Aspiration Syndrome (MAS) Respiratory disease of term, postterm, and small newborns caused by inhalation of meconium or meconium-stained amniotic fluid into the lungs; characterized by mild to severe respiratory distress.

Meconium-Stained Fluid Amniotic fluid that contains meconium because fetal distress has caused increased intestinal activity and relaxing of the fetus's anal sphincter.

Meningomyelocele Congenital defect of the central nervous system of the baby. Membranes and the spinal cord protrude through an opening or defect in the vertebral column.

Menstruation Regular or periodic discharge of a bloody fluid from the uterus.

Microcephaly Abnormally small development of the head in the developing fetus.

Milia Tiny white spots appearing on the face of a newborn as a result of unopened sebaceous glands; they disappear spontaneously within a few weeks.

Miscarriage The spontaneous loss of a pregnancy before the fetus can survive outside the uterus.

Mittelschmerz Pain that coincides with release of an egg from the ovary.

Mongolian Spot Dark, flat pigmentation of the lower back and buttocks noted at birth in some infants; usually disappears by the time the child reaches school age.

Morning Sickness Nausea and vomiting, with ill health, found primarily during the first trimester of pregnancy. Suggestions for easing nausea include eating small, frequent meals, eating a high protein snack before bed, eating saltine crackers or fruit bars before getting out of bed, avoiding unpleasant odors, eating slowly, decreasing fat in diet, avoiding liquids thirty minutes before and after meals, taking prenatal vitamins at night, and adding vitamin B_6, peppermint tea, pressure point wrist bands, ginger capsules. See *Hyperemesis gravidarum*.

Mucus Plug Secretions in cervix; often released just before labor.

Multiple Pregnancy A pregnancy in which there are two or more fetuses.

Neonatologist A pediatric specialist who cares for premature or sick newborn babies.

Neural Tube Defects Abnormalities in the development of the spinal cord and brain in the fetus. See *Anencephaly; Hydrocephalus; Spina bifida*.

Nonstress Test (NST) A test in which fetal movements felt by the mother are recorded along with changes in the fetal heart rate using an electronic fetal monitor.

Nurse Midwife Nurse who has received extra training in the care of pregnant patients and the delivery of babies.

Obstetrician Physician who specializes in the care of pregnant women and the delivery of babies.

Oligohydramnios Lack or deficiency of amniotic fluid.

Ossification Bone formation.

Ovulation Cyclic production of an egg from the ovary.

Oxytocin A drug used to help bring on contractions.

Palmar Erythema Redness of palms of the hands.

Pap Smear Routine screening test that evaluates for cervical cancer.

Paracervical Block The injection of a local anesthetic into the tissues around the cervix to relieve pain during childbirth.

Pediatrician Physician who specializes in the care of babies and children.

Pelvis The lower portion of the trunk of the body bounded by the hip bones, coccyx, and sacrum.

Perinatologist Physician who specializes in the care of high-risk pregnancies.

Perineum The area between the vagina and the rectum that is cut during an episiotomy to help widen the vaginal opening during delivery.

Phospholipids Fat-containing phosphorous. The most important are lecithins and sphingomyelin which aid in the maturation of fetal lungs before birth.

Pica The urge to eat nonfood items during pregnancy.

Placenta Organ inside the uterus that is attached to the baby by the umbilical cord; provides nourishment to and takes away waste from the fetus. It is also called afterbirth.

Placental Abruption Premature separation of the placenta from the uterus.

Placenta Accreta Placenta that attaches to muscle of uterus.

Placenta Previa Low attachment of the placenta, covering or very close to the cervix.

Posterior Fontanel Small triangular area between the occipital and parietal bones of the skull, generally closes by eight to twelve weeks of life.

Postpartum After childbirth or delivery.

Postpartum Blues Mild depression after delivery.

Postpartum Depression Depression after delivery.

Postterm Pregnancy A pregnancy that extends beyond forty two weeks.

Preeclampsia Combination of symptoms significant to pregnancy, including high blood pressure, edema, swelling, and changes in reflexes.

Pregnancy The condition of having a developing embryo or fetus in the body after fertilization of the female egg by the male sperm.

Pregnancy-Induced Hypertension (PIH) A hypertensive disorder including preeclampsia and eclampsia, characterized by the three cardinal signs of hypertension, edema, and proteinuria.

Premature Delivery Delivery before thirty-seven weeks gestation.

Preterm Born before thirty-seven weeks.

Prolactin A hormone secreted by the anterior pituitary that stimulates and sustains lactation in mammals.

Prolapsed Cord Umbilical cord that becomes trapped in the vagina before the fetus is delivered.

Prolonged Labor Labor lasting more than twenty-four hours.

Prostaglandins A hormone that has profound effects on pregnancy as well as many other body systems. Prostaglandins break down the collagen in the cervix, softening it for dilation.

Proteinuria Protein in urine.

Pruritis Gravidarum Itching during pregnancy.

Pubic Symphysis Bony prominence in the pelvic bone found in the midline. Landmark from which the doctor often measures during pregnancy to follow growth of the uterus.

Pudendal Block Local anesthesia during labor.

Pulmonary Embolism Blood clot from another part of the body that travels to the lungs. Can cause closed passages in the lungs and decrease oxygen exchange.

Pyelonephritis Serious kidney infection.

Pytalism Excessive salivation.

Quickening Feeling the baby move inside the uterus.

Reflex An involuntary response.

Relaxin A water-soluble protein hormone secreted by the corpus luteum that causes relaxation of the pelvic bones and cervical dilatation.

Respiratory Distress Syndrome (RDS) A condition of some preterm babies in which the lungs are incompletely developed.

Retracted Nipple A nipple that has pulled inward.

Rh Factor Antigens present on the surface of blood cells that make the blood cell incompatible with blood cells that do not have the antigen.

Rh-Negative Absence of the rhesus antibody in the blood.

RhoGAM An anti-Rh (D) gamma-globulin given after delivery to an Rh-negative mother of an Rh-positive fetus. Prevents the development of permanent active immunity to the Rh antigen.

Rh Sensitivity See *Isoimmunization.*

Rhythm Method The timing of sexual intercourse to avoid the fertile time associated with ovulation.

Round Ligament Pain Pain caused by stretching ligament on the sides of the uterus during pregnancy. This pain is often eased by bringing the legs up toward the abdomen.

Rupture of Membranes Loss of fluid from the amniotic sac. Also called "breaking of waters."

Seizure Sudden onset of a convulsion.

Semen Thick whitish fluid ejaculated by the male during orgasm and containing the spermatozoa and their nutrients.

Sexually Transmitted Disease (STD) Infection transmitted through sexual intercourse.

Sickle Cell Anemia Anemia caused by abnormal red blood cells shaped like a sickle or a cylinder.

Skin Tag Flap or extra buildup of skin.

Spina Bifida A neural tube defect that results from improper closure of the fetal spine.

Spinal Block A form of anesthesia that numbs the lower half of the body.

Station Estimation of the descent of the baby.

Sterility Inability to conceive or to produce offspring.

Steroids Group of medications of hormone origin. Often used to treat various diseases and given to enhance fetal lung maturity. Includes estrogen, testosterone, progesterone, and prednisone.

Stillbirth Delivery of a baby that shows no signs of life.

Stretch Marks Areas of the skin that are torn or stretched. Often found on the abdomen, breasts, buttocks, and legs. Mineral oil, lanolin, aloe vera oil, and lotion may help.

Sucking Reflex The infant's tendency to suck on any object placed in the mouth.

Sudden Infant Death Syndrome (SIDS) The unexpected sudden death of any infant or young child in which the cause of death is unknown.

Surfactant Phospholipid present in the lungs. Controls surface tension of lungs. Premature babies often lack sufficient amounts of surfactant to breathe without assistance.

Syphilis Sexually transmitted venereal infection caused by *treponema pallidum.*

Systemic Lupus Erythematosus (SLE) Connective-tissue disorder common in women in the reproductive ages. Antibodies made by the person act against his or her own tissues.

Tay-Sachs Disease Inherited disease characterized by mental and physical retardation, convulsions, enlargement of the head, and eventually death. Trait is usually carried by Ashkenazi Jews.

Teratogens Agents that can cause birth defects when a woman is exposed to them during pregnancy.

Thrombosis Formation of a blood clot (thrombus).

Thrush Monolial or yeast infection occurring in the mouth or mucous membrane of a newborn infant.

Tocolysis Stopping contractions during premature labor.

Tocolytic Agents Medications that stop labor.

Toxemia See *Preeclampsia.*

Transducer A device that emits sound waves and translates the echoes into electrical signals.

Transverse Lie Fetus is turned sideways in uterus.

Trichomonal Vaginitis Vaginal infection caused by trichomonas, sometimes causing internal itching.

Trimester Any of the three 3-month periods into which pregnancy is divided.

Tubal Sterilization A method of female sterilization in which the fallopian tubes are closed by tying, banding, clipping, or sealing with electric current.

Ultrasound A test in which sound waves are used to examine internal structures. During pregnancy, it can be used to examine the fetus.

Umbilical Cord Cord that connects the placenta to the developing baby. It removes waste products and carbon dioxide from the baby and brings oxygenated blood and nutrients from the mother through the placenta to the baby.

Umbilicus Belly button.

Uterus The organ in which the embryo/fetus grows. Also called a womb.

Vacuum Extraction The use of a special instrument attached to the baby's head to help guide it out of the birth canal during pregnancy.

Vagina The tube or passageway located between the external genitals and the uterus of the female.

Varicose Veins Blood vessels (veins) that are dilated or enlarged. The discomfort may be lessened with resting with the legs elevated, avoiding crossing the legs when sitting, exercising regularly, alternating standing positions, resting in bed on your side, and wearing support hose.

Vasectomy A method of male sterilization in which a portion of the vas deferens is removed.

Vena Cava Major vein in the body that enters into the right atrium of the heart. It returns unoxygenated blood to the heart for transport to the lungs.

Vernix Caseosa A white, cheesy, waxy substance that coats babies' skin in late pregnancy.

Vertex Head first position.

Zygote Cell that results from the union of a sperm and egg at fertilization.

REFERENCES

Ament, L.A. "Maternal Tasks of the Puerperium Reidentified." *Journal of Obstetric, Gynecologic, and Neonatal Nursing.* 1990, 330–335.

American College of Obstetricians and Gynecologists. "Management of Diabetes Mellitus in Pregnancy." *Technical Bulletin,* Number 92. 1992.

———. *Planning for Pregnancy, Birth, and Beyond,* 2d ed. Washington, D.C., 1995.

Blackburn, S.T., and D.L. Loper. *Maternal, Fetal, and Neonatal Physiology: A Clinical Perspective.* Philadelphia: W.B. Saunders and Co., 1992.

Clark, S.L., et al. *Handbook of Critical Care Obstetrics.* Cambridge, Mass.: Blackwell Scientific Publications, 1994.

Creasy, R.K., and R. Resnik. *Maternal Fetal Medicine: Principles and Practice,* 3d ed. Philadelphia: W.B. Saunders and Co., 1994.

Cunningham, F.G., et al. *Williams Obstetrics,* 19th ed. Norwalk, Conn.: Appleton & Lange, 1994.

Curtis, G.B. *Your Pregnancy Week-by-Week.* Tucson, Ariz.: Risher Books, 1994.

Eastman, N.J., and K.P. Russell. *Expectant Motherhood.* Boston: Little, Brown, 1970.

England, M.A. *A Colour Atlas of Life Before Birth: Normal Fetal Development.* Aylesbury, Bucks, England: Hazell Books, 1990.

Evans, C.J. "Description of a Home Follow-Up Program for Childbearing Families." *Journal of Obstetric, Gynecologic, and Neonatal Nursing.* 1991, 113–118.

Fischbach, F.T. *A Manual of Laboratory Diagnostic Tests,* 3d ed. Philadelphia: J.B. Lippincott Co., 1988.

Glanz, W.D., ed. *Mosby's Dictionary,* 3d ed. St. Louis, Mo.: C.V. Mosby Co., 1990.

Heppard, M.C., and T.J. Garite. *Acute Obstetrics: A Practical Guide.* St. Louis, Mo.: Mosby-Yearbook, 1996.

Keppler, A.B. "Postpartum Care Center: Follow-up Care in a Hospital-Based Clinic." *Journal of Obstetric, Gynecologic, and Neonatal Nursing.* 1995, 17–21.

Newman, M.A. *Health as an Expanding Consciousness.* St. Louis, Mo.: C.V. Mosby Co., 1986.

Nilsson, L., and L. Hamberger. *A Child Is Born* (C. James, trans.) New York: Bantam Doubleday Dell, 1990.

Norr, K., and K. Nacio. "Outcomes of Postpartum Early Discharge, 1960–1986: A Comparative Review." *Birth,* 14(3), 1987, 135–141.

Olds, S.B., et al. *Maternal Newborn Nursing. A Family Centered Approach,* 3d ed. Menlo Park, Calif.: Addison-Wesley, 1988.

Rogers, C. *Freedom to Learn for the Eighties.* Columbus, Oh.: Charles E. Merrill, 1983.

Rubin, R. "Puerpural Change." *Nursing Outlook,* 9(12), 1961, 743–755.

Scott, J.R., P.J. Disaia, C.B., Hammond, W.N. Spellacy (eds.). *Danforth's Obstetrics and Gynecology,* 7th ed. Philadelphia: J.B. Lippincott Co., 1994.

Varney, H. *Nurse Midwifery,* 2d ed. Boston: Blackwell Scientific Publications, 1987.

Youngkin, E.Q., and M.S. Davis. *Women's Health: A Primary Care Clinical Guide.* Norwalk, Conn.: Appleton & Lange, 1994.

INDEX

A

accreta, 233
ACE inhibitors, 111-112
afterpains/cramping, 51, 52-53
amniocentesis, 123-124, 127,
    134, 196, 219
amniotic fluid, 21-22, 29, 30, 36,
    39, 40, 219
  leaking, 41-42, 189-190
anemia, 171
anesthesia, and cardiac changes,
    63
antibiotics, 68, 71, 163
antibodies, 118-119, 120, 126-127,
    157
antibody titers, 122-123
antiphospholipid antibody
    syndrome, 154-156
  concerns and risks, 155
  labor, delivery and postpartum,
    156
  prenatal care, 155-156
aortic stenosis, 71-75
arteries, 60
arthritis, rheumatoid, 163-164
atrial septal defects, 64, 77-78
autoimmune diseases, in
    pregnancy, 149-167. *See also*
    specific disease
autonomic dysreflexia, 144-145

B

babies
  after birth, 49-50
  of diabetic mothers, 133-134
  first few days, 49-50
  large, 137-138, 204, 206-207
  premature, breast-feeding, 242,
    244-245, 246
  premature, during labor, 46
  small, 174-175
backaches, 35
balance, sense of, 20-21
bedrest, suggestions for, 177,
    191-192, 197
betamethasone, 196, 220
biophysical profile, fetal, 137, 206
birth, 47. *See also* labor, delivery,
    and postpartum *under specific
    medical conditions*
  cesarean, 48-49
bladder, 94
bladder infections. *See* urinary
    tract infections
bleeding with pregnancy, 225-238
  about, 225-226
blood clots, 62, 68, 76
blood pressure. *See also* hyper-
    tension, chronic
  diastolic, defined, 60
  systolic, defined, 60

blood types, 117-118
blood vessels
 characteristics of, 60-61
 normal changes during
  pregnancy, 61-62
"bloody show," defined, 237-238
Braxton-Hicks contractions, 38
breast changes in pregnancy, 12
breast-feeding, 241-247
 benefits of, 242-243
 complications with, 246, 247
 disadvantages of, 243-244
 medications to avoid while,
  245-246
 with multiple babies, 180-181
breast pumps, 243-244
breathing, focused, 45, 46, 199-200
breech extraction, 179
brethine, 192-193

C

calcium supplementation, 31
cardiovascular system, in
  pregnancy, 57-92
cerclage, 187
cervical dilation, 38, 43
cervical effacement, 38-39, 43
cervix, incompetent, 176
cesarean section, 48-49
 diabetic mothers and, 137
 hemolytic disease and, 127, 129
 for multiple births, 173, 178,
  179-180
 placenta previa and, 232-233
 preeclampsia and, 221-222
 procedure, 180
 recovery from, 48-49

colostrum, 243, 245
constipation, postpartum, 53-54
contractions, 20, 188
 of labor, 38, 42, 43-44, 45, 46,
  47, 199-201
convulsions. *See* seizures in
  pregnancy
cordocentesis, 125
corpus luteum, 11, 17

D

deformities, and diabetes, 133-134
delivery. *See* labor, delivery, and
  postpartum *under specific
  medical conditions*
dental hygiene, 27
depression, postpartum, 52, 54
dexamethasone, 221
diabetes, 103, 203-207
 White's Classification, 132-133
diabetes, gestational, 131
 about, 204-206
 labor, delivery, and postpartum,
  206-207
 risk factors, 204, 207
 testing for, 204-205
diabetes, Type I, in pregnancy,
  131-132, 132-138, 207
 concerns and risks, 133-136
 labor, delivery, and postpartum,
  137-138
 precautions against complications, 136-137
diabetes, Type II, 131, 207
diseases, contagious, and breast-
  feeding, 246
diuretics, 112

Down syndrome, screening for, 25
due date, 10

E

echocardiogram, fetal, 136, 152
eclampsia, 212-213
ectopic pregnancy, early signs of,
  14
edema, 32, 36, 49, 211, 213
  cerebral, 213
  pulmonary, 211, 222
Eisenmenger's syndrome, 64,
  81-83
embryo, 12
  cell layers, 12
  normal development, 12, 14,
  17-18
endometrium, defined, 17
episiotomy, 47, 51, 53, 201
estrogen, 12-13, 13, 36, 37, 40
examination, first comprehensive,
  15-17

F

fertility drugs, 169, 170
fertilization, 10-11
fetal echocardiogram, 136, 152
fetal heart monitoring, 206
fetal monitoring, 42-43, 194, 195,
  nonstress test, 136-137
fetal testing, 123-124, 125
fetus
  at end of first trimester, 21
  at week eleven, 17-18
  at week fifteen, 24
  at week twenty-one, 28-29

at week twenty-seven, 34
at weeks twenty-eight to thirty,
  36
fluid intake, 12, 14, 33
food, and nausea, 13-14

G

genetic abnormalities, 175
genital warts, 22
gestational age, defined, 172
gestational diabetes. *See* diabetes,
  gestational
girdle, for pregnancy support,
  177-178
glomerulonephritis, 104
Grave's disease. *See* hyperthyroid
  diseases

H

Hashimoto's thyroiditis, 165-166
headaches, postpartum, 51, 53
heart, structure and function,
  57-61
heart block, congenital, 152
heartburn, 23, 31
heart disease, congenital, of
  mother, 76-86
heart disease, in pregnancy, 64-92
  congenital problems, 64-65, 76-
  86
  diabetic mothers and, 134
  myocardial infarction, 86-87
  peripartum cardiomyopathy,
  90-92
  prognosis for pregnancy and,
  65-66
  valve problems, 66-76

HELLP syndrome, 158, 214-215, 318
hemolytic disease of infancy
 labor, delivery, and postpartum care, 128-129
hemolytic disease of the newborn, 120, 121-122, 123, 125, 129
hemorrhage. *See* bleeding with pregnancy
hemorrhoids, 26, 51, 53
hormones, 11, 17, 18
 in first trimester, 12-13, 17, 18
hospitalization
 for placenta previa, 230-231
 for preeclampsia, 217, 218-219
human chorionic gonadrotropin (HCG), 11
hypertension, chronic, 93-116, 104, 109-113
 concerns and risks, 110-111
 lifestyle and, 110
 medications, 111-113
hypertension, pregnancy-induced. *See* preeclampsia
hyperthyroid diseases, 166-167, 168
hypothyroid diseases, 165-166
hysterectomy, 233

I

idiopathic/autoimmune thrombocytopenia purpura, 156-160
 concerns and risks, 157-158
 labor, delivery, and postpartum, 159-160

immune response, and RH disease, 118-119
immune system and pregnancy, 98, 118-119
indocin, 194
indomethacin, 194
induced labor, 43-48
insulin, 138, 203-204
insulin-dependent diabetes. *See* diabetes, Type I
intrauterine fetal transfusion, 126-127
intrauterine growth retardation, 172

J

jaundice, newborn, 122, 123-124

K

Kegel exercises, 26, 27
kidney failure, 225
 acute, 108-109, 214
 chronic, 104-109
 labor, delivery, and postpartum, 114-115
kidney problems, in pregnancy, 93-116
 and/or high blood pressure, 93-116
 causes of, 103-104
 infections, 97-100, 101, 102
 kidney failure, 103, 104-109, 114-115, 214, 225
 preeclampsia and, 214
 risks of, 104-105

kidneys
  importance of, 96-97
  normal changes in pregnancy,
    95-96
  structure and function, 94-95

L

labor, 41-48. *See also under
    specific medical conditions*
  contractions of, 42, 43-44, 45,
    46, 47, 199-201
  focused breathing during, 45,
    46, 199-200
  induced at thirty-eight weeks,
    43-48
  pushing phase, 44, 46-47, 200-
    201
  stages of, 44
  visualization during, 44-45, 199
laboratory tests
  between fifteen and eighteen
    weeks, 25
  first prenatal, 16-17
lactation specialists, 180, 241,
    244, 245
lifestyle, and hypertension, 110
liver, and HELLP syndrome, 158,
    214-215, 221
lupus. *See* systemic lupus
    erythematosus
lupus-like syndrome, 154-156
lupus nephritis, 151

M

macrosomia, 204
magnesium sulfate, 193-194, 197,
    220-221

Marfan's syndrome, 65, 87-90
maternal serum alpha feto protein
    test, 25, 210
meconium, 29, 42, 50
medications
  antiseizure, 140-141, 142
  breast-feeding and, 245-246
  for hypertension, 111-113
  for myasthenia gravis, 162
  for preeclampsia, 220-221
  to stop contractions, 192-194
mitral regurgitation or
    insufficiency, 69-70
mitral stenosis, 66-68
mitral valve prolapse, 70-71, 79
moles, 22
moodiness, 22-23
mucous plug, 41, 45, 189
multiple pregnancies, 169-184
  about, 169-171
  care of mother and babies,
    174-175, 176-178
  concerns and risks, 171-176
  death of fetus in, 175
  labor, delivery, and postpartum,
    178-182
  preeclampsia and, 210
multiple sclerosis, 146-147
  labor, delivery, and postpartum,
    147
myasthenia gravis, 160-163
  care of mother, 162
  concerns and risks, 161
  labor, delivery, and postpartum,
    162-163
  medications, 162
myocardial infarction, 86-87

N

nausea in pregnancy, 13-14
neural tube defects, screening for, 25
neurological problems, high risk. *See* multiple sclerosis; seizures in pregnancy; spinal cord injury
nifedipine, 193

O

ovaries, 10, 11
oxytocin, 38, 44, 49

P

patent *ductus arteriosus*, 64, 80-81
perinatologist, 68, 195, 218
peripartum cardiomyopathy, 65, 90-92
placenta, 11, 17
    structure and function, 226-227
placental abruption, 216, 226, 233-238
    complications of, 237
    risks of getting, 234-235
    signs and symptoms of, 235
    treatment of, 236-237
placenta previa, 226, 228-233
    cesarean section and, 232-233
    hospitalization for, 230-231
    risks of, 228-229, 232-233
    risks of getting, 229
    signs of, 230
    treatment of, 230-232
plasmaphoresis, 161, 222

polycystic kidney disease, 104
polyhydramnios, 174
postpartum period, 49-54.
    See also labor, delivery, and postpartum *under specific medical conditions*
    cardiovascular changes during, 63-64
    first week, 50-54
preeclampsia, 31, 111, 113, 115, 135, 156, 158, 209-223
    about, 209-210
    delivery and postpartum, 221-223
    delivery as cure for, 209, 219, 223
    diagnosis of, 218, 219
    effects on mother and baby, 209-223
    in multiple pregnancies, 176
    risk of getting, 210, 217, 223
    risks to mother and baby, 210-216, 220
    signs and symptoms of, 216-218
    theories of, 211
pregnancy, high-risk
    inducing, 43
    "red flags" for, 3-4, 6-7
pregnancy, normal, 9-54. *See also* pregnancy, high-risk
    first trimester, 10-22
    second trimester, 22-34
    third trimester, 34-40
pregnancy-induced hypertension. *See* preeclampsia
premature delivery
    breast-feeding and, 242, 244-245, 246

labor, delivery, and postpartum, 197-202
preeclampsia and, 209, 219
premature labor and delivery, 129, 161, 185-202
about, 185-186
care for mother and baby, 190-194
concerns and risks, 190
defined, 171
hospital stay for, 195-197
multiple births and, 171-172
risk factors for, 186-187
triggers for, 187
warning signs for, 188-190
warning signs of, 197-198
prenatal care, 111
preterm labor. *See* premature labor and delivery
procardia, 193
progesterone, 11, 17, 22-23, 31, 38, 95

R

red blood cells, 117-118, 121-122
relaxation/visualization technique, 199
rest. *See* bedrest
retinopathy, 135
Rh disease, 50, 117-130
care plan, 124-129
defined, 119-120
immune factor and, 118-119
prevention of, 120-121
rheumatoid arthritis, 163-164
concerns and risks, 164
labor, delivery, and postpartum, 164

Rh factor, 118
Rh immunoglobulin (RhoGAM™), 28, 50, 120-121, 130
risk factors, 3-4, 6. *See also under specific medical conditions*
ritodrine, 193

S

seizures in pregnancy, 140-143
concerns and risks, 140-141
from eclampsia, 13, 211
labor, delivery, and postpartum, 143
medications, 140-141
prenatal care, 141-143
septic shock, 99-100
sexual intercourse, avoiding, reasons for, 19-20
sexuality, in first trimester, 18-20
sleep patterns, 34-35
of baby, 52
spina bifida, screening for, 25
spinal cord injury, 143-146
concerns and risks, 144-145
labor, delivery and postpartum, 145-146
station, 39
synthroid, 166, 167, 168
systemic lupus erythematosus, in pregnancy, 150-154
concerns and risks, 151-152
diagnostic criteria, 150
labor, delivery, and postpartum, 154
prenatal care, 152-154

T

terbutaline, 192-193
tetralogy of Fallot, 64, 84-86
thrombocytopenia purpura,
    156-160
thyroid disorders, 165-168
    labor, delivery, and postpartum,
    168
    types, 165-168
thyroid releasing hormone,
    196-197
thyroid storm, 167, 168
toxemia. *See* preeclampsia
trauma, and placental abruption,
    235
triplets. *See* multiple pregnancies
twins, 172-174. *See also* multiple
    pregnancies
    resources for parents, 182
twin-to-twin transfusion
    syndrome, 172, 173-174, 176

U

ultrasound examination, 30, 125,
    136, 142-143, 196, 218, 232
    of cervix, 176
ureters, 94
urethra, 94
urinary incontinence, 51, 144
urinary tract infections, 12, 33,
    97, 98-100, 144
    prenatal care and, 100-102

V

vaginal discharge, 22, 28
    changes in, 188-189
valve replacement surgery, 75-76
vasa previa, 237
vasospasms, 211-214, 215, 216
    veins, 60
ventricular septal defects, 64, 78-80
vernix caseosa, 29, 40
vision, 36
visualization/relaxation
    technique, 44-45, 199
vitamin K, 141

W

warning signs of problems, 6-7
warts, 22
weight gain, 24, 28

Y

yeast infections, 22
yutopar, 193